"Josef Sorett and a team of scholars, practitioners, artists, and thinkers—blended at the intersections of their expertise—present readers with an invitation to explore and feel our way through important discussions of Blackness, sexuality, and church/spiritual politics. Written and presented as a communal practice of listening, learning, and 'reasoning together,' this book illuminates what matters today in Black religious discourse."
—THELATHIA NIKKI YOUNG, AUTHOR OF *BLACK QUEER ETHICS, FAMILY, AND PHILOSOPHICAL IMAGINATION*

"I am a Same-Gender-Loving African American Woman, Pastor, Bishop, Teacher, Preacher, Mother, and evolving Pentecostal Justice Warrior! I find my whole self and my community deeply situated in *The Sexual Politics of Black Churches*, a collection of experiences and studies focused on the Black Church and Sexuality. It was a joy to be part of the conversations, and the finished product is filled with scholarship and liberation power!"
—REV. DR. YVETTE A. FLUNDER, PRESIDING BISHOP OF THE FELLOWSHIP OF AFFIRMING MINISTRIES

"*The Sexual Politics of Black Churches* is not only timely—even overdue—but especially rewarding intellectually, politically, and ethically. Advancing conversations on sexuality and Black Christianity, this work is essential reading for anyone interested in Black Christianity in general, in religion and sexuality, in studies of religion and race, and in accounts of theology and politics in the United States. A wonderful achievement."
—ANTHONY PETRO, AUTHOR OF *AFTER THE WRATH OF GOD: AIDS, SEXUALITY, AND AMERICAN RELIGION*

THE SEXUAL POLITICS OF BLACK CHURCHES

RELIGION, CULTURE, AND PUBLIC LIFE
Series Editor: Matthew Engelke

The Religion, Culture, and Public Life series is devoted to the study of religion in relation to social, cultural, and political dynamics, both contemporary and historical. It features work by scholars from a variety of disciplinary and methodological perspectives, including religious studies, anthropology, history, philosophy, political science, and sociology. The series is committed to deepening our critical understandings of the empirical and conceptual dimensions of religious thought and practice, as well as such related topics as secularism, pluralism, and political theology. The Religion, Culture, and Public Life series is sponsored by Columbia University's Institute for Religion, Culture, and Public Life.

For a complete list of titles, see page 263.

The Sexual Politics of Black Churches

EDITED BY
Josef Sorett

Columbia University Press
New York

Publication of this book was made possible in part
by funding from the Institute for Religion, Culture,
and Public Life at Columbia University.

Columbia University Press
Publishers Since 1893
New York   Chichester, West Sussex
cup.columbia.edu

Copyright © 2022 Columbia University Press
All rights reserved

Library of Congress Cataloging-in-Publication Data
Names: Sorett, Josef, editor.
Title: The sexual politics of Black churches / Josef Sorett, editor.
Description: New York : Columbia University Press, [2021] | Includes index.
Identifiers: LCCN 2021030088 (print) | LCCN 2021030089 (ebook) |
ISBN 9780231188326 (hardback) | ISBN 9780231188333 (trade paperback) |
ISBN 9780231547772 (ebook)
Subjects: LCSH: African American churches—Doctrines. |
Sex—Religious aspects—Christianity. | African American churches—
Political activity.
Classification: LCC BR563.N4 S485 2021 (print) | LCC BR563.N4 (ebook) |
DDC 264.008996073—dc23
LC record available at https://lccn.loc.gov/2021030088
LC ebook record available at https://lccn.loc.gov/2021030089

Cover design: Milenda Nan Ok Lee
Cover image: Hisham Ibrahim / PhotoV / Alamy

*This book is dedicated in memory of Janisha Renee Gabriel
Colleague, Friend, Believer in the fullness of Black Lives
(October 15, 1980 ~ September 6, 2020)*

Contents

Acknowledgments
Josef Sorett xi

Introduction
Josef Sorett 1

PART I   A Call to Conversation

1. Religion, Race, and Sexuality in American Culture:
A Public Conversation
*featuring Victor Anderson, Serene Jones, and Barbara Savage;
moderated by Cathy Cohen and Josef Sorett* 17

PART II   Sacred Texts, Social Authority, Sexual Difference

2. Jephthah's Daughter and #SayHerName
Nyasha Junior 41

3. An Inconsistent Truth: The New Testament,
Early Christianity, and Sexuality
Michael Joseph Brown 50

PART III   Historical and Cultural Formations of Black
(Christian) Sexual Politics

4. "Have the Sons of Africa No Souls?" Manliness, Freedom, and Power in
the Cultural Roots of Afro-Phallic Protestantism
Jonathan Lee Walton 67

5. Everybody Knew He Was "That Way": Chicago's Clarence H. Cobbs,
American Religion, and Sexuality During the Post–World War II Period
Wallace Best 78

6. Interrogating the Passionate and the Pious: Televangelism
and Black Women's Sexuality
Monique Moultrie 104

PART IV Identity and Inclusion in Black Churches

7. The Self-Interested Politics of Collective Religious Transformation:
Issues of Family Definition and LGBT Inclusion in Black Churches
Melynda J. Price 119

8. Intersectional Invisibility and the Experience of Ontological Exclusion:
The Case of Black Gay Christians
Valerie Purdie Greenaway, Richard Eibach, and Nick Camp 128

PART V Theological and Pastoral Visions of Inclusive Black Churches

9. Gay *Is* the New Black, Theologically Speaking
Monica A. Coleman 147

10. Flesh That Needs to be Loved:
Wounded Black Bodies and Preachin' in the Spirit
Luke A. Powery 159

11. Aiding and Abetting New Life:
"Sex-Talk" in the Pulpit, Pew, and Public Square
Brad R. Braxton 173

12. An Experiment in Inclusion:
A Conversation with Christine and Dennis Wiley
Interview by Derrick McQueen 190

Epilogue
Josef Sorett 209

Notes   217
List of Contributors   243
Index   249

Acknowledgments

JOSEF SORETT

It is customary to reiterate, in acknowledgments, the truth that no book reaches print solely by the efforts of a single author. All books are the productions of multiple people, connected by various webs of relationships. This fact is all the more true for an anthology such as this one, which consists of twelve chapters and eighteen contributors. Moreover, as acknowledged in both the volume's introduction and epilogue, this book began and took shape in the context of an event that evolved into a set of conversations that eventually took the form of a center at Columbia University—the Center on African-American Religion, Sexual Politics and Social Justice (CARSS). This anthology, like CARSS, is a community affair that includes a range of individuals who have done everything from attend a single event, serve on a panel, present a paper, and write or comment on a chapter, to those who have offered sustained support and guidance to all of CARSS's work, including the work that preceded the center, over the past decade. To be clear, this volume stands on its own, but it took shape in the context of a set of conversations that led to the founding of CARSS. Without the community of people that have participated in and supported CARSS's work in various forms, this book never would have seen the light of day. Accordingly, these acknowledgments necessarily express appreciation both to CARSS's extended community, and to those who helped move this book project forward in more specific ways.

First and foremost, I owe debt of gratitude to Fred Davie, who while serving as president of Public/Private Ventures first hired me as a researcher to lead a study of sexuality in the context of black churches back in 2007. Fred then brought that project with him to the Arcus Foundation, where he funded the convening where most of the book's chapters were first presented as short reflections. Fred only appears briefly in the book's opening conversation, but his support of this volume been consistent ever since. With support from Jon Stryker and the Arcus Foundation, and crucial guidance from Tom Kam and Roz Lee, Derrick McQueen and Jennifer Leath joined the project. Both Derrick and Jen participated in shaping the contours of the early conversations where the idea for this book first emerged. Derrick also appears in this volume, interviewing pastors Christine and Dennis Wiley in the final chapter, and he continues to play a key role, as associate director, in CARSS's ongoing work.

Working together, we assembled a small group of scholars, clergy, and activists—Brad Braxton, Michael Brown, Mandy Carter, Barbara Savage, Christine Wiley, and Dennis Wiley—who eventually became known as the planning team. Together, they helped organize a series of three convenings that took place in 2011, in Chicago and Houston, of the Roundtable on the Sexual Politics of Black Churches. This larger group—once again of scholars, clergy, and activists—included the planning team as well as Roderick Belin, Kelly Brown Douglas, Leslie Callahan, Keri Day, Yvette Flunder, Eric Lee, Ray Owens, Benjamin Reynolds, Mykal Slack, Eboni Marshall Turman, and Michael Walrond. Jarvis McInnis also played an essential role by taking detailed notes at each of the roundtable's gatherings. At the first meeting, we were fortunate to have five guests who graciously helped to set the context and course for our conversations: gratitude here goes Cedric Harmon, Candy Holmes, Sharon Lettman-Hicks, Leslie Malachi Watson, and Carlton Veazey. The purpose of these gatherings was to develop strategies for advancing a more inclusive vision of black churches that affirmed "the moral and civil equality of LGBTQ persons and communities," and for supporting individuals and institutions interested in or already doing this work in the context of black communities.

Following three convenings of the roundtable, we handed over a "black church strategy" to the Arcus Foundation. This report was intended to help guide the work that Arcus would do in support of black churches, community organizations, and leaders who either embraced or were open to a vision of black churches and communities that was inclusive of and publicly affirmed gender and sexual difference—and lesbian, gay, bisexual, trans and queer black folks, specifically. It is important to note that, at the time, the Arcus Foundation's stated policy priority was achieving marriage equality. That said, the strategy that we developed was organized around a vision of black churches, communities, and families wherein black LGBTQ folks felt safe, fully affirmed, included, empowered, and, most simply, at home— where, in practice, #AllBlackLivesMatter, as the now common refrain goes. I continue to appreciate the fact that the Arcus Foundation deferred, in this regard, to the wisdom of this group of black clergy, scholars, and activists. Moreover, much gratitude goes to Melinda Weekes-Laidlow and Curtis Ogden, who helped turn a more than sixty-page report that captured the roundtable conversations into a clear and compelling seven-page strategy document that we submitted to Arcus. Following the strategy, CARSS was founded at Columbia and launched in the fall of 2014 with the conference, "Are the Gods Afraid of Black Sexuality? Religion and the Burdens of Black Sexual Politics." Along with Jennifer Leath and Derrick McQueen, Laura McTighe brought years of expertise and experience as an organizer to help us plan this international event, which gathered scholars, religious leaders, and activists (yet again) from around the world to both map a scholarly agenda and intervene in public debates.

Since its founding, CARSS has received guidance from a community of advisors at Columbia and around the country—including members of the planning team and roundtable participants, but which also includes the Reverend Jewelnel Davis, Katherine Franke, Janisha Gabriel, Farah Jasmine Griffin, Bishop Yvette Flunder Fredrick Harris, Janet Jakobsen, Darnell Moore, Mignon Moore, Alondra Nelson, and Kendall Thomas. CARSS continues to take cues from the range of ideas and ambitions voiced at that 2014 conference, with the goal of advancing "research, education and public engagement at the nexus of religion, race and sexuality with regards to black communities in the U.S. and the African Diaspora." This volume falls within that purview even as it focuses on a more specific formation; namely, the sexual politics of black churches. It has benefited not only from all of the work that has been invested in CARSS but also from the more traditional kinds of feedback and investment that go into the making of a book. In additional to helping plan "Are the Gods Afraid," Laura McTighe commented on early versions of chapters as the authors first submitted them. Participating in the 2011 Seminar on Debates on Religion and Sexuality at Harvard Divinity School was also helpful in thinking through this volume at an early stage. A special thanks goes to the seminar participants, instructors, and faculty director Mark Jordan. More recently, Jana Reiss offered a close and critical reading of the entire manuscript and provided individualized feedback on each chapter to all of the authors. Jana's comments were incredibly helpful at the stage right before the book went back out for external review with Columbia University Press.

As then director of Columbia's Institute for Religion, Culture and Public Life (IRCPL), sponsor of the series in which this book appears, Mark C. Taylor supported the project early on. Now led by Matthew Engelke, IRCPL's investment in this volume has been steadfast. The editorial and marketing team at CUP, including Wendy Lochner, Lowell Frye and Marisa Lastres, has been a pleasure to work with throughout the process—from proposal to publication. And the two anonymous readers the press provided offered really important questions, criticisms, and recommendations; all of which helped clarify and better weave together the range of voices and visions (unwieldy by design) articulated in the volume into what, I hope, reads more like a shared conversation. The production process benefited greatly from the steady guidance of Ben Kolstad and team at KnowledgeWorks Global LTD. Finally, Barbara Savage (who appears as a panelist in chapter 1), gave a close read of a penultimate version of the entire manuscript and provided helpful suggestions at just the right time.

While, as editor, I cannot claim credit for any the insights in each of the volume's chapters, I am proud to stand by the anthology as a whole and, even more, I appreciate the trust (and patience) that all of the contributors extended to me in sticking with the volume over the long haul.

THE SEXUAL POLITICS OF BLACK CHURCHES

Introduction

JOSEF SORETT

Gay vs. Black—and Other Odd, Yet Persistent, Oppositions

"I came to tell you about sin," preached Kim Burrell in a January 2017 sermon at Love and Liberty Fellowship Church International, the Houston church she founded and where she is pastor. "That perverted homosexual spirit, and the spirit of delusion and confusion, it has deceived many men and women," she continued.[1] In 2017, Burrell, a popular gospel musician, had recently achieved a new level of celebrity, appearing on the soundtrack to *Hidden Figures*, a popular movie that grossed over $230 million in 2016 and garnered a Screen Actors Guild (SAG) award. Her place on the movie's soundtrack had led to performances alongside Pharrell Williams on several popular daytime and late-night talk shows, including NBC's *Today* and the *Tonight Show*. Kim Burrell was poised to convert an already successful career in gospel music into a new level of mainstream acclaim—until an unnamed parishioner filmed Burrell in the midst of her antigay litany and released the footage on social media. As her sermon went viral, Kim Burrell's invitations began to disappear, including a prompt disinvitation from *Ellen* and, shortly thereafter, the cancellation of her radio show *Bridging the Gap*.

So much about the complicated workings of race, religion, and sexuality in contemporary society crystallized in the fierce fallout occasioned by the airing of Kim Burrell's sermon. However, instead of provoking a productive

[1]

conversation about the complicated racial and sexual politics of American culture, media coverage of Burrell's fall from grace quickly took the shape of a familiar fascination with the culture and politics of black churches. African American clergy and congregations have long been figured as morally and socially conservative, especially on matters of sex and sexuality, even as they have been appealed to as both sources of progressive politics (e.g., Martin Luther King Jr.) and as sites of an eroticized aesthetic of Christian worship (e.g., gospel music; embodied, emotional worship; etc.). Afro-Protestantism, in the popular imagination, has long been a source of excessive and transgressive sexuality and politics. Except when it's not. The rapidly shifting landscape of race, gender, and sexual politics during the first decades of the twenty-first century only amplified a longstanding concern—really, an affective ambivalence—with black churches.

At least since "Gay Is the New Black!" appeared on the December 16, 2008, cover of the *Advocate*, African Americans have figured as the public face of resistance to a then-rising marriage equality movement.[2] By 2017, data from the Pew Research Center confirmed that African Americans were evenly divided concerning gay marriage. However, the vocal opposition of a small group of black preachers has garnered significantly more attention.[3] Indeed, the image of African American clergy and congregations has been etched into the American political imagination as a stand-in for all religious opposition to same-sex marriage. Even in 2008, the *Advocate* article offered a much more complicated account of the relationships between racial identity and sexual orientation than the headline implied. Written by Michael Joseph Gross, the cover story was one of the first efforts to unpack the significance of what had taken place at polls across the nation just one month earlier, when California joined with the nation as a whole in electing Barack Obama as president of the United States yet also voted to pass Proposition 8, which denied LGBTQ couples the right to marry. While the ballot initiative passed only by a slim margin (52.3 percent to 47.7 percent), early commentary noted that African Americans, motivated by religious commitments, overwhelmingly voted for Obama *and* voted against marriage equality, solidifying what became a popular media trope: "gay versus black."

As Gross pointed out in his 2008 article, which carried the equally provocative subtitle "The Last Great Civil Rights Movement," the logic that pitted black against gay was no more helpful (or accurate) than the many facile connections that had been drawn in recent years between black and gay political organizing and identity politics. "Persons who are in the closet serve on the deacon boards, serve in the ministry, serve in every capacity in the church," Rev. Dennis W. Wiley, pastor of Covenant Baptist United Church of Christ in Maryland, said of black churches. "I do believe a certain hypocrisy is there."[4] Such formulations, generally speaking, posited that the logical extension (or culmination) of the black civil rights movement of the 1960s was the more recent gay liberation movement, which by the 1990s had evolved into an LGBTQ lobby that increasingly set its targets on marriage as the measure of equality and inclusion.[5] Foreshadowing Rev. Wiley's quote, black people were not only cast as standing in opposition to progress—which had come to be defined as LGBTQ equality vis a vis marriage—but they were also judged as hypocrites in the shadows of their own tradition of racial justice.

Despite Gross's arguments, which highlighted the tensions and complexities attendant to the juxtaposition and entangling of black and gay identities, the "gay vs. black" talking point has held firm, arguably, to the present day. In the years since 2008, the familiar opposition was invoked all too often and to varying ends. "Gay vs. Black" evolved from a provocative 2008 headline employed by the premier LGBTQ publication into a political wedge strategy deployed on the Right by the National Organization for Marriage, an anti–gay marriage conservative outfit.[6] Along the way, some dissenting voices declared, "Gay ain't the new black," or variations on this theme. Critics in this vein often called attention to the elisions of real difference at stake in drawing equivalences or generalized comparisons between race and sexuality. After all, these movements—for black freedom and for gay liberation—took shape in different moments and were organized around distinct experiences of racial and sexual difference and their attendant social exclusions.[7] Each movement, in this view, required analysis rooted in the specific historical experiences of each community.

To be sure, justice was no less at stake in either moment or movement; but what presumably falls under the rubrics of "gay" and "black" can be no more conflated than the years 1965 and 2015. Nor were the two categories ever mutually exclusive or entirely separable. This fact is readily apparent in the figure of Bayard Rustin, a black *and* openly gay man and a practicing Quaker who is generally credited as a leading strategist of the civil rights movement. Nevertheless, a neat thread linking the two narratives persisted in the years that followed. The linguist and public intellectual John McWhorter affirmed the original *Advocate* proposition in his *New York*

Daily News column in January of 2013. "Gay Really Is the New Black," McWhorter opined, adding that the history of racial oppression placed a "special responsibility" on African Americans to support LGBTQ rights.[8]

That same year, Yoruba Richen's powerful documentary *The New Black* teased out some of the complexities that lay behind the formulation. Richen's film chronicled the campaign for marriage equality in Maryland, illuminating how a ballot initiative was debated by the predominantly black residents of Prince George's County. Of course, the perspectives of most black voters on same-sex marriage—and matters of sexuality more broadly—are more complex than a simple "yes" or "no" vote. As Richen later explained, her appeal to the phrase "the new black" was intended to capture (as well as to encourage) what she observed to be novel yet robust conversations taking place within black communities where matters of (homo)sexuality were no longer being relegated to "the closet."[9] That these conversations took place within campaign cycles—that is, as part of actual struggles over political power in a shifting social landscape—suggested that the "gay vs. black" formulation had traction beyond popular imaginings and provocative headlines. This was proven to be the case when the United States' highest court delivered three monumental and related decisions during the summer of 2013.

On June 25, 2013, the court voted to dismantle key protections provided by the Voting Rights Act of 1965, clearing the way for the removal of federal oversight and leading to the rise of new voter identification laws in many of the same states where black voters had previously been disenfranchised. A day later, the court ruled that the 1996 Defense of Marriage Act was unconstitutional, and it overturned California's 2008 ballot initiative, Proposition 8, as well. Together, these last two decisions effectively affirmed marriage equality for same-sex couples at the federal level. At least in the Supreme Court's assessment, black civil rights (i.e., voting protections) were no longer a pressing concern, and LGBTQ equality (insofar as marriage could secure it) had become the cause célèbre. Perhaps gay was the new black, after all.

That black churches found a prominent place in the story of marriage equality's seemingly rapid ascent to legal affirmation, from the initial passage of Proposition 8 in 2008 to its undoing by the Supreme Court in 2013, suggested a more concrete example of continuities with the 1960s. If LGBTQ rights were to be endorsed as "the last great civil rights movement," then the religious connection mattered all the more. In this view, civil rights mythology, organized around the iconic figure of the Reverend Doctor Martin Luther King Jr., was considered compromised in light of African Americans' support for Proposition 8, which was credited to homophobia incubated in black churches. While gay rights were being framed as an extension of a civil rights movement in which black clergy played prominent roles, black churches were now being figured as the primary opponents to social justice. In truth, black ministers played leading roles on both sides—that is, on campaigns both for and against marriage equality—around the nation and especially, at this time, in Washington, DC, and Maryland.

In this regard, black churches' involvement in the fight for marriage equality was not a conservative diversion from a singularly progressive black church tradition, and was instead much more in keeping with the historical record than most supposed.[10] As archives and denominational records show, during the 1960s black churches were divided over the question of what posture to adopt concerning the civil rights movement as it was building steam. King's position represented only a small contingent of the largest black denomination, which led to a physical fight at the annual meeting of the National Baptist Convention followed by the formation of a new denomination. True to historical form, with regards to marriage equality, Afro-Protestantism has been characterized more by contest than by consensus. That is, black churches and their clerical leaders were both the homophobic foil to *and* a formidable voice for LGBTQ equality. Religious arguments in favor of progressive politics and others in favor of the status quo—in this case, LGBTQ inclusion and exclusion—have abounded all at once, both then and now.[11]

Religion, Race, and Sexuality in American Culture

In contemporary conversations regarding religion and sexuality, one of the more common generalizations is that Christian churches are institutions that cultivate and legitimate a culture of homophobia. Across a diverse spectrum of American congregations, black churches, in particular, are often observed to be especially hostile to the concerns of LGBTQ people and communities. For example, surveys by the Pew Research Center for People and the Press have documented that while a majority of American churchgoers were opposed to same-sex marriage and claimed to have heard sermons citing biblical laws against homosexuality, African American Protestant congregants ranked among the highest subgroups in both of these categories.[12] Confirming the appeal of this popular assumption and preliminary evidence, on the same day that the nation elected its first black president, roughly 70 percent of African Americans in California voted in favor of Proposition 8.[13]

The accuracy of the Associated Press's exit poll was subsequently disputed, raising the question of how much such polls and survey instruments can actually tell us about the cultural politics of black churches. However, the general logic of this analysis—that black people were particularly loyal to their churches and thus voted to make same-sex marriage illegal in California— stuck. More generally, African American Christians were cast as wholly against extending several rights (e.g., marriage, adoption, and partner inheritance) to LGBTQ people across the country.[14] Meanwhile, Catholics and Mormons were largely left out of the narrative, despite their funding of campaigns in support of ballot initiatives such as Proposition 8.[15] In short, the argument went, because black churches tend to be socially conservative, African Americans are easily enlisted in political causes (particularly social issues) championed by the "religious right," such as opposition to marriage equality. While there is perhaps some truth in this observation, it is premised upon the familiar assumption that black churches and the communities they serve are especially unsympathetic when it comes to matters of sexual difference in comparison to other Christians and U.S. citizens in general.[16] As these assumptions about black churches became widespread, short shrift was given to the white Christian communities that funded such ballot initiatives in the first place. Given all that is at stake in legislative campaigns, such as Proposition 8 and in the making of social policy in general, this book's more detailed investigation of these matters is both merited and overdue.

To be sure, much of the public discourse and policy debates regarding gender and sexuality have shifted since 2008. After marriage equality became the law in several states and Washington, DC, it was achieved at the federal level in 2013. It was then upheld by the Supreme Court in 2015 with the *Obergefell* decision. The landscape moved dramatically during Barack Obama's two-term presidency. Subsequently, Donald Trump's one-term presidency sought to undo many of the protections established under the previous administration. President Joe Biden, who is newly in office as this book goes to press, has already begun to reclaim the protections established during the Obama years. Rather than a steady stream of progressive policymaking, the pattern has been more of a push and pull—especially when viewed through the prism of black life. For instance, within a couple of days in May 2012, President Obama affirmed marriage equality, which many credited with having a major impact on African American opinions on the issue, and North Carolina voters passed Amendment 1, revising the state constitution to preclude the possibility of same-sex marriage. During the Obama administration, the military ended its Don't Ask, Don't Tell policy, and the Supreme Court determined that Defense of Marriage Act was unconstitutional. Yet as marriage equality was achieved, many prominent black LGBTQ activists questioned whether marriage was the most pressing issue in the communities where they lived and worked—namely, black communities—even as many of these same black LGBTQ activists (alongside white LGBTQ activists) remained supportive of Obama and other black politicians who supported gay rights. For instance, many black LGBTQ activists have wondered what marriage equality has done to redress violence enacted on black trans women, or to protect black queer youth who are disproportionately represented among homeless populations—two issues that have not improved, and in some instances have gotten worse, in the years since marriage equality was won.

In recent years, the increased visibility of antiblack police violence; the 2015 slayings at Mother Emmanuel AME Church in Charleston, South Carolina; the rise of the #BlackLivesMatter movement; and the public resurgence of organized white supremacist groups (given renewed legitimacy by a Trump presidency), which reached an apex with the insurrection at the Capital building in January 2021, have brought renewed attention to a host of issues that, some would suggest, make marriage a much lesser concern within black LGBTQ communities. Meanwhile, studies have shown that lines to the altar in black communities have grown increasingly short in recent years, with some arguing that "marriage is for white people."[17] There is much evidence to suggest that marriage—gay or straight—was never *the* issue for black voters. Even still, the prominent participation of and preoccupation with African American churches (and black clergy, in particular) in contests over same-sex marriage helps to clarify the degree to which the institution still matters, both symbolically and economically. It also reveals how a concern with marriage must be understood in relation to other issues that impact black communities, such as education, housing, mass incarceration, and police violence. Moreover, while a few prominent black clergy members stepped up to affirm civil marriage as a legal right for same-sex couples, even most of those preachers stopped short of endorsing full LGBTQ equality on theological or moral grounds. The rules, privileges, and protections associated with citizenship and church membership were clarified, in this case, to be different matters. One might ask, then, how are the relationships between racial identity and association, religious belief and practice, public deliberations and political participation, church membership and citizenship, to be understood? And how are we to understand the relationship between the cultural politics of black churches and the ways black churches (and their members) participate in the formal processes of electoral politics?

In short, the political or public significance of black churches ought not to be confused with the sexual politics of black churches. Clarifying this difference does not serve to erect a false division between public and private or between culture and politics. The intramural dynamics of black life and politics of race in America should neither be conflated nor understood as mutually exclusive. Indeed, more can be done to tease out the complex relationship(s) between the cultural politics of black churches and the business of electoral politics more generally. With this basic premise, this volume's contributors begin their work; and they do so with the benefits of, and by bringing together, scholarship that has been forged across many fields.

Studying Religion and Black Sexual Politics

Scholars from many disciplines have recently paid significant attention to topics such as the fallout over Proposition 8, the sexual politics of black churches, and their salience for American cultural and political life. Like the public commentary on black voting patterns on LGBTQ rights, many academics also begin from the assumption of a religiously motivated black hyperhomophobia. While journalists and bloggers found evidence for their arguments in voting patterns, scholarly efforts in the fields of religion and theology have been driven largely by anecdotal evidence and theoretical concerns.

Within the fields of religious and theological studies, the existing scholarship typically moves quickly from evidence to offer an ethical critique of the perceived shortcomings of churches. Kelly Brown Douglas's book *Sexuality and the Black Church* (1999) is a pioneering work on this topic and is illustrative of this approach. In Douglas's view, homophobia within black churches and the communities they serve is a result of African Americans having bought into the binary logic of Western theology (e.g., gay/straight, body/spirit). Moreover, it reflects the degree to which racial stereotypes have fostered a culture of silence where African Americans are unwilling to talk frankly about sexuality or their bodies. Dwight Hopkins and Anthony Pinn's *Loving the Body: Black Religious Studies and the Erotic* (2004) extends Douglas's discourse analysis to offer a constructive interdisciplinary model for theorizing "the body" in African American religion. More recent works from Horace Griffin (2010), Roger Sneed (2010), and Pamela Lightsey (2016) also provide critical analysis while foregrounding black LGBTQ experience within church and society.

The second category of relevant scholarship, more squarely in the social sciences, explores black cultural and political practices. The works in this category help to account for how certain black political strategies have helped underwrite homophobia, and they also explain how such tactics have further marginalized black LGBTQ people. Cathy Cohen's *The Boundaries of Blackness* (1999) is helpful here. According to Cohen, black consensus politics are based on downplaying differences within African American communities, which then lead to what she calls the "secondary marginalization" of subpopulations perceived to be beyond the pale of mainstream, middle-class American values. Because of the common association of HIV/AIDS with homosexuality and intravenous drug use, Cohen surmises, black institutions such as churches and the NAACP responded slowly to the health crisis. In other words, because sexuality is perceived to be a dividing issue, many African American leaders and institutions are reluctant to address related social problems. A more recent anthology, Sandra Barnes and Juan Battles's *Black Sexualities* (2010) offers a rich and broadly sweeping portrait of sexuality in African American life, including two essays that focus on religion. And Angelique Harris has provided an important sociological study of black church responses to AIDS (2010).

Many new books work at the intersections of black identity, gender and/or sexuality, and queer theory, including E. Patrick Johnson and Mae G. Henderson's *Black Queer Studies* (2005) anthology, Muriel Miller Young's *A Taste for Brown Sugar: Black Women in Pornography* (2014), Jeffrey McCune's *Sexual Discretion: Black Masculinity and the Politics of Passing* (2014), C. Riley Snorton's *Nobody is Supposed to Know: Black Sexuality on the Down Low* (2014), and Ashon Crawley's *Blackpentecostal Breath: The Aesthetics of Possibility* (2016). All of these works are tremendous resources, but they still leave open—and even create—space for this volume. *Passionate and Pious: Religious Media and Black Women's Sexuality*, by Monique Moultrie (a contributor to this volume) is, to date, one of very few books published by a university press (either edited volumes or single-authored monographs) that provides sustained attention to the subject of religion and black sexual politics.

Scope and Overview

Recent scholarship and debates around same-sex marriage over the past two decades have both helped set the context for and served as a key impetus for this anthology. That being said, *The Sexual Politics of Black Churches* directs its primary focus on the intramural dynamics of life within black churches and the communities they serve, rather than focusing on the larger social debates in which they have been figured as significant. The volume does so with the clear conviction that a more rigorous—empirically, critically, and theoretically driven—examination of the sexual politics of black churches can contribute to more helpful conversations about the relationships among black churches, the communities they serve, and American public life.[18] The chapters that follow are meant to model an interdisciplinary and wide-ranging conversation that is simultaneously guided by descriptive and prescriptive concerns. Indeed, the highs and lows of recent struggles for the full inclusion and civil protection of LGBTQ people within American society—and how black communities have figured therein—highlight the gains that have been made even as they reveal the complexities of the challenges that remain.

The essays in this volume span the humanities (including history and cultural studies), the social sciences (cultural psychology and political science), and the fields of theological and religious studies (e.g., biblical studies, ethics, homiletics, and theology) to shed light on this situation. The book begins and ends with chapters that began as a public conversation and interview, respectively. These bookends capture the spirit of the book as a whole and its ambitions to both document and model a more inclusive conversation about the sexual politics of black churches. Each chapter represents a distinct entrée into the dialogue rather than one step in a larger, shared argument. What they do share is that all contributors were invited to address the same basic question: How do various developments in your field provide resources to help us understand the way(s) that black churches have figured in recent debates about religion and sexuality in American culture? This rather straightforward question does not suggest a simple or single answer—all the more so, given the range of expertise and experience represented by the authors in this collection. Though every reader will not equally appreciate every chapter, I hope that different kinds of readers—from humanists and social scientists to theologians and Bible scholars; to practitioners, clergy and lay; as well as some segment of generally interested readers—will be able to find insights in the chapters that they find to be most interesting or relevant.

The essays in this volume draw on a range of evidence, including ethnographic, historical, and textual sources, as well as focus groups, interviews, and survey data. A fair reading of this rich milieu of materials and methods begins with the basic (yet often ignored) understanding that African American churches are not a monolith and cannot be spoken of simply in the singular. As Barbara Savage (a participant in the conversation that opens the book) argues in the introduction to her 2008 book, *Your Spirits Walk Beside Us: The Politics of Black Religion*, there is no such thing as the "Black Church."[19] Even if they are lumped together under the weight of America's racial history, black churches have responded to this social and political reality in myriad ways, and they have employed a range of strategies to negotiate issues of race politics, and of gender and sexual difference, specifically. For example, much of the data detailed herein seems to suggest that an unspoken code of "don't ask, don't tell" operated within black churches long before it became a 1990s military policy that has since been overturned.

Another important perspective shared by the following essays is that, despite the very specific racial history that facilitated their emergence, black congregations are part and parcel of American culture. Although some recent public discussions, such as the one that ensued in the aftermath of the 2015 slayings in Charleston's Emmanuel AME Church, often frame these institutions as if they occupy an altogether alternative social sphere, black churches share many of the same norms, values, and theologies as white congregations. These essays confirm that the interpretations of scripture that black churches adhere to—and the gender and sexuality norms they prescribe and proclaim—cannot be adequately understood without a discussion of American evangelicalism, generally, or something like "muscular Christianity," specifically. Collectively, *The Sexual Politics of Black Churches* seeks to account for such complexities with a sense that there is much at stake in the subtle yet significant distinctions between homophobia, heterosexism, and heteronormativity and the multiform role that churches of varying races and ethnicities play in each of these formations. Such distinctly American complexities are no less apparent if the focus of inquiry is squarely situated within black churches.

As the book progresses, the chapters shift back and forth from descriptive to prescriptive concerns, as well as from theological and theoretical queries to more practical matters. Some authors are more concerned with an audience of academic experts, while others address various publics—black and white, clergy and lay, churchgoing and otherwise. The larger narrative of the volume is organized by the idea that moving from caricature (e.g., sound bites, personal experience, or anecdotal evidence) to nuance, in the realm of analysis, is a necessary condition for producing more helpful public conversations and scholarly inquiry. It is important to note, as a baseline, that contributors to this volume share a commitment to an intellectual vision that affirms the full humanity of all persons, including the diverse specificities of identity and subjectivity as it relates to sexual orientation, gender identity, and gender expression. At the same time, each chapter reflects the specific training and commitments of individual contributors. Each author's contribution reflects the range of theological commitments, political positions, and practical strategies that they feel are most effective toward realizing such a vision of human difference within religious communities and society at large. Most are in agreement, however, that dispassionate analysis may not be enough.

Several chapters attempt to chart out strategies for reshaping public debates and congregational life in directions that are more affirming and inclusive of sexual difference. These chapters might take the form of a theological model that links civil rights struggles of the 1960s with the present movement for LGBTQ equality, for example, as Monica A. Coleman does. Or they might involve rereading gender and sexuality in the Christian Bible to recognize differences (within texts *and* interpretive contexts), rethinking church-based responses to HIV/AIDS, or reimagining the educative role of the sermon. In his chapter on the Reverend Clarence Cobb, Wallace Best draws on the archives to present what might be read as an alternative (or queer) history of black clergy. Brad Braxton draws on the wells of his personal experience while discussing his efforts to preach his congregation toward a more open discussion of sex, in general, and sexual difference, specifically. In this regard, *The Sexual Politics of Black Churches* constructively theorizes and historicizes the actual practices of black churches. The book also aims to provide some resources, albeit limited, for individuals concerned not only with understanding black churches but also with increasing their ability to substantively address various concerns associated with sexual politics, including public health crises, hate crimes, and social and theological inequality. No simple solutions are proposed here. Each chapter can be read as a resource for understanding the past and present and for reimagining the future.

Ultimately, through an interdisciplinary approach informed by empirical, interpretive, and constructive commitments, *The Sexual Politics of Black Churches* attempts to intervene in academic debates in a manner that also addresses public deliberations. With sexual politics as its central subject, this is a study of African American churches and their relationship to the broader cultural and political terrain of black communities and the United States more generally. It is written not only for students and scholars of religion in America but also for readers who claim a stake in the future of Christian churches. In addition to academia, it is written for those who are on the front lines of debates about religion and sexuality in American public life. In many ways a performance of the very dialogue that it seeks to deepen, *The Sexual Politics of Black Churches* begins with a public conversation and ends with the more intimate genre of interview. This narrative arc speaks to how debates around religion and sexuality take place at the nexus of public and private, in election campaigns as well as in congregational life. Where the public conversation helps to clarify questions and key issues, the interview offers a glimpse of one local effort to reimagine the terms of the dialogue.

As a whole, by building on the insights of existing scholarship, *The Sexual Politics of Black Churches* helps to clarify that debates around marriage and sexual difference are deeply informed by theological positions, cultural practices, and political strategies. This anthology deepens academic and public conversations in several regards. First, it nuances the approach to studying black churches by treating them as not inherently in isolation from, in opposition to, or enthralled with American/Western culture. In short, black churches are distinctively black iterations of a decidedly American experience. Second, drawing on archival, ethnographic, and survey data, as well as anecdotal and first-hand observations, adds a significant and sustained empirical, yet multidimensional, approach to the dialogue. Third, as a model of interdisciplinary and collaborative work, the insights of religious and theological studies are put in conversation with the humanities and social sciences more broadly. As an academic and public intervention, *The Sexual Politics of Black Churches* analyzes the politics of sexuality within black churches and the communities they serve, and it also analyzes how these churches have participated in recent conversations about issues such as marriage equality, reproductive justice, and transgender visibility in American society. In so doing, it figures (racialized, gendered, and sexualized) black bodies (individual bodies and collective bodies) as sites of religious imagination and anxiety, as sources of social and political contestation, and as agential subjects that influence society across the spheres of culture, political, social, and religious life. While the push for marriage equality is no longer shaping the national debate and Proposition 8 now seems like a distant memory, *The Sexual Politics of Black Churches* still offers a timely and unique contribution to academic and popular conversations concerned with the shape of black churches and the communities that they serve.

PART ONE
A Call to Conversation

CHAPTER 1

Religion, Race, and Sexuality in American Culture

A Public Conversation

FEATURING VICTOR ANDERSON, SERENE JONES, AND BARBARA SAVAGE

MODERATED BY CATHY COHEN AND JOSEF SORETT

June 30, 2010, New York City

When the public conversation that stands at the center of chapter 1 one took place in June of 2010, President Barack Obama was approaching his first set of midterm elections, and vibrant, often vitriolic, debates were taking place about what was then referred to as "same-sex marriage." Black churches figured significantly, in many ways, in these debates, often as a bridge between two of the major movements for social change in twentieth-century American history—the modern civil rights movement that culminated in the 1960s and the gay liberation movement that followed, which eventually became organized around the fight to legalize same-sex marriage. In this narrative, black and gay identities and communities were often framed as mutually exclusive, at best, and pitted as fundamentally opposed to each other, at worst. As detailed in the introduction, "gay vs. black," "is gay the new black?" and "gay ain't the new black!" were just some of the phrases that emerged to account for these juxtapositions. And black churches were made to serve a range of arguments on all sides of the debates.

Wading into these debates, with support from the Arcus Foundation, Columbia University convened a group of scholars in New York City in June 2010 to better understand the role of black churches in the contemporary social and political landscape and in the specific context of debates about marriage. This convening began with an opening conversation at Union Theological Seminary. (The following day, a group of scholars continued the discussion downtown at what was then the Desmond Tutu Center, to present a series of reflections that over time developed into most of the chapters that follow.) While over a decade has passed since this gathering, and the political debates and social issues that define our conversations about sex and sexuality have significantly changed, much of what was shared reads as incredibly relevant, full of insights and fresh analysis, for the current moment.

This conversation was edited for length and clarity.

JOSEF SORETT: Good evening. I want to thank you all for coming out this evening for our public conversation on religion, race, and sexuality in American culture. It is good to see such a *good* turnout on this hot New York City night. Given that it was the summer months, we didn't know quite what to expect, but we figured it was better to have a room overflowing than a half-full room.

My name is **Josef Sorett**. I'm a member of the faculty here at Columbia and a comoderator on this evening's panel. I want to welcome you on behalf of our cosponsors, [including] of course, our host institution, Union Theological Seminary; and its dynamic president, Serene Jones, also a member of our panel; the Institute for Religion and Culture and Public Life at Columbia, directed by Mark C. Taylor; and the Institute of Research in African-American Studies, at Columbia, directed by Fredrick Harris. And, of course, our funder, the Arcus Foundation, which is supporting this important work.

We want to jump right into our conversation. It is indeed a privilege to introduce this distinguished panel, and I simply will give you their titles. And then we'll move right into conversation, as their CVs are too long to list all of the details. First, my comoderator this evening is **Cathy Cohen**. She is the David and Mary Winton Green Professor of Political Science and the College at the University of Chicago, as well as she is the principal investigator of the Black Youth Project. Closest to me here, we have **Victor Anderson**, professor of Christian ethics at the Divinity School and professor of African-American Studies and Religious Studies in the College of Arts and Sciences at Vanderbilt University, followed by **Barbara Savage**, who is a Geraldine R. Segal Professor of American Social Thought and professor of history at the University of Pennsylvania. And then we have President **Serene Jones**, our host this evening, who is the sixteenth president of the historic Union Theological Seminary in the City of New York.

There are so many directions that a conversation on religion, race, and sexuality could go, and rather than offering some set-up comments, I will simply pose a general question that our presenters will be invited to respond to in any way they like: In your scholarship, and in your life, and in light of recent events in American society, what is it about the intersections of the categories of religion, race, and sexuality that you find most troubling, most pressing, most encouraging, or most significant as we think about moving our conversation forward?

VICTOR ANDERSON: I'm glad to be here and to see so many friends I haven't seen in a long time. While waiting at the airport to fly here yesterday from Nashville, I overheard two voices behind me. As I listened to them —yeah, I was being nosy—the voices had a familiar sound that verged on stereotyping. I recognized the texture of the sounds. I knew that the two voices behind me were African Americans and that they were young. But I also recognized another texture in their voices, one that I've heard many times before in the close company of other gay friends. It was the sound in their voices that gave them away. I guess my "gaydar" really got into motion there—[slight laughter]—and I knew that seated behind me, also waiting for the flight, were two gay African American males. So I turned to look for other signs of whether my intuition was correct. I looked at their clothing, and they were dressed alike. Their white shorts were similar, and so was their white shirts. And I said, "Mm. That would be a kind of sign." When they got up from their seats, I notice the way they walked. They walked pretty normally, pretty much like me. But it had a kind of, a kind of *lift* to it, and I said, "that might be, that might be another sign!" [Audience laughs.] But when I got on the plane, and the plane got quiet, I had to go to the bathroom; as I got to the bathroom, I looked over at their seats in particular, and I saw their heads on each other's heads, and they were holding hands. And I said, "Wow. That's neat." I said to myself, "Oh, if that were only possible in the era in which I grew up. If such expressions of love and affection were ever possible in the years that I grew up." And then a more sinister thought came to me. It was this: "I wonder if they grew up in the church?" [Audience acknowledges Victor's point.] I don't know why I thought immediately that such expressions would be characteristic of someone *not* in the churches that I grew up in, whether Pentecostal, Assemblies of God, or Baptist.

Such wonderings have been going on within me for a very long time. I was a young minister, a youth minister, a pastor of two churches, and a brother, having a brother who was openly gay—myself having gone into the closet—because I was the minister of music at my church and an ordained associate minister. I was so envious of my brother that it caused a deep rift in my family. Sadly, my brother and I did not speak for years because I was jealous and resentful that he got a chance to come out, and I had to go deep into the closet to maintain the mask that my church placed upon me as the one in charge of religious worship and especially tasked with cultivating the spiritual formation of youths.

Now, as I was flying on the plane, looking at these two young brothers holding hands and clearly embracing each other with reciprocal affection, it occurred to me that times have changed—and times have not changed.

Times have moved on, and times have not moved on. I mean, rather than talking positively about love and intimacy between same-sex loving people, which I saw expressed by the two young black gay men on my plane as the shape of our religious discourse, I still find myself in discussions on the sexuality of black gay males theologically held under "the shadow of death"—in venues where I am present as a community educator focused on the sexual health of our communities. I try to move our discussions about black young gay people on from HIV and AIDS as a *disease* that stands over them as a "threat and shadow of their non-being," as if their sexualities are a perpetually menacing danger. And yet, I still find it very difficult in such an environment to move the discussion to liberatory or emancipatory practices beyond the shadow of death.

In our politics of church and society, it seems that if the church can render the beauty, intimacy, and affections that I witnessed between these two black gay men on the plane and turn their love into something diseased or sick, then somehow the gospel of Jesus Christ would make more sense regarding homosexuality because now being sick, they too can sit at Bethesda's pool. [A biblical reference to the healing miracle in John 5: 1–15.] Now, they too can sit at the pool. Now they too could wait for the promised "age to come" and participate in something miraculous, being touched by sacred healing water. And then, maybe, even for them, some angel may put their poor sick souls into the water, and they would be healed. Only if we were sick, the church seems to say, then the church could deal with us. But the politics that I want to talk about this evening is beyond HIV, AIDS, and death.

I wonder if it's possible in the black church and black religiosity to move our politics away from death and the shadow of death towards the politics of liberatory love. I'm not talking about mere acceptance; I've seen how mere acceptance works. I've seen it as a choir director and church musician, a gospel performer. I've seen how the stereotypes circulate and bind other people to the kinds of closets within the churches that make them acceptable. I'm talking about real, genuine expressions and displays of affection and care for each other; I'm talking about intimacy. The black church—like the one I grew up in—has a long ways to go before such displays of intimacy that I think are most characteristic of the gospel are actuality. Not the gospel in its *ideal promises*, but the gospel in its concrete actuality. My primary concern is this: What is the meaning of the gospel today? Not for people who are sick, people who are diseased, people who are dying, but what is the meaning and the message of the gospel for those of us who want to love one another as the expression of our being, as displays of intimacy for one another? My other concern is whether our spiritual communities are capable—no, not capable, but capable and *willing*—to put at risk their roles as regulatory police over black sexuality? Whether our black churches are capable and willing to, in fact, follow the way of the cross? That is the way of self-denial, the way of self-giving, and perhaps even the way of self-dying. Whether the black church is capable and willing to come up to that point where Jesus on the Cross had to come, namely, to the very place of self-negation, for the Kingdom of God's sake? [Audience acknowledges point.]

"What is the meaning and significance of these kinds of questions of religion, culture, and race?" It takes a new vision, but it also takes new power. It takes a new infusion of love. I'm thinking of bell hooks's book, *Salvation: Black People and Love* (2001). I think she got something right in that book. The salvation of black people will be very much tied to the extent and the power to which we can extend love—not only for its most privileged members but for whosoever will.

That's my opening comment.

BARBARA SAVAGE: Thank you. I certainly want to thank everybody for coming out tonight. And with this sort of general question, I want to approach it in a much less *eloquent* way. And perhaps, a much less moving way, as well. But I feel like part of what we're being asked to talk about and to deal with tonight also has to do with thinking about strategies; or trying to think more specifically about how African American churches can better approach a number of issues that come from intersections between religion, race, and sexuality. And one of the encouraging things about this gathering, and some of the work that's been done that preceded it, is an attempt to disaggregate black public opinion in a way that represents the *vast* diversity among African Americans—and among African American religious people and religious organizations. This move away from monolithic thinking, I think, is absolutely the first step in beginning to deal with the complexities that black people themselves share and live with around this debate, and this issue, and a number of issues as well. It is also a moment where we might think about African American churches, and their responses to issues around sexuality, within the broader context of American religion and American religious institutions. Black churches certainly have been pulled out and especially criticized—and I don't think unfairly, but criticized—for their *failings* on this issue. But it is important to remember that some of this is also shared very much with American religious institutions much more broadly. I just want to stake that out.

The other thing that I want to have us think about some is the importance—and I say this as a historian—of thinking with historical specificity about some of these issues as part of our strategic planning. Because in the past, with a number of issues (including marriage and even "Don't Ask, Don't Tell"), there has been a tendency to overlook the differences in other social movements—especially social movements involving African Americans. And to move so deftly to comparisons and analogs that are often misfits can lead to even greater misunderstandings. And I think we'll have an opportunity to talk about that, as well.

For me, the most pressing issues in this conversation really have to do with the role and the work of black people who are gay and who are willing to stand up and do something from *within* African American churches. I think part of what we're all hoping for is a lesbian and gay rights movement that is more racially and economically inclusive. That's one of the overall goals of the foundation, and I'm very supportive of that. But it really led me to begin to think: Is there a black LGBT agenda? What does it look like? Is it different from or similar to or overlapping with the ways in which we've thought about those issues in a larger context? And more specifically: Could there be a specific agenda formulated by *religious* people who are also lesbian and gay and transgender? And what would that look like? Is there a special, particular role for black religious gay and lesbian people to play within African American churches? To ask questions from within and to work within? And what would those issues look like? Would those issues look more like some social service or economic issues, also included in these broader concepts of justice, that are driving a set of the larger issues that we're familiar with?

And it also seems to me there's another big question if we're going to think about what can be done from *within* African American churches. Is there not a special and particular role that black women—gay *and* straight—have to play, must play, can play in this debate? And there are other subsets within that, having to do with generation and class, that complicate that picture even more. And so those are the questions that came to my mind.

But I do feel this is a moment of encouragement—just looking at this room, and certainly this work that's been done. Reports have been written; attempts have been made to really deal with some hard questions having to do with notions of black masculinity, which is always on the table, which is always at stake in these debates, in very complicated and historically specific ways. But I would still then ask the question about the role of black women, in particular, and in part because they represent such an *enormous* part of African American religious life and culture. And their voices are so very overlooked, silenced, missing, from this broader debate—among ourselves, but certainly in the larger debates as well. So those are the questions and ideas that came to me from the broad opening.

SERENE JONES: I just want to begin by saying how important, over the last thirty years, the work of Cathy and Barbara and Victor has been in this whole area, in this collective wisdom and wrestling with this. What I want to talk about, very briefly, is this question in the context of Union Theological Seminary. I've been here now for two years. And it's a *powerful* question to ask in this context because if you were to ask most people who know something about the history of theological education, they would say that Union Theological Seminary is the place in which *black* theology was birthed. And then they would go along and say, "And it is also the place where *queer* theology was birthed. And where LGBT issues came to the fore for the first time." You look at the timeline of our school's history, and both of these tracks, next to each other, have a long history of "firsts" in this school. What that means in terms of our present-day experience is fascinating. And I'm going to talk about the present student body—and there's enough of them here that I'm sure that all the things that I say that are wrong they will quickly correct. [Audience laughs.]

I echo Victor's comment about how much has changed and how much hasn't changed. At one level, much *hasn't* changed. We don't have anywhere near the level of racial diversity on our faculty that it would take to make this a truly excellent institution with regards to engaging these questions. And in our student body, while it's a very diverse student body, wrestling with questions of race and sexuality continues to occupy a lot of energy and time in very positive ways with respect to the constant *wrestling* and argumentation that takes place in Old Testament courses and ethics courses and theology courses. It's here all the time. I want to add that students who have been active in the black caucus and the LGBT caucus both confront the fact that when they leave this place, it's a challenge to figure out what kind of pulpit they will step into. They've come here to get a professional degree, and there's not a world waiting to embrace them. So, for instance, for the LGBT students, we've created our own commissioning service where we give them a ritual of a kind of quasi-ordination in a context that most of them will never experience. So, much hasn't changed. But, much *has* changed. And there are three indications of this that I want to put before us to reflect on where the future is going.

While we still have a very vibrant black caucus and LGBT caucus, the three caucuses that actually on an ongoing basis claim the most attention of the students are the arts caucus, the interfaith caucus, and a program called the "edible churchyard," which has to do with environmental issues. When those caucuses meet, the room is jam-packed with people. And so it raises a question about identity configuration and what it means that these three categories have come to the fore in terms of how people actually identify their deepest pleasures and interests.

Secondly, we are experiencing at Union the effects of the demographic shifts in religion in North America that are being felt everywhere. Being in New York City and where we are located, I think we feel them more acutely; and we're probably about five years ahead of the rest of the country. But our two largest-growing groups are Latino and African American Pentecostals—many of whom are also Roman Catholic—and others who are "unaffiliated," or who have left traditional churches and are yoga instructors. I use that as an image for them. And what's *fascinating* is that these two groups, while they appear to be on the opposite ends of the social and political spectrum, actually share a lot more in common than the group that Union ten years ago would've claimed at its center. Which would have been mainline African American and traditionally white Protestant churches. What these two communities share in common is that their religious experience is very *embodied*. And it's about the rituals of pleasure and embodiment. It's about everyday practices and how one connects with the earth and the people around you. It's focused on languages of beauty and of pleasure. And this is where the question of sexuality, I think, becomes quite interesting. They both exist in a realm of a theology that is deeply erotic, as opposed to the theological vocabulary and traditions of the mainline that has been here historically. So in both of these worlds, sexuality is coming to play a central role in ways that have not even been considered on the stage of religiosity in North America today. And race and religion and sexuality are all at the center of that.

What I want to say in conclusion is that there is a *huge* generational gap in theological education. The students coming in today are living in a theological imaginative world that is profoundly different than the students that came here twenty years ago. And it's more than just a twenty-year gap; it's probably more like a hundred-year gap with respect to what it demarks. The theology that is driving these areas of growth has—and this is going to sound very theological (I'm a theologian, so I'll just jump right into it)—it has a metaphysics driving behind it that needs to be profoundly engaged and hasn't been. The line between God and the world is fluid. The metaphysics between the body of the self and the other is fluid. And the whole logic of pleasure is being turned inside out and upside down. And finding that theological language is fascinating. So, that's just a bunch of issues to put on the table, but I think it frames in the present-day context the things we're wrestling with here.

CATHY COHEN: Not to make a comment, but just to ask the next question. I have to say, this feels much like church because I see people with hand fans. [Audience laughs.] Or at least it feels like *my* church! Except I haven't heard any "amens," and I figure they *all* deserved that. So I'll go onto the next question—and I want to kind of *push* on this question of the "generational gap." Because I think often we're looking at their ability to embrace a different type of *liberatory* theology. However, in work that we've done through the Black Youth Project, we've found, for example, that a majority of young black people [ages] fifteen to twenty-five state that homosexuality is *always* wrong. A majority of [them in] polls oppose same-sex marriage, and a majority believe that the government should promote heterosexual marriage. And they are the *only* group of young people for which a majority agree with these statements.

Now, some have said this is the "*black* church effect." That the reason these young people feel this way is that they've been brought up and socialized in or near black churches. So I guess I'd like you to speak to first of all, is this a "black church effect"? And, if it's not, that's fine. But if it is, what are the possibilities, theologically and in practice, for intervening around these attitudes having to do with LGBT issues and race?

BARBARA SAVAGE: I would just say we both credit and discredit "the black church" with powers that it does and does not have. So, is this a church effect or is this a *hip-hop* effect?

CATHY COHEN: Can I push back on that? Actually hip-hop has a positive correlation with *positive* attitudes [toward LGBT issues]. So, actually the more hip-hop they listened to, the more, in fact, they're willing to be embracing of homosexuality. And religion has a *negative* effect. So, the more religious they are, the more, in fact, they're oppositional to the equality of LGBT folks.

BARBARA SAVAGE: Okay. So you *did* set me up for that. [Audience laughs.] That's very surprising and disappointing. Because I think we do assume that it is a generational shift, and certainly in other groups it is a generational shift. Do you think it has anything to do with the ferocity of youthful religiosity? That's there's something about them being young and religious that's different?

VICTOR ANDERSON: Cathy, your findings don't surprise me. In my work in the community, I find fifteen to twenty-four-year-olds to be some of the most conservative regarding their attitudes about partnership, about sex—even if they don't live up to their conservative sexual values. This is especially so for those who identify as born-again Christians when compared to others who appear rather moderately evangelical. So, some of their attitudes may well reflect their churches' attitudes about sex and sexuality. Some may think of themselves as conservative, but I talk to a good number who are more worried about having transgressed their own conservative moral values, either by engaging in same-sex sex, or having premarital sex, or doing what used to simply be called "being freaky." In their sexual practices, they may, in fact, be doing the very things that they say they wouldn't do. But I find in talking with them, they tend to be very conservative. I'm not sure whether they're saying what I want to hear or if they're really reflecting, in their own language, their moral judgments.

What Ann Rich has called "compulsory heteronormativity" requires a measure of conformity of them for their own sustainability within the community. I saw this in the church of my youth. Our pastor just didn't believe [and many still don't] that there is a sex orgy-like mentality among kids in high school and in the church. And the church turns a blind eye to this possibility because it says, "not our kids." That gives them a certain luxury, a certain privilege. If the church surmises that they're not capable of doing such things, then they can enjoy the privileges of the church. But they also enjoy the privilege of transgression. And so, more often than not, when I intervene, it's usually at the level where they're coming in for testing.

SERENE JONES: Just to put an exclamation point on what you've just said, Victor, I'm always cautious of equating what people say they *believe* religiously with they actually *do*, religiously. And, while this statistic is not related to the black church, specifically, in the evangelical world, the gap between expressed opinion about premarital sex and *actual* premarital sex means there's more premarital sex in the evangelical world than the liberal world. Statistically, it's a higher percentage. It gives you pause, in terms of what this statistic means. Which then turns around and suggests that if one *doesn't* accept that, what kinds of practices are going to actually intervene on the ground where people live and find the language that holds them? That is the challenge.

JOSEF SORETT: Another follow-up question. More generally, in recent years, there's been an effort to draw comparisons, theoretically and practically, between the modern civil rights movement of the 1960s and the more recent LGBT rights movement of the last decade or two. I'm interested to hear the panel's thoughts on the possibilities and problems posed by this connection. As well as, more generally: What might those engaged in the fight for full acceptance and inclusion of LGBT persons learn from the successes and *failures*—right?—of the 1960s? We live in a moment that, on one hand, elects the first black president, but then we've also witnessed the stark racial disparities of the prison industrial complex. So, I guess, most shortly: How do these claims of postracial America sound for those of us who might imagine "posthomophobic" America?

BARBARA SAVAGE: I'll do one part of it, which is the civil rights analogy. Again this goes back to my earlier concern about the importance of historic specificity and the ways in which *the* civil rights movement exists as something that has quasi-sacred status among African Americans who associate it with a very finite period and set of political issues. I think to the extent that there is some historical attachment to that term, there has been a *tremendous* disconnect and resentment—whether fair or not—about the use of the term "civil rights." Which I think is used to mean "human rights," and the kinds of rights that the state grants—what one expects from the state. But ignoring, I think, the kind of historic attachment African Americans have for the term has just caused a tremendous amount of misunderstanding and resentment. Or it at least has been a stated reason for disagreement around some gay and lesbian issues. The disagreement may have been there anyway and regardless, but I do think that exacerbated at least the difference between the two communities.

The other thing to be reminded of, of course, is the religiously conservative nature of the civil rights movement. And let me be clear that, for people like King and others who were at the forefront of that movement, it's always important to be reminded that that cost King his membership in the National Baptist Convention. And that there was only a minority of black religious people who were abiding with the kinds of claims that King and others were making.

This is something I *always* have to remind my students of. I think that black churches have benefited from the association with the successes of the civil rights movement. But in fact, it was a minority of a minority of a minority *movement* itself.

And the other caveat when you're talking about social reform movements is that there are analogies to be drawn. I had a reporter call me the other day for a story he was doing on "Don't Ask, Don't Tell." And he said, "What about all those people who are saying, 'the arguments against gays and lesbians in the military are *exactly* the same arguments that were raised against the desegregation of the military for African Americans?'" I said, "of *course* they're the same arguments. But that doesn't get us anywhere." Saying that then doesn't mean African Americans kind of fall in line and follow. Nor does that, as I said, constitute a strategy; it's an observation, and there are limits to it.

VICTOR ANDERSON: My dear friend, the late Vincent Harding, changed for me the whole question of whether this ought to rightly be called a "civil rights issue." His book *Hope and History* (1991) was written to teach high school students the historical significance of telling the story. He believed that the story hasn't changed. So the question about a postracial society in America might be best understood as a fantasy or a dream.

But even so, professor Harding argued that "it is a misnomer to refer to the kinds of association we're talking about in terms of civil rights." He says that the civil rights movement was, in fact, a "third freedom movement," and that we would do well to understand that what was happening there was not simply the affirmation and articulation of a set of rights that are to be distributable among citizens. For him, "nothing was more at stake than the freedoms to exercise those kinds of rights." And so, the questions for same-sex-loving, same-gender-loving people about marriage, about enjoying those same benefits as heterosexual people, are not simply about articulating the right to *have* such rights. Rather it's the right to *enjoy* those kinds of privileges and rights that belong to all citizens. And for him [Harding], telling the story of the civil rights movement or the freedom movement of the 1950s and '60s has to go on for *generative* purposes. Not for regulative purposes but for generative purposes. It's important to keep telling the story, lest we forget and become indifferent to the most powerful force of American citizenship—namely, the right to enjoy the free exercise of those privileges that belong to every citizen. In that sense, it's not just about civil rights (and I think it is) that affect same-sex-loving people but also the liberty to enjoy those privileges that every other citizen enjoys.

SERENE JONES: Josef and I were recently in a conversation with a group of theologically minded people in which you could see *the* storyline of the civil rights movement. If you take it, and put it in a biblical text, it's the story of Exodus. And it has a certain kind of imaginative framework within which you could understand certain kinds of conflict. And you have a particular way of identifying who is who in that scenario, which at some level was helpful but at some other level just stopped the whole conversation from moving forward. Because there was not a larger pool of imaginative resources to be deployed around race and sexuality. Those other storylines wouldn't *displace* that story.

CATHY COHEN: I'm going to ask one last question, and then we're going to open it up. In reading the report from the convenings and focus groups, I was struck by the fact that a number of respondents agreed that the discourse on "sin"—in particular where we communicate *tolerance of sin* as "we love the sinner, but we hate the sin." That discourse on sin would always limit really significant inroads to LGBT activism in churches. So I'm wondering how you might help us think about and deal with the dominant framework of sin in churches and religion.

SERENE JONES: All right, I'm going to go first because I have a very strong opinion. First of all, I don't think the language about sin, in its totality, is the problem. I actually *like* "sin." I like the language of "sin." I like both the sinner and the sin. [Audience applauds and laughs.] I think the sin language in the church has done a lot of good across time and space.

One of the challenges is to figure out where you locate the fact that human beings are capable of doing profound and sustained harm to one another, and fail to even acknowledge that they're even doing it. That's what "sin" marks. And so we don't want to lose that category, but we need to rethink what it means to engage in it and move out of it, through grace. So, I think we need to revitalize "sin language."

BARBARA SAVAGE: Well, maybe one way of thinking about this is by examples: I don't mean the definition of what a sin is. One place in particular to do this is to talk about shifting attitudes towards divorce, which has required a *tremendous* amount of change within churches. I mean, Jesus speaks about divorce, but he never speaks about homosexuality. And yet, in the early twentieth century, when there was a liberalization of divorce laws in this country, it was a tremendous church-state conflict. So there were questions about, for example, whether someone who was divorced could be a bishop or a preacher; and this was a tremendous debate, certainly in the Methodist church and other churches as well.

And so, if you chart out a particular set of *examples*, and talk about the process by which what was considered sinful was renegotiated over the course of "X" number of decades and debates to where it was no longer considered a sin, that may be at least a way to foster some discourse.

VICTOR ANDERSON: That leads me to talk about "sin" as transgression. That is, the very idea of defining sin as a set of practices is a very difficult thing. This is why we can never come to any theological agreement on just what is a sin. We're constantly revising our understanding of what sin is. Basically, the language of sin, or "sin talk," is a way of regulating practices. And some of the ways that we regulate our practices are death dealing, bringing about so much guilt and shame that many of young people are even driven to suicide or near suicide. I know because I was one of those kids teetering on suicide. Some of the ways in which sin operates and circulates are not only death dealing but also life-*denying*. That is, we live our lives under the shadow and the weight of sin such that the fulfillment of life—the abundance of life that Christianity was to bring in, usher in—is cut off. *That's* sin. That's transgressing the very will of God—which is that we enjoy our lives to the fullest through the very gifts that God has given us, in our bodies and through our bodies, to love one another. Transgression is allowing the languages of sin to destroy and negate the love with which God has endowed us, in and through our bodies: that's sin.

Questions and Answers

AUDIENCE MEMBER: Good evening. My name is Michael and I'm a graduate student at Union Theological Seminary. I have a question because of an episode that occurred at my church not too long ago. I petitioned to have a license to preach, and the following week a gospel singer appeared at our church. She talked about Jesus, Jesus, Jesus, and said that her brother died five years ago. Well that's very sad, and that's very unfortunate. But he wrote a book, and one side of the book was about "race." That was interesting. But then she flipped the book and said, "he was delivered from homosexuality." So, what happened was that it caused a murmur in the church because we don't talk that kind of language from the pulpit. Which affirmed my earlier research and my thesis that the black church has become more homo-*intolerant* than homophobic: we've learned some lessons from the majority community. We found out in my research and in talking to people that it appears that certain people from evangelical Christian communities have come into black churches and used key words: *Jesus* and *race*. And then they influence homosexuality. How can we address the intersection between the black church and white evangelical churches on that particular issue?

VICTOR ANDERSON: I think part of it has to do with the *over*-articulation of what constitutes the mind of the traditional black church. I'm often amazed by how many people think that the black church is revolutionary, radical, fundamentally prophetic, and liberationist. [Audience snickers.] Ok? I don't recall that church in my experience.

Growing up in Chicago, we listened to Moody Bible Institute as much as we listened to Black Radio Sunday Church Broadcasts. Many teachers from Moody Bible Institute would come to our churches and hold classes. Our churches were very open to what I would call a mild evangelical confluence, which has always *been* there in the black churches. Black churches are basically evangelical in orientation.

But I have become increasingly amazed by how many black churches today are increasingly fundamentalist—[audience acknowledges point]—which is not characteristic of the ethos that characterized traditional black churches. So, I want to shift a little bit. It's not so much the evangelical influence that becomes so *dangerous* to traditional black churches. There is an increasing fundamentalism—an increasing literalism—that has taken hold in many of our black churches and pulpits. We have to ask about the role of increasing fundamentalism.

NEXT AUDIENCE MEMBER: Just a quick question about family and marriage and sexuality and black communities in general. None of you touched on that issue, and it seems to me that sexuality in the black communities, in general, is a taboo subject. I mean, we can't talk about HIV AIDS; we can't talk about anything. I remember sitting in the back of the congregation and the conversation was about gay and lesbian rights, and one person whispered, "I don't even know how to talk to my own kids about sex. Now how am I supposed to talk about homosexuality or whatever?" So I would like to see if the panel could address that issue.

BARBARA SAVAGE: I think that's a really good question. I think it's something we need to be reminded of, because it's not as if there is this fluid conversation that goes on about other issues that are related to sex. There is a way in which silence and secrecy around sexuality in general has been especially been carried over into the ways in which African American churches have responded to the question of homosexuality.

I guess the broader question is: How do you then break the taboo against talking about the taboo? It's difficult to figure out where the entry point is, in the face of that. But I think you're absolutely right that it is an ethos. And it's *there*. It's important to be reminded of the general unease we're talking about in matters having to do with sex and sexuality.

SERENE JONES: I think it also needs to be said that you can have churches that are very LGBT friendly and still don't talk about sex at all. I mean, the discourse of sexuality is completely absent. I also think the Bible is one way in, because there is every kind of sex imaginable! All *over* the place. [Audience laughs.]

NEXT AUDIENCE MEMBER: I'm Kendall. I want to describe, very briefly, two possible responses to the problem that's called "homophobia in black churches." One response is the example of someone who is a child of the Church of God in Christ: Bishop Yvette Flunder, who decided, I think prophetically, a few years ago to go establish the Fellowship of Affirming Ministries. I've attended a couple of their services; the meetings are almost overwhelmingly same-gendered loving people. They are profoundly spiritual. And very central is the message of embracing the exile.

The other is a much more explicitly political and secular response. That is to say, it does not try to respond to the politics of the black church in the language of sin or with a better theological argument that recognizes that the black church, like the Christian Church in general, is in a position of power. And that what we need is a secular politics of resistance that resists the claims of *any* church, right?

I'm a child of the black church—my grandfather was a Baptist preacher. I left his church. And even though I go to another church, I have embraced a secular politics. So, of those two possible responses, which do you think at this particular moment would be the most effective response to this increase in fundamentalism that you've identified? That's a relatively recent historical phenomenon, because I do remember the progressive black church in which women were allowed leadership roles and we marched from the church to the courthouse, when I was a kid.

BARBARA SAVAGE: Those are two very difficult polar positions to think about. In thinking about the secular politics of resistance, it's a church-state question. It's a conflict between a belief in religious freedom—however abhorrent we might think those beliefs are—and the ability of the state to resist the import of those beliefs into policies. The most vivid examples have been around gay marriage issues and the *inability* of most people to separate civil marriage as opposed to marriage as the religious ritual.

SERENE JONES: Another dimension to it is the subject of choosing. In religious communities actually, it's not often a matter of thinking about where you are in that choice. Another way of saying this is that this church-state religious freedom language may not hold in its entirety the real complexity of that question. It happens outside of that frame.

BARBARA SAVAGE: Except when the state actually, you know, passes a proposition.

SERENE JONES: Right. Right. Which is about choice.

VICTOR ANDERSON: This is such an existential question for me. As a minister in the church, I baptized kids and families in the church. For years I served as the chaplain of a funeral home and did funerals for gay people in the community whose churches rejected them and refused to perform their funeral and burials. As chaplain of the funeral home, it was my duty to make sure that they had the decent respect due to any human being, to give an honorable account of their living and their dying.

And since having become an expatriate from the church, I lived with a certain kind of anxiety of displacement for years. Because the question for me wasn't just about the freedom to pack up my bags and move to another camp that was more accepting. Usually, when I did things like that, I found the camp I found myself in even more intolerable than the camp I left, on a whole lot of subjects. [Audience laughs.] Nonconformity in those camps can seem kind of like discipline and punishment for not really being among the saints. I'm not saying that's what drove me back to the traditional church, to which I have recently returned. But I think people are in churches for a lot of reasons. The question is really similar to this: Why do same-sex-loving people stay in the churches that abuse them all the time? And the answer is complex.

Because for some of us, it's a matter of our memories; for some of us, we're there not because of the preaching. Some of us are there for prayer. Some of us are there because there are things we grew up with that we're accustomed to, that we take delight in, and they fill our memories with what is familiar. So there are a lot of subjective reasons and values that are not simply transferable by taking one's bags and moving to another camp. Sometimes the other camp can't fill the gap that displacement from those familiar values leaves.

There followed a series of rapid questions from the audience.

NEXT AUDIENCE MEMBER: It seems to be from the perspective of the United States. But yet, you know, there's also the exporting of hate, when you look at Uganda and you look at Malawi. Could you talk a little bit about the connection that's happening overseas, where they're legislating putting people to death because you're LGBT?

NEXT AUDIENCE MEMBER: I have questions of how you define *black churches*. Are they [determined by the] percentage of people within the churches or by ideology or is it, "you know when you're there?"

NEXT AUDIENCE MEMBER: Generally, how do we get away from discussing homophobia every time we talk about sexuality? Because I think that when we do that, we are reverting to talking about heterosexism, and not talking about the embodied living of gay people, right? So how do we talk about gay people's experience within the church and the construction of churches? And how they, in fact, liberate themselves?

NEXT AUDIENCE MEMBER: We are talking about opening dialogue [about black LGBT issues] within the churches. We are also thinking about other strategies. I'm wondering how effective you feel such things would be?

JOSEF SORETT: Professor Hendricks in the back. You will have the final question. And then our panelists will have three minutes to respond to any of this final series of questions.

OBERY HENDRICKS: I'd like to comment on Matthew 25. Jesus speaks very clearly about the poor and the least of these. And there's no denying that LGBTQ today would fall into the category of those whom society deems "the least." And if you don't care for them, you're going to hell. This is the strongest judgment that Jesus gives us.

My question is this. A lot of people will point to scriptures that appear to explicitly speak disparagingly about LGBTQ folks. We've all heard people say something to the effect of, "I know the Bible says this, that and the other." It's tough to get people to look beyond passages such as these.

And because there does not seem to be a similarly explicit or concrete affirmation of LGBTQ folks in the Bible, how do we get beyond the impasse of those passages that appear to do precisely the opposite?

SERENE JONES: All right. I will answer one of the questions. I think that as a biblical scholar, you have framed that well. But what it also points to, in terms of Scripture, is how important it is as a context for imaging. It suggests patterns that are provocative. And this is why Bible professors are so important in the midst of all this. I mean, just what you just did is a witness to the importance of your question. That's a nonanswer, isn't it?

OBERY HENDRICKS: I like it though. [More laughter.]

BARBARA SAVAGE: I'll just speak to the question of strategies from within black churches. And whether and how gay men and lesbians and transgender people who are within churches can organize themselves and find the courage to speak truths to the power within the churches they claim as "home." And in what ways we can help empower ourselves to be willing and able to do that. And to then take the consequences of that. Which may include being forced into exile and alienation. I think that's what's at greatest risk.

But what would it mean if everyone in a church who was gay stood up one Sunday morning, said that, and forced a different kind of conversation? What would that strategy look like? What would we be asking for? I mean, what would that kind of agenda look like from within African American churches? That's an unanswered question, but it's one that really holds a certain amount of hope and promise. But one that would require a great deal of courage.

VICTOR ANDERSON: I'm going to try and take at least two of the questions that I heard and put them in the context of globalization. We once thought of the United States and a lot of the North Atlantic world as *the only* center of the world. Everything else was peripheral. Well, we live in a polycentric environment today. There are multiple centers, and they're emerging all over the world. We're having African evangelists come to the United States only to remind us that we have fallen; they come as prophets, urging us to take up our mantle again and be the city that sits on a hill. We [black Christians and churches] have to broaden our conversation on religion, race, and sexuality to realize that that there are multiple centers we enter into and others outside our circles of direct influence, each making demands on our individual loyalties. The vision of black church as an all-comprehensive institution may have served its purpose. But our lives have been changed by many competing centers that we participate in, give our loyalty to, and intersect among ethnicities beyond our own local tribes. The world has, in some sense, been embodying that kind of change—we call it globalization, but it's really another kind of expansionism. And so we have to be on guard then. For both the good and the evil that world brings. For sure, more freedom is spread, but at the same time, more domination, hurt, pain, and suffering also accompany it.

We have to also be doubly aware of how democratic powers have the power to be demonic, to control and determine the kinds of relationships we have. And so, it's more of a warning to always be on guard. I see that as a kind of Christian duty—to be aware, to keep both eyes open, for the thief cometh but to kill and destroy. And so we have to understand that when we take the role of the thief, the danger lies within—as in all fascisms. Be on guard for the propensity of our own capacities to participate in evil.

JOSEF SORETT: Let's close on that sobering note. [Audience laughs.] Thank you for your participation! And let's give our panel and our hosts a round of applause.

PART TWO

Sacred Text, Social Authority, Sexual Difference

CHAPTER 2

Jephthah's Daughter and #SayHerName

NYASHA JUNIOR

In my experience as a member of church communities, I have never heard the biblical narrative of the unnamed daughter of Jephthah (Judges 11:29–40) preached from a pulpit or read in Bible study.[1] As a teacher of undergraduate and graduate students in religious studies, it is rare that a student has heard of this text. It is not part of the canon within a canon. Although it appears as part of the biblical canon, it is not a text that is frequently engaged. In contrast to Judges 11, Genesis 22, the binding of Isaac or "Aqedah" is a much more familiar text. In this text, Abraham nearly sacrifices his only son Isaac but, miraculously, a ram is caught and serves as the sacrifice.[2]

I assigned the story of Jephthah's Daughter to a Hebrew class once, and after we read it together, a student yelled out, "This is not uplifting!" He was right. The story of Jephthah's Daughter does not involve a miraculous healing or longed-for pregnancy. There is no water from a rock. There is no last-minute ram in a bush that saves a (male) child whose name is included in the text (Isaac) from being sacrificed by a father (Abraham). There is no joyful family reunion or happy ending in Judges 11. The story of Jephthah's Daughter is an intentional, deliberate killing.

Comparisons between the unnamed woman in Judges 11 and Isaac in Genesis 22 have become commonplace among biblical scholars from across the political and ideological spectrum.[3] This essay revisits this comparison as an interpretative strategy for reading the story of Jephthah's daughter. I consider how contemporary activism for black girls and women who have been victims of police brutality may highlight some of the benefits and drawbacks of interpreting her story based on this comparison. First, I give a brief overview of the story of Jephthah's Daughter in Judges 11. Second, I provide background on the #SayHerName campaign and the biblical narrative of Jephthah's daughter. Third, I consider the types of questions raised when we examine the comparison of Judges 11 and Genesis 22 in light of the #SayHerName campaign. Fourth, I explore how the comparison of these two texts may obscure the state-sanctioned nature of the violence against Jephthah's Daughter that does not meet resistance from the community. I conclude with further discussion of the implications of this work, especially for black churches.[4]

Jephthah's Daughter

In the Bible, the book of Judges is set during the period of the judges, also referred to as chieftains.[5] According to a biblical chronology, this is a transitional era after the exodus from Egypt but before the rise of the Israelite united monarchy. Various judges rule over the Israelites, but no single leader is governing all of the tribes. The Israelites are fighting Philistines, the Canaanites, and other groups who regard the Israelites as invading enemies and seek to defend their territory. In addition, the Israelites are engaged in intertribal conflicts. This is a period of instability as characterized by Judges 17:6: "In those days there was no king in Israel; all the people did what was right in their own eyes" (cf. Judges 18:1; 19:1, 21:25).[6]

Jephthah, one of the biblical judges, is a crafty negotiator who has talked his way into a leadership position with the Israelites. The majority of Judges 11 focuses on his rise to power (vv. 1–10) and his role as a warrior (vv. 11–33). When negotiating a land dispute with the Ammonites, he declares, "Let the Lord, who is judge, decide today for the Israelites or for the Ammonites" (Judges 11:27b). When he eventually goes into battle with the Ammonites, he makes a vow to the Lord, which would be standard practice in the ancient Near East, to influence the judgment of a deity in one's favor (cf. Numbers 21:2–3). He promises, "If you will give the Ammonites into my hand, then whoever comes out of the doors of my house to meet me, when I return victorious from the Ammonites, shall be the Lord's, to be offered up by me as a burnt offering" (Judges 11:30–31). When he returns from his victory, his only child, a daughter, comes to greet him. When Jephthah sees her, he tears his clothes as a sign of mourning and claims that he cannot renege on his vow. She acknowledges his vow and requests a two-month reprieve with her friends. After two months, she returns. According to the text, Jephthah fulfills his vow, but the text does not provide details regarding the sacrifice of Jephthah's Daughter. The text does not narrate the death of Jephthah's Daughter. It explains simply that after a two-month reprieve, "she returned to her father, who did with her according to the vow he had made" (Judges 11:39).[7]

In a text about her experience, Jephthah's Daughter remains marginalized. We are not told how she died or given information on her burial. Jephthah's Daughter is yet another narrative of the expendability of women and their bodies. #SayHerName asks us to center the victim of the narrative. It demands that we acknowledge and remember black girls and women who have been victims of police brutality and state-sanctioned violence just as we do with their male counterparts.

#SayHerName

The murder of unarmed black men and boys by police is not a new phenomenon in the United States, but in response to the 2013 acquittal of George Zimmerman in the shooting death of Trayvon Martin, Patrisse Cullors, Alicia Garza, and Opal Tometi popularized the hashtag #BlackLivesMatter. In doing so, they launched what has become a global #BlackLivesMatter movement.[8] The online and offline use of the #BlackLivesMatter hashtag and hashtags of the names of the deceased assisted in galvanizing protests, community organizing, and ongoing advocacy efforts for racial justice and criminal justice reform.[9] The deaths of Trayvon Martin, Michael Brown, Eric Garner, and others would likely have remained local incidents without significant national and international press coverage without social media's collective efforts to publicize their murders and subsequent legal cases against their assailants.[10]

In popular media, black men and boys are regarded as the victims of police profiling, the school-to-prison pipeline, and mass incarceration. Although police violence affects black women and girls disproportionately, they are often not included in narratives surrounding police violence. We do not hear women and girls' names such as Aiyana Stanley-Jones, Sandra

Bland, Korryn Gaines, Tanisha Anderson, Natasha McKenna, and Rekia Boyd as part of the standard litany of victims of police brutality. Furthermore, when black women are victimized, there tends to be more media victim-blaming than with black men. Police-involved incidents with black women are more often treated as local, isolated incidents rather than as part of the national phenomenon of police violence. Also, when police-involved incidents related to black women are linked to domestic violence and intimate partner violence, they are regarded as private issues.

Founded by Kimberlé Williams Crenshaw, the African American Policy Forum launched the #SayHerName campaign.[11] On May 20, 2015, the campaign began in New York City at an event called #SayHerName: A Vigil in Memory of black Women and Girls Killed by the Police. The campaign aims to document the disproportionate police brutality experienced by black women and girls. It advocates for an end to police violence, including sexual assault and sexual harassment. Also, it seeks a more gender-inclusive approach to gain justice for victims of racialized police violence and highlights issues of race, gender, and sexuality among victims of police brutality. #SayHerName acknowledges this sometimes selective outrage; black women defend black communities, but black women victims do not receive the same number of protest marches, vigils, petitions, or crowdfunding as their male counterparts. The aim of these advocates is not at all to dismiss or discount the experiences of black men and boys but to call attention to the experiences of black women and girls.

#SayHerName and Comparisons of Genesis 22 and Judges 11

Scholars compare Genesis 22 and Judges 11 for several different reasons. For example, Jack M. Sasson uses the comparison to portray Jephthah as playing a high-stakes game of "chicken" with God. Sasson writes, "Jephthah will go eyeball to eyeball with God, fully expecting him to blink first—just as God did for Abraham when the life of Isaac was at stake."[12] Susan Niditch uses it to make a point about theological views in ancient Israel. She writes, "The authors of Genesis 22 and this passage understand that all life is God's to bestow or take back."[13] J. Alberto Soggin uses it as evidence for views about human sacrifice in ancient Israel. He writes, "Here we have one of the very rare cases of human sacrifices attested in the Old Testament, which not only is not censured in any way, but is even considered necessary as the fulfillment of a vow. We have another case in Gen. 22.1ff., but there, as is well known, in the end Isaac is not sacrificed."[14] Phyllis Trible uses it to contrast the fates of Isaac and Jephthah's Daughter. She writes, "How different is this story from Abraham's sacrifice of Isaac. . . . At the last moment, the angel of the Lord negates the divine imperative, 'Kill your child,' by another command, 'Do not lay your hand on the lad or do anything to him' (Gen, 22:12a, RSV). But in the story of the daughter of Jephthah, no angel intervenes to save the child."[15] Along these lines, reading the comparison in light of the #SayHerName campaign raises its own set of concerns. It asks why one story is widely known while the other is hardly remembered. Why do we know the name of the male victim of Abraham's (near) human sacrifice but not the female victim of Jephthah's completed human sacrifice?

#SayHerName requires being loud and vocal about death. In the case of Jephthah's Daughter, we cannot say her name since we do not know her name. For the ancient scribes and editors who preserved this text, her name was not important enough to include. She is known only as the Daughter of Jephthah like so many women who are known only by their role or their relationships to others.[16] In the case of Jephthah's Daughter, to those who wrote and edited these texts, her name was less important than her death. #SayHerName calls out the name of any black woman and girl who is victimized. #SayHerName activism insists that we call all the names of those who have been victimized, including queer and trans black women. #SayHerName vigils and commemorations provide strategies of resistance. Speaking up and out, saying the names of victims, and gathering together indicate that the victim's death did not go unnoticed. It demands that we remember the names of female victims of violence and notice their stories rather than depicting it as a terror that endangers only boys and men.

#SayHerName and Comparisons of Jephthah and Abraham

When scholars interpret the story of Jephthah's Daughter through a comparison to the near-sacrifice of Isaac, they imply a comparison between Jephthah and Abraham. In both texts, a father sacrifices or nearly sacrifices his child. In both texts, the children refer to the men as "father" (Genesis 22:7; Judges 11:36; cf. 11:27, 39). Abraham repeatedly refers to Isaac as "my son" (Genesis 22:7, 8; cf. 22:2, 3, 6, 9, 10, 12, 13, 16), and when Jephthah's Daughter comes out to meet him, he cries out "Alas, my daughter!" (Judges 11:35). Yet, despite this familial terminology, there is an important difference in the roles that Abraham and Jephthah play in these two texts that are often obscured by the comparison of Genesis 22 and Judges 11.

Abraham acts in his capacity as a father in Genesis 22. Specifically, God commands him to sacrifice Isaac because he is Abraham's son. In Genesis 22:2, God tells Abraham, "Take your son, your only son Isaac, whom you love, and go to the land of Moriah, and offer him there as a burnt offering on one of the mountains that I shall show you." Abraham nearly sacrifices Isaac because of a direct divine command to a father. He is not performing a ritual (cf. the prohibitions in Leviticus 18:21; 20:2–5; Deuteronomy 12:31; 18:10). He is not killing, or nearly killing, his son to fulfill a curse or influence a deity in the context of war (e.g., 1 Samuel 14:24–46; 2 Kings 3:26–27). He is not functioning as a warrior, although he may act in these capacities elsewhere in Genesis (e.g., Genesis 14:1–16). In Genesis 22, Abraham is a father who nearly kills his son Isaac.

This contrasts sharply with the role that Jephthah plays in Judges 11. While he is obviously the father of his daughter, he makes and carries out his vow in his capacity as a warrior. Niditch refers to Jephthah's vow as a "war vow" and writes, "The vow (11:30) is another piece of the preparation for war. As in Numbers 21:2–3, the warrior promises a sacrifice of some sort to God in exchange for victory in battle."[17] Unlike Abraham in Genesis 22, Jephthah acts as a warrior in Judges 11, and his carrying out his vow is part of warrior activity. Jephthah's Daughter is the victim of warrior-related violence. Yet, comparisons of Judges 11 to Genesis 22 amplify Jephthah's role as a father while obscuring the fact that he kills his daughter because he is acting in his capacity as a warrior.

Both Judges 11 and contemporary police violence against black women and girls involve state-sanctioned violence. Israel as depicted in the Bible was not a nation-state with a police force. Still, Jephthah is a military commander, and Jephthah's Daughter's fate is decided by a vow made to ensure military success. The violence against Jephthah's Daughter is not simply a private, domestic, or family issue. This is not only because the distinction between private and public life was not constructed in the same way as in the contemporary United States. The text does not state that Jephthah's vow was made privately. Moreover, other biblical texts suggest that such war vows were made in public.[18] For example, Numbers 21:2–3 refers to Israelite warriors collectively as "Israel" when they make a war vow in public with conditions that are strikingly similar to Jephthah's vow in Judges 11:30. The text reads, "Then Israel made a vow to the Lord and said, 'If you will indeed give this people into our hands, then we will utterly destroy their towns.' The Lord listened to the voice of Israel, and handed over the Canaanites; and they utterly destroyed them and their towns; so the place was called Hormah."[19]

In this sense, Jephthah's war vow was not a private or family matter but a form of state-sanctioned violence that could involve the killing of humans, even if Jephthah tries to depict the killing of his daughter as an unanticipated tragedy when, upon seeing his daughter, he cries out, "Alas, my daughter! You have brought me very low; you have become the cause of great trouble to me. For I have opened my mouth to the Lord, and I cannot take back my vow." (Judges 11:35).[20] It is not a tragic accident but a predictable outcome of his vow, considering that Israelite women greet warriors upon their return from a victorious battle in other texts.

The tragedy is not that Jephthah's Daughter's death was accidental but that no one who knew of the vow spoke up to save her life. It did not have to end this way. Authors of the Hebrew Bible could imagine scenarios in which the community would protest the killing of a child after a military leader declared a curse in the context of a war. According to 1 Samuel 14:24, Saul "had laid an oath on the troops, saying, 'Cursed be anyone who eats food before it is evening and I have been avenged on my enemies.'" After his son Jonathan violates the curse, Saul vows to kill his son (1 Samuel 14:44).[21] But the people immediately protest. 1 Samuel 14:45 reads, "Then the people said to Saul, 'Shall Jonathan die, who has accomplished this great victory in Israel? Far from it! As the Lord lives, not one hair of his head shall fall to the ground; for he has worked with God today.' So the people ransomed Jonathan, and he did not die." Rather than staying silent, the community advocated for Saul's male child against a culture that would sanction Saul's war-related curse and the killing of Jonathan. By contrast, in Judges 11, the community did not protest or resist the state-sanctioned violence against a female victim. No one calls Jephthah out. Jephthah's Daughter becomes collateral damage in her father's military career within an unquestioned warrior culture system that failed her.

#SayHerName questions a system that supports police who are often not charged or convicted for acts of violence. It asks who are the police protecting and serving in committing acts of brutality. #SayHerName activism asks who was involved not only in the particular incident of violence but what personnel, officials, and systems were involved, and how did they fail the victim. It causes us to ask who was present when Jephthah made the vow. It forces us to consider who failed Jephthah's Daughter. It considers not just individuals and particular incidents but systems of oppression. Reading Judges 11 through the prism of the #SayHerName campaign and similar efforts in support of black women and girls rather than through a comparison to Genesis 22 illuminates this point. In making this point, I am not offering a simple parallel between the warrior culture depicted in the Bible and the contemporary police state but focusing attention on Jephthah's Daughter and highlighting issues of naming, victimization, and possibilities for resistance.

Black Church Reflections

It may seem that Judges 11 is a text that does not "preach." That is, it does not provide an uplifting, easy-to-grasp parallel to contemporary life. #SayHerName asks why don't we know the names of these black women and girls. Looking at Judges 11, why don't we know this text? This is not a text that is usually covered in Sunday school or preached from the pulpit. It makes us consider who is writing the curriculum, creating the lectionary, and deciding the sermon topics. Biblical texts could serve as resources for engaging issues such as state-sanctioned violence and other issues that are affecting our communities. Engaging texts in this way could assist readers by increasing their ability to substantively address concerns associated with sexual politics—including public health crises, hate crimes, and social and theological equality—both within their congregations and in the broader society. Biblical material such as Judges 11 is a part of canon, but those in leadership have to set it before readers.

As a biblical scholar, I caution my more theologically minded students not to seek easy answers or neat parallels in search of a present-day application of biblical texts. Yet, I believe that ancient texts can help us ask new questions about our contemporary lives. It is important to help readers get comfortable with struggling with the text and to expect that struggle, even and especially with texts that we presume to know. I hope that this essay offers some space to reflect on whose lives and deaths matter in our lives, neighborhoods, and faith communities. For all of those who continue to do justice work in memory of Jephthah's Daughter, for black women and girls, and for all of those whose names we don't say, Audre Lorde's "A Litany for Survival" reminds us:

> So it is better to speak
>   remembering
>   we were never meant to survive.[22]

CHAPTER 3

An Inconsistent Truth

The New Testament, Early Christianity, and Sexuality

MICHAEL JOSEPH BROWN

It is terribly difficult, I think, for the Christian who takes the Bible seriously and regards it as providing guidance for daily life, to find a clear-cut, concrete directive which can be followed consistently.

LUKE TIMOTHY JOHNSON,
SHARING POSSESSIONS: WHAT FAITH DEMANDS

Sexuality has been a difficult topic for Christianity to discuss from the beginning. It is not that it was a taboo subject, for example, in the environment of the early church. On the contrary, it was quite the opposite. Compared to the modern climate of the United States, people in the world of the first Christians were surrounded by many more images, opportunities, and discussions of sexuality than the average person today could imagine. Nevertheless, the early Christian movement seemed uncomfortable discussing the topic and appeared to be of more than one mind on the matter.

As we will see, certain Christian thinkers and their followers felt that the practice of sexuality demonstrated a lack of self-control—a newly created Christian virtue (see Gal 5:23) that accompanied the reception of the Holy Spirit. Simply put, these Christians believed that engaging in sex meant diverting one's attention from the Lord. If Christianity called for single-minded devotion to Christ and His mission in the world, then only abstinence, virginity, and like-minded forms of sexual renunciation were appropriate ways of living the Gospel faithfully.

By contrast, as Christianity continued to attract followers, not everyone was convinced that it was advantageous or even possible for followers of Jesus to live so far outside of the social mainstream—specifically the social expectation that individuals would marry (and have children) as soon as the opportunity presented itself. To these Christians, living faithfully to the

Lord meant conducting their lives in a way that would not invite suspicion or ridicule. Some have argued that this perspective on sexuality represents the transformation of the *ekklēsia* (church) from more of a movement to an institution (e.g., the preoccupation with religious offices, like bishops and deacons, in the pastoral epistles). Although such an understanding is not entirely without merit, it appears that the "logic" of this position predates the conjectured maturation of the church from a movement to an institution.

As Christianity continued to develop, the institution faced a couple of related problems. Most immediately, the church had to wrestle with the delay of the Second Coming of Jesus. In the time of the apostle Paul, some twenty to thirty years after Jesus's death and resurrection, expectations for the Second Coming ran high. This appears to be part of the apostle's rationale for telling his congregations to focus on the Lord and not on marriage (and all that goes with it). Over one hundred years later, in the time of Clement of Alexandria, this rationale became increasingly difficult to defend, much less promote for the average Christian. Since it did not appear that Jesus would return as soon as some had expected, the church's conundrum was how to conduct itself in the meantime. Nevertheless, no positive argument had been made on behalf of Christian sexuality generally and marriage in particular. Clement was among the first Christian intellectuals to make such an argument. His treatise on behalf of marriage—*Stromata* III—laid the foundation for a Christian doctrine of sexuality that largely persists into our modern world.

As Christianity developed its understanding of sexuality, the dominant conversation (or debate) centered on how sex and sexuality fit into a proper Christian lifestyle. Moreover, the conversation's context appears almost exclusively confined to the realm of marriage. Other forms of sexual expression did flourish alongside marriage, of course. However, these are discussed scantly, if at all, in the early Christian writings. When they are discussed, simple declarations are generally made, and depth is usually absent. Nevertheless, such declarations do have a context and a history that need to be brought forward and examined before determining their adequacy.

Just Don't Do It: Paul and His Communities on Sexuality

Most people begin discussions about early Christian social practices by going straight to an examination of the scriptures. My experience, however, has taught me that such conversations are not helpful unless the participants understand the historical context in which the text under discussion was written. This is especially important when we are talking about someone as influential as the apostle Paul. Outside of Jesus, there is probably no other figure in early Christian history as significant as the one-time persecutor of the church, who later turned into one of its greatest champions. Just a cursory examination of the New Testament proves the apostle's influence. In this respect, understanding Paul is necessary to understand what the second half of the Bible is trying to say to us.

Paul believed strongly—at least at the beginning of his career—that Jesus would return in his lifetime. This strong belief shapes the "what" and "why" of many of Paul's statements in his letters. This is particularly true when it comes to what Paul has to say about sexual relations. Moreover, all of Paul's letters are what scholars call "occasional" letters. By this, we mean that they were written to specific Christian communities regarding specific issues that confronted those assemblies of believers. This is most definitely true when it comes to a document like 1 Corinthians, the letter in which Paul conducts his longest discussion of how Christians should handle themselves sexually.

The letter we call 1 Corinthians is mislabeled somewhat. It is not, in truth, Paul's first letter to that church. The first letter Paul wrote to Corinth is lost to us. We know it existed because he refers to it in what we call 1 Corinthians (e.g., 1 Cor 5:9: "I wrote to you in my letter . . ." [New Revised Standard Version]). We also know that the Corinthian congregation responded to Paul's initial letter with one of their own because, again, he refers to it (e.g., 1 Cor 7:1: "Now concerning the matters about which you wrote . . ."). So, what we have in 1 Corinthians is an ongoing conversation between Paul and a church that has a lot of questions for its founder. In effect, we join in not at the beginning of the conversation but somewhere after. So there is much that we do not know about how this discussion between the apostle and his congregation began. For example, why is sex such a large part of this letter when it is barely discussed in any of Paul's other letters?

Three interesting sexual conversations arise early in the letter. I would like to address two of them quickly and then look at the third in more depth. The first is somewhat odd. In 1 Corinthians 5, Paul begins with an air of disgust: "It is actually reported that there is sexual immorality among you, and of a kind that is not found even among pagans; for a man is living with his father's wife" (5:1). The Greek term *porneia* is what Paul uses and is translated by the phrase "sexual immorality." There has been a great deal of debate as to what the term means *specifically*. As best we can tell, it refers to any kind of sexual activity considered outside the realm of the acceptable. In other words, it was a fluid concept; something regarded as porneia in one time and place may not be viewed the same way in another. Nevertheless, the situation described by Paul is strange.

Notice that Paul does not say that the man is living with his mother but with "his father's wife." This suggests that this woman was not the unknown man's mother but his stepmother. Second and even third marriages were not an uncommon occurrence since life expectancy was so short. In addition, calling the woman "his father's wife"—and not his widow—suggests that the man's father was still alive. This situation would have been a clear-cut case of adultery. Unlike what we mean today, which is any sexual infidelity in a marriage, adultery specifically meant sleeping with another man's wife in Paul's day. This would have been a serious violation of law and custom, what the Greeks called *nomos* and the Romans called *lex*. Depending on when it happened and who committed it, the punishment for adultery could be death.

Paul does not seem to be interested in what those outside the church may think about the situation, nor does he expect Christians to cut off their relationships with those who are immoral outside the body of Christ. He says, "I wrote to you in my letter not to associate with sexually immoral persons—not at all meaning the immoral of this world . . . since you would then need to go out of the world" (5:9, 10). His concern is entirely in-house. As he says, do "not associate with anyone who bears the name of brother or sister who is sexually immoral. . . . Do not even eat with such a one" (5:11).

The second discussion of sex may strike us as odd as well, but in truth, it would not have been unusual in Paul's day. The apostle writes, "Do you not know that your bodies are members of Christ? Should I therefore take the members of Christ and make them members of a prostitute? Never!" (6:15). This statement strikes us as odd because patronizing prostitutes is almost always illegal and morally reprehensible in our culture. And it most definitely goes against contemporary Christian moral teaching. So, we think, why would Paul have to tell these Christians not to patronize prostitutes?

The simple answer begins with "it was a different time." Although prostitutes themselves were not held in high esteem—they were usually slaves—prostitution was practiced openly. It was taxed like any other business. Moreover, houses of prostitution were quite common in seaports like Corinth. I pointed out earlier that adultery meant having sexual relations with another man's wife, which means it did not apply to relations with prostitutes. (It especially did not apply to slaves, who were legally not considered persons but property under the law.) This is another instance where Paul calls what is going on porneia, translated this time as "fornication" (6:13). Thus, it may not have been apparent to these Christians in Corinth that frequenting houses of prostitution was somehow wrong or immoral.

Again, the apostle admonishes those believers who do such things. It is how he does it that is odd. First, he quotes Genesis 2:24, "The two shall be one flesh," a scripture almost always associated with marriage and not sex with prostitutes. Second, he tells them that their bodies are "temple[s] of the Holy Spirit" and invokes the metaphor of slavery— "You are not your own. . . . You were bought with a price"—an irony since most prostitutes were, in fact, slaves (1 Cor 6:19, 20).

The last incident I would like to address is a little more familiar, although modern readers often misunderstand it. The question on the table is: Should a believer marry or not? Moreover, if a believer is already married, should he or she remain married, especially if the spouse is an unbeliever? Although we assume that marriage is a fundamental Christian value, it was a lifestyle that was up for debate in Paul's day. Again, this was a matter that involved *porneia*, on this occasion translated as "sexual immorality" (7:2).

The discussion begins, "Now concerning the matters about which you wrote: 'It is well for a man not to touch a woman' " (7:1). It may not be readily apparent, but Paul is quoting from the letter sent to him by the church in Corinth. So for some reason, they believe that Paul wants them to renounce sex. This is, in truth, a slight misunderstanding of what the apostle teaches. They believe that marriage is a state of life advocated by Paul because of the potential problem of porneia. In some ways, this is correct. However, Paul advocates a traditional Jewish understanding of marriage: each partner in the marriage should satisfy the other's sexual needs (7:3–5). This arrangement can be modified at times "by agreement," but it should not be carried out too long "because of your lack of self-control." And that is what gets at the heart of the matter for Paul, which is why he says, "This I say by way of concession, not of command" (7:6).

Marriage and the sexual relationship that accompanies it is an expression of a Christian's ability to practice self-control. As Paul says, "I wish that all were as I myself am," implying that he can practice self-control over his sexual desires (7:7). This self-control would be the ideal life choice for the Christian, allowing the unmarried person to be "anxious about the affairs of the Lord, how to please the Lord," and not how to please his or her partner (7:32). Nevertheless, as the apostle says, "Each has a particular *charisma* [i.e., spiritual gift] from God, one having one kind and another a different kind" (7:7). Thus, he lays down a set of pastoral practices that he thinks believers should follow. First, unmarried men and widows should remain unmarried. The exception, of course, is if they lack self-control (7:8–9). Second, those already married should heed the Lord's injunction against divorce, which we find in the Gospels as well, and if they are separated, they should attempt to find some way to reconcile (7:10–11). Third, if a believer is married to an unbeliever and the unbelieving spouse wishes to stay in the relationship, then the couple should remain married. This also guarantees the sanctity of the spouse and the children, as well as the legitimacy of the children (7:12–14, 16). However, if the unbelieving partner wishes to divorce, this is not a problem for the believing partner (7:15). The apostle then outlines in greater detail why he thinks believers should follow such rules, which he concedes are mainly his opinions on the matter (7:25–35). Fourth, for those on the verge of marriage and experiencing sexual desires, marriage is not necessary if they can practice self-control (7:36–37). He sums up this section by saying, "So then, he who marries his fiancée does well; and he who refrains from marriage will do better" (7:38).

As I pointed out earlier, this is often a difficult discussion for modern readers to understand because Paul does not provide a ringing endorsement of marriage, which we have come to expect since contemporary Christianity sees marriage as a fundamental good. What we come across with the apostle is a complicated relationship to the institution of marriage based on whether or not the believer has the spiritual gift of self-control. As a general rule, however, Paul advocated that people not marry because it distracted them from serving and pleasing the Lord, which was the very definition of worship in his day.

Be Like Everyone Else: Christians Trying to Negotiate Sexual Expectations in the Second and Third Generations

"But [*porneia*] and impurity of any kind, or greed, must not even be mentioned among you, as is proper among saints," says the author of Ephesians (5:3). In many ways, this statement is typical of the growing desire to be respectable in the second and third generations of the Christian movement. Already we have seen Christians grappling with social expectations around marriage in Paul's discussion with the Corinthians. This is primarily because the world in which Christians lived emphasized—if not demanded—that people marry and procreate, even after the death of a previous spouse. Paul's desire that Christians remain single, practice self-control, and devote their time to the Lord made some Christians feel odd. Many probably believed that it drew undue attention to themselves and the movement. And so, advocates of marriage and traditional households can be heard through the pages of the New Testament as well.

I am sure others could point out several examples. I would like to discuss two. The first involves the expectations for individuals who assume the church offices of deacon and bishop. In many respects, the expectations outlined in 1 Timothy 3:1–13 are similar to others found in what is known as the household codes in other parts of the New Testament (e.g., Col 3:18–4:1; Eph 5:22–6:9; 1 Tim 2:8–15; 6:1–2; Tit 2:1–10; 1 Pet 2:11–3:7). By comparison and most likely by necessity, the expectations for church office are more detailed than those of being a good "head of the household." Notice, as well, that we are talking about "households" and not "families." This is because the Latin term *familia*, from which we derive our modern word *family*, is not the same type of social institution. When we speak of families in our modern world, we usually describe a close-knit arrangement consisting, first and foremost, of a father, mother, and children. When individuals two thousand years ago spoke of a *familia* (Latin) or *oikia* (Greek), they were describing a more dynamic social arrangement consisting of the "head of the household" (in Latin *paterfamilias*), wife, children (and their spouses and children if they had them), other relatives who may have been in need, slaves, former slaves, clients, and possibly others. It is not quite the same as our idea of the "extended family," but that may be a helpful way to think about it. This is why these verses speak of household management; a familia could consist of a large group of people. This explains why the author asks, "If someone does not know how to manage his own household, how can he take care of God's church" (1 Tim 3:5)?

When we look closely at the expectations for a bishop or a deacon, we begin to see that they are similar to those character traits expected of a *patrona*, a socially acceptable Roman man. Cicero, for example, discusses the ideal qualities that a good man should possess:

> What situation can be more splendid than the government of the state by excellence and virtue? When the man who rules others is not

himself a slave to any base emotions, when he himself cherishes all those things in which he instructs and to which he beckons his fellow citizens, then he does not impose on the people laws which he does not himself obey, but rather offers to his fellow citizens his own life as a model of lawful behavior. If a single individual could accomplish all these things satisfactorily, we would have no need of more than one ruler (*About the Republic*, 1.34.52).

This is not to say that everyone did or could live such virtuous lives, but the expectations were there nevertheless. Further, as we have seen, we can also find these expectations in the early church's thinking about offices. Of course, in the Roman mind, this included having and managing a familia. Thus, respectability and social conformity became the implicit sexual norms in the second and third generations of the church, at least around the conduct of men seeking office.

The second example is found later in the same letter (1 Tim 5:3–16). It begins, "Honor widows who are really widows" (5:3). On the surface, this sounds odd. By definition, a woman is a widow if her husband has died. Yet, this scripture wants to qualify appropriate widows over against those who should not be considered widows. The influence for this stance appears to come from both inside and outside the church. Inside the church, the financial burden of taking care of widows seems to have been an institutional concern, which prompts the epistle's author to define the requirements for qualifying as a widow in the church. The woman has to be no less than sixty years old, which is an amazing age requirement considering that less than 5 percent of the female population ever reached such an age in that period.[1] She is only married to one man, another interesting requirement in an era when second marriages and blended families were normal (5:9). She must be well attested for her good works, devoting "herself to doing good in every way" (5:10). In effect, these expectations sound eerily reminiscent of the ideal *matrona* (Roman mother) cast in an ecclesial mode. As one writer says, "We ought to revere as a goddess the mother who has given us birth, especially a mother as good and virtuous as ours" (*Sammelbuch* 6263 [*Select Papyri* 121]). In this way, the church appropriated the social expectations of the larger society to determine who would qualify for its financial assistance.

Outside the church, society essentially demanded that women remarry after the death of a spouse. Of course, a woman of sixty might not feel such pressure since she was well beyond childbearing age. However, for younger women, the obligation was strong. Our text identifies such women as having "sensual desires," being idle, and worse: "they are not merely idle, but also gossips and busybodies, saying what they should not say" (5:11, 13). Thus, the author recommends that they marry and have children to guarantee social acceptability (5:14). This coincides with the stance taken by the Julian Laws (23 BCE) and others which demanded that widows remarry: "The Julian Law allowed a woman to be exempt from marriage for one year after the death of her husband, for six months after a divorce. The Papia-Poppaean Law allowed two years after a husband's death and eighteen months after a divorce" (*ADA*, 187). Thus, in line with the larger social expectations of the surrounding society, the church (or at least parts of it) decided to appropriate and advocate for sexual practices and marital positions that made its members just like everyone else.

Nevertheless, this did not quell the debate that still went on in the church regarding the role of sexuality in Christian discipleship. There were still those who followed Paul's admonition that believers should devote themselves entirely to God and renounce sexual desire (e.g., Matthew's idea of "eunuchs for the kingdom of heaven" [Matt 19:12]). Others believed that disciples should fit into the larger society by promoting sexual practices, like marriage, that supported larger social goals. Moreover, very little, if anything, is said in the New Testament about sex outside of marriage. Neither does it speak about domestic violence, which we know was widespread (see, e.g., Augustine, *Confessions* 9.9). The seed of one resolution to the problem can be found earlier in the letter we just considered. First, Timothy 2:14–15 refers to the creation story, as did Paul in 1 Corinthians, and uses it as a basis for women's subordination. Yet, it also points to the potential legitimacy of sexual activity within a certain realm, since "she will be saved through childbearing, provided they continue in faith and love and holiness, with modesty" (2:15).

Do It for the Lord: Christians Attempting to Make Sense of the Demands of the Gospel and Their Place in the World

As we have seen, the New Testament does not fully explain or resolve how early Christians handled human sexuality. Further discussion would be needed. A century after Jesus's death, the church had developed into what scholars generally call the patristic period (100–450 CE). The expectation that Jesus would return soon—so crucial to Paul's message—had begun to wane, and Christians sensed the need to develop an understanding of human sexuality that would last in the period before the Second Coming. At this point, the interpretation of the Bible became an even more central concern for the church and its intellectuals. Arguments abounded regarding the precise meaning and possible application(s) of scriptural statements, especially those contained in the Old Testament. Fitting Old Testament conceptions of sex and sexuality into a later (now Greco-Roman) framework was not as simple as some may initially assume, as we have already seen in earlier examples.

Clement of Alexandria was one of those Christian thinkers. Although he left a substantial body of writing, we know very little regarding the life of this theologian. We know that he was one of the leading thinkers of his time and headed a school in Alexandria, Egypt, that instructed new believers in the Christian faith. He was also one of the first Christian writers to pen an essay on sexuality. To accomplish this, he attempted to integrate biblical ideas and statements regarding sex with current Greco-Roman understandings of what it meant to be a human being.

In addition to the Bible, three other factors influenced Clement's development of a doctrine of Christian sexuality: mortality, marriage patterns, and the advocacy of Pauline instruction that Christians should avoid sex. Like Jesus and Paul, Clement lived in an era where very few people ever experienced old age, at least as we know it. And although we have already touched on this issue in our earlier discussion, it plays (I believe) a larger role in Clement's approach than we can determine from our earlier examination. Life expectancy was around twenty-four years.[2] Since people died so young on average, some people—generally women—were forced to marry at much earlier ages than in most modern societies. According to census data, women began to marry around the age of twelve. By contrast, men, who often outnumbered women, generally had to wait until their twenties before they could marry. At least a quarter of these marriages ended because of the death of one spouse, usually the wife. And so, multiple marriages and "blended" families were a common occurrence in the early church.

Not only did men wait longer than women to get married, but they were also often forced to consider life options other than matrimony. Among the religiously (and philosophically) minded, asceticism was an appealing alternative to married life. According to this way of life, individuals needed to isolate themselves from aspects of life that might arouse desire, especially if those desires were considered unnecessary. An unnecessary desire was something considered potentially dangerous to the individual's personal development. In this case, Christians thought eating certain foods, drinking wine, and engaging in sexual intercourse were dangerous.

Sex involves desire. Desire is the source of pleasure, but in early Christian thought, it is also an indicator of a deficiency on the part of the individual (*Strom*. 3.5.42.1). As Clement says, "The human condition involves some things which are natural and necessary, [and] other things which are merely natural" (3.1.3.2). Food, for example, is both natural and necessary because we would die without it. Yet, as the Christian theologian determines, "all this business of sexual intercourse is natural but not necessary" (3.1.3.2). We only think it to be necessary because of the presence of desire, a product of the influence of Satan. It can only be counteracted by self-discipline and self-control, an idea we already heard from the apostle Paul. Self-control, in this case, means indifference to all the things that may attract us, including sexual intercourse.

Although one might think that Clement would eschew marriage, his stance was simple yet complicated. In a key portion of his essay on Christian sexuality (*Stromata* 3), Clement outlines his central argument that marriage is a proper social state for Christians—a clear blow against his detractors, who argue that Christians should go back to Paul's idea of avoiding marriage. Drawing upon the apostle's statement in 1 Cor 7:5, Clement claims that sex in marriage is a prophylactic against the devil's influences (3.12.82.1). He justifies marital sex as a practice condoned in the Old Testament for "the breeding of children" (3.12.81.5). As such, it is an option for Christians as an expression of the will of God. The same is true in the case of a second marriage, which, as I said, was common in the early church. Clement believed that marriage was important to the Christian life because many people lacked the self-control Paul advocated. Moreover, Clement viewed marriage as a proper and legal social arrangement intended by God for procreation. He defines it as follows: "Marriage is a union between a man and a woman; it is the primary union; it is a legal transaction; it exists for the procreation of legitimate children" (2.23.137.1). Any sexual union outside of marriage was wrong for three reasons, according to Clement. First, it was a defilement of one person's body through a partnership with an alien body (3.12.89.2). Second, it established a union, whether legal or not, for purposes other than the procreation of children (3.12.90.1). Third, it misunderstood the Old Testament and rejected the will of God (3.12.90.2–4). Although Clement was a strong advocate of marriage, he did not go so far as to see it as a moral obligation incumbent upon all Christians. He could not do this and remain faithful to Paul's statements in 1 Corinthians.

An "Effeminate" Man Cannot Enter the Kingdom of God: The Clash of Sexual Visions in Christianity

As we have seen throughout this short overview of early Christian sexuality, the church struggled with the proper role sex should play in the lives of its members. Some renounced sex altogether because it took time away from the Lord. Others advocated marriage and procreation because they fit into the larger expectations of the society in which they lived. Consequently, other forms of sexual expression were either not addressed or dismissed because they did not fit into the emerging views of sexuality the church debated. For example, although the apostle Paul repudiated sex with prostitutes, he said nothing of the practice of masters having sex with their slaves, which was just as prevalent. Something similar is true when it comes to homosexual practices. It is given cursory consideration and then dismissed. The primary reason for this goes back to two human experiences that have run through our entire conversation: desire and self-control. Sex for pleasure or satisfaction (i.e., desire) was considered illegitimate because it demonstrated a lack of the Christian virtue of self-control. Furthermore, homosexual sexual practice was dismissed because it questioned an implicit vision of masculinity that the church never challenged.

In Paul's letter to the Corinthians, one can find one of the most famous statements on this topic: "Do you not know that wrongdoers will not inherit the kingdom of God? Do not be deceived! Fornicators, idolators, adulterers, male prostitutes, sodomites, thieves, the greedy, drunkards, revilers, robbers—none of these will inherit the kingdom of God" (1 Cor 6:9–10). Of course, it would be easy to read these words from Paul and nod in agreement as if they are self-evident aberrations. However, the apostle goes on to make it clear that "this is what some of you used to be" (6:11). So we should reserve severe judgment before looking more carefully at what the text is trying to tell us.

The first person excluded from the kingdom named in this list is the *pornos*, translated as "fornicator." It is usually the designation of a male prostitute. Still, many scholars think it is being used here more generically to refer to any sexually immoral man who cannot practice the proper degree of self-control. The third person, the *moichos* or adulterer, is excluded on the same grounds. Adultery in the New Testament and early Christianity meant having sexual relations with another man's wife, an apparent demonstration of a lack of self-control. The fifth person, the *arsenokoitēs*, is a man who has sex with other men, generally younger ones. Again, this exposes the absence of self-control. In other words, all of these behaviors would call into question a man's masculinity, at least according to Roman social norms. As one scholar makes clear, "The belief that a man who cedes control over his own desires and fears is less than fully masculine surfaces in many [Roman] contexts. . . . Masculinity was not fundamentally a matter of sexual practice; it was a matter of control."[3]

The odd translation here is "male prostitute" for *malakos*, which means "soft." In this case, it refers to the effeminate (or "soft") man. In this case, most translators assume that this refers to the man who plays the receptive or effeminate role in a male-to-male sexual encounter. Yet, a closer examination of the term displays it is much more than that. The correlate Latin term for the Greek *malakos* appears to be *cinaedus*. It refers to any man who does not fit into the predominant stereotype of masculinity. Moreover, it has nothing to do with whether the effeminate man has sex with other men or with women. It is a matter of public appearance. The malakos/cinaedus is the man who is a public entertainer, who is overly concerned about his looks, who cannot control his desires, who does not choose to participate in the "rough and tumble" of public life. He allows himself to be publicly humiliated or seen as "womanish" by another, a metaphorical "insertion into" or "softening" of his manhood. Certainly, eunuchs—a favorite image in the Gospel of Matthew—were considered unmanly because of their inability to procreate. Men who chose a lifestyle other than marriage faced the same sort of public labeling, a problem that would present itself with the rise of the monastic movement in early Christianity. Men who allowed their manhood to be disgraced by another without challenge would be placed in the same category (e.g., Matt 5:38–42). In other words, some Christian virtues would have qualified as effeminate according to the larger society. This may be why translators seek to narrow the meaning of malakos in 1 Cor 6; it clashed with the dominant understanding of masculinity at the time, which placed a heavy emphasis on the domination and penetration of others. Furthermore, the problem for us as twenty-first-century readers may be that most modern conceptions of masculinity would not measure up to this ancient one, particularly when we consider the emerging trend toward more fluid gender identities that can be observed, especially among young people, in the United States and across the world. By ancient standards, many, if not virtually all, modern men would be considered effeminate in some form or another.

Many Voices, Inconsistent Truths, and a Contemporary Understanding of Christian Sexual Practice

What it means to be a human being and how one practices self-control have been central to the Christian understanding of sexuality. Yet, these understandings have been influenced heavily by factors external to the church and its cherished writings. Thus, the "push" and "pull" we find in the New Testament and early Christian writings regarding sexual activity reflect the larger debate Christianity had around the subject. Some would think that Clement settled the matter: sex in marriage for the procreation of legitimate children has been the Christian standard. Yet, it is not clear that procreation won the day, as many proponents of procreation were themselves unmarried (e.g., priests and intellectuals). Nor did Clement advocate heterosexual marriage as the standard for all believers.

The truth is that we can find many, often contradictory, voices on sexuality in the Bible. Judah can have sex with a prostitute in Genesis 38 without regret, while Paul will condemn such activity. Jacob can marry two sisters and procreate with their slaves as well, while Jesus and others advocate monogamy as the only guarantor of legitimacy. Moreover, very little of the discussion about sexuality focuses on sex as such. And so, any honest reader of the Bible is left with an entire set of unanswered questions. For example, what is the purpose of sex? Is it solely for the procreation of children, as strongly suggested by the early church? If so, how can we ignore all of the other emotional benefits that accompany the act? If not, then is there a bias in our writings toward procreation such that any other form of sexual activity is automatically demonized because it does not lead to the bearing of legitimate children? (I think there is.) Infertile women, homosexuals, prostitutes, and slaves have all carried the stigma of such sexual encounters without any thorough consideration of what it means to promote a standard of activity that few Christians (ancient and modern) follow(ed) in the first place. For far too long, a veneer of consistency has been placed over a set of inconsistent statements and practices. What needs examination is how the various forms of sexual expression found in the Bible and the early church manifested themselves and how they allowed human beings to flourish (or not). If, as we have come to understand, sexuality is at the core of our experience of our humanity, then it needs more thoughtful consideration than it is often given in the early church.

PART THREE

Historical and Cultural Formations of Black (Christian) Sexual Politics

CHAPTER 4

"Have the Sons of Africa No Souls?"

Manliness, Freedom, and Power in the Cultural Roots of Afro-Phallic Protestantism

JONATHAN LEE WALTON

Scholars across many disciplines are concerned with the historical roots and the most recent manifestations of what is widely accepted as a tradition of muscular Christianity. Historians have illumined muscular Christianity's rise in Victorian England and its influence in Progressive-Era America. And sociologists, theologians, gender theorists, and performance studies scholars have been preoccupied with the resurgence of hypermasculine social movements in America over the past couple of decades.[1] Many are sounding the alarm as they sense the stale bread of male dominance seemingly served on new plates of benevolence and theological complementarianism. But despite the scholarly attention directed toward white male evangelicals in recent years, the ways African American men purposefully appropriate, construct, embrace, and perform their own male-centered Christianity has been obscured at best and ignored at worst. Several works examine gender hierarchies within black Protestant communities and the many ways African American women carved out spaces that both affirm their humanity and perform the work of the church on behalf of the race in general and black women in particular.[2] Much less has been written about the ways black men willfully engaged and purposefully influenced notions of domesticity and gendered conceptions of morality.[3] This is indeed an important distinction. The former can unwittingly leave persons and institutions with specific interests in maintaining a gendered status quo unnamed. More importantly, the former allows the inert yet fluid gender ideologies that circulate within operative power relations to remain intact. On the other hand, the latter can reveal gendered conceptions of domesticity, morality, and virtue as anything but natural toward demystifying the inner logic of institutional apparatuses that can manifest in any given moment.

Toward this end, my approach is both genealogical and theological. It is genealogical insofar as it seeks to trace the emergence of particular conceptions of masculinity within racial and religious discourse among African American Protestants in the nineteenth century. I understand masculinity as an ideology that, though negotiated, contested, and extended in particular historical epochs by human subjects responding to material conditions, nonetheless maintains a logic that transcends those human subjects. Hence, my reading resists viewing masculinity as either transhistorical (always and already) or merely a tool of economic and political realities. Rather, the gender ideology of masculinity within racial and religious discourse can be historically negotiated, culturally reflective, autonomously generative, and socially transformative.

My approach is theological in that it understands this ideology to be religious. Here, I am simultaneously borrowing from and extending theologian J. Kameron Carter's insights on the theopolitical dimensions of the development of the conception of race to particular constructions of gender. For Carter, whiteness developed as both a philosophical and religious problem in the modern era. Early constructions of race and modern identity were bound up with superseding the perceived inferior racial other.[4] Thus, whiteness comes to possess a sacral dimension, a racial ground of all beings, from which the rest of the world must be measured. I argue that something similar can be said of masculinist ideals among nineteenth-century African American Protestants. We will see that ideas about gender circulate within metaphysical discourses of ultimate concern and are naturalized as reflecting divine order. Thus, ignoring the theological grounds and implications of such discourse allows a large dimension of their authoritative resonance to be unnamed. Yet, by historicizing the social constructions of both race and gender, this chapter seeks to unpack meanings of racial and gender ideologies at a particular moment in history.

Afro-Phallic Protestantism

Afro-phallic Protestantism is a particular form of masculinized, predominantly evangelical Christianity operative within historically black churches and denominations. The term *phallic* here signifies male privilege yet speaks to the interests of both black men and black women in promoting gender ideologies, which are believed to advance the interests of all who espouse them. Afro-phallic Protestantism's development has been informed by, and is often responding to, three major historical developments of the mid-nineteenth and early twentieth centuries that also constitute the history of Protestant muscular Christianity among the white middle class: Victorian sentimentality and small-scale competitive capitalism, the Western imperialist urge and its accompanying civilization discourse, and a growing fascination with sports and male physicality.

Muscular Christianity is typically traced to the novels of Thomas Hughes and Charles Kingsley in the mid-nineteenth century.[5] Their response to the perceived effeminacy of the Anglican Church is noteworthy since it signaled the shifting concerns and heightened anxieties among men. For decades, women constituted the majority of church attendees among Protestants in England and the United States. That churches were morally gendered as female-dominated spaces similar to the domestic spheres seemed not a problem for men who exercised their authority in "public" realms such as politics and business. The home and churches were sites for cultivating virtue and moral control, dispositions that were innately attributed to women. On the other hand, self-discipline, self-mastery, sobriety, thrift, and honesty (intellectual virtues marked by one's rational capacity to purposefully regulate natural passions) were viewed as the path to middle-class masculinity.

The masculine reassessments of such social understandings were impelled by Victorian sentimentalism among ministers and women on the one hand and changing economic realities on the other. Middle-class white women took their embrace of innate morality to the next logical conclusion. Many women's temperance and suffrage movements, along with cultural productions in literary mass culture, were based on the assumption that virtuous women must extend the boundaries of domesticity to eradicate prevalent social ills—slavery, labor disputes, alcoholism, and overall family disillusionment. This newfound authority pushed the interests of male Protestant ministers away from Calvinist patriarchal models of assumed religious authority toward the highly gendered concerns of social activism and mass culture.[6]

Emerging women's movements challenged white male middle-class dominance of the public sphere at the very moment opportunities for middle-class advancement were diminishing. The rise of corporatism and low-level clerical occupations in the postwar era placed professional ceilings over the heads of "industrious" men. Self-restraint and discipline became increasingly incongruent with the prevailing cultural trend toward consumer capitalism and the aesthetics of leisure. Thus, a perceived "crisis in masculinity" developed by the turn of the twentieth century. As American men were inundated with romantic images of domesticity defined by consumption and leisure, the rungs on the ladder of social advancement grew further apart, and, for most men, became unattainable. In short, the gendered Protestant system of morality tied to economic advancement no longer served the interests of masculine identity.[7]

Like many other aspects of the modern era, the marriage between Victorian gentility and entrepreneurial impulse received its philosophical license from the writings of Immanuel Kant. For Kant, a moral capacity necessitates a self-legislating and self-determining free will. Actions are deemed moral not according to the purpose they were meant to (or do) bring about but according to the motivating principle (maxim) that guides the activity. Autonomy of the will and free will, then, are the same; both are a priori concepts that characterize rational (read: moral) beings in the intelligible world. Conversely, heteronomous subjects lack independent rational capacity and are dependent on internal forces and pressures. For the most part, society perceived women of the nineteenth century as bound to the laws of nature that governed the sensible world. This is to say, women were heteronomous subjects governed by their natural emotions (good or bad) and the rules of cause and effect. This helps to explain why masculinist critiques of late-nineteenth-century Protestantism complained that the church had become too emotional; to counteract this, men were to govern it according to the rational dictates of business principles.[8]

By the turn of the twentieth century, psychologist G. Stanley Hall emerged as a central contributor to developing new ideologies of male power linking new representations of white male power to racialized civilization discourses. Hall was, by and large, responding to the masculine paradox created by the pervasive "diseases" of neurasthenia among white middle-class men. According to physicians of the day, when highly civilized white male bodies overspent their vital energies through the work of civilization—akin to overspending one's sexual energy through masturbation—men became ill-equipped to ward off the effeminizing and crippling effects of overcivilization. In cultivating civilized character by developing self-mastery over their passions, men were forced to squelch latent savagery and short-circuit their natural tendencies. The educator Hall set out to develop a pedagogy that could allow white men to continue on the path of higher civilization without having manliness malnourished by their success. Rather than viewing savagery/civilization and self-mastery/passion as oppositional, Hall framed them as evolutionary developments. Thus males could move away from savagery on a civilizing trajectory from boys to men. Yet it was possible, Hall averred, to hold on to healthy reserves of passion and nervous forces. By encouraging young white males to cultivate aspects of their "savagery" by fighting, engaging in sporting activities, or reading stories of war and bloodshed, teachers helped boys to build up their manly immunity to combat the emasculating effects of civilization associated with mature adulthood.

Consider the perceived role of athletics. Many social reformers regarded competitive sports as an essential feature of socializing young men in urban spaces such as New York and Chicago. Physician Luther Halsey Gulick, an early architect of athletic competition in the YMCA, outlined his advocacy of competitive sports for boys in his book *Philosophy of Play*. Sport is a vehicle through which young men can safely express their primeval masculine traits. In a chapter entitled, "Masculine and Feminine Differences," Gulick contends that the strongest instinct within young men is an attraction to gang culture. "The gang," Gulick writes, "is the modern representative of the tribe, the germ out of which club and society develop."[9] Athletics, he avers, converts the gang instinct from activity that is evil to behavior deemed moral and righteous. This worldview was so widespread that most educators took it for granted. Athletic competition was the domain of masculine expression, with schools, church leagues, and neighborhood associations continuing to offer predominantly male athletic leagues up to the present. That many of these athletic leagues remained racially segregated—and even heightened racial tensions—for the majority of the twentieth century reveal the ways race and masculinity were coactive concepts.

These three developments constitute the reasons the term *muscular Christianity* overdetermines white middle-class Protestantism and obscures the particularities of emerging gender ideologies among black Protestant communities. This is not to suggest that African American reflections on gender take place within a racially closed system. Black women and men in Christian leadership were simultaneously resisting, embracing, and redefining the prevailing gendered moral frameworks. As we will see, compared to white male Protestants, African Americans expressed arguably less anxiety about themes of domesticity. Many regarded domesticity as a masculinist means of inclusion within the dominant civilization narrative—a narrative that black denominational leaders incorporated into their emigration efforts and storylines of African redemption. Moreover, the framing of black bodies bound to the sensible (irrational) world governed by emotions and passions reflected a "brawn over brains" conception of black labor, religion, and family life. African Americans, then, were less concerned with the supposed effeminizing dynamics of "overcivilization" and a need for organized sports as markers of manliness. Rather, by demonstrating a mastery of the written and spoken word coupled with performances of moral refinement, African Americans could challenge "scientific" findings and a priori conceptions concerning their supposed moral and intellectual deficiency.

Masculinity, Freedom, Power, and Moral Agency

Debates over the presence and persistence of slavery in early nineteenth-century America were highly gendered insofar as ideals of freedom, equality, and manhood were bound up with notions of bondage, racial inferiority, and women's subordination. Many prominent abolitionists extended the struggle for emancipation beyond the matter of racial equality to that of manhood. "O Americans! Americans!! I call God—I call angels—I call men, to witness, that your DESTRUCTION *is at hand*, and will be speedily consummated unless you REPENT," declared David Walker in his classic jeremiad *Appeal to the Coloured Citizens of the World*. Yet Walker's ultimate goal was not the divine destruction of the nation but rather full inclusion based on manly equality. "Treat us then like men, and we will be your friends. And there is not a doubt in my mind, but that the whole of the past will be sunk into oblivion, and we yet, under God, will become a united happy people," Walker concluded.[10]

This relationship between freedom and manliness can be identified in the writings and speeches of several other influential abolitionists, most notably Frederick Douglass. In a chilling account offered in both his *Narrative* and *My Bondage and My Freedom*, we learn that Douglass first identifies himself as a slave during a moment of perverse sexual violence. While literally trapped in a closet, Douglass witnesses his Aunt Esther being savagely whipped by the overseer Aaron Anthony. For Douglass, the overseer signifies both his slaveholding father and his white racial self, while his aunt represents his blackness and bondage.[11] To identify with his aunt and thus acknowledge his reality of enslavement is to embrace an emasculated subjectivity under white masculine domination and control. From an early age, Douglass's existence is situated racially and sexually along a binary with whiteness, manliness, power, and freedom on one side and blackness, femininity, impotence, and servitude on the other. It is no wonder, then, that upon attaining his freedom, Douglas writes, "Personal independence is the soul out of which comes the sturdiest manhood." Although there is evidence that Douglass understands his struggles for manhood as directly related to the full equality of women, he did little to unhinge his conception of masculinity from the doorframe of freedom. Despite offering his aunt, grandmother, half-sister, and several other women early in his autobiographies as representatives of an enslaved life, only one out of fifty-three chapters in Douglass's final autobiography acknowledges a positive female influence. In the concise but compelling words of literature scholar Jenny Franchot, in Douglass's autobiographies, "one knows women in slavery and men in freedom."[12] In the social context in which Douglass came to embody freedom, his bourgeois virility seemed to necessitate the eradication of enslaved femininity.

Henry Highland Garnet offers an instructive example of one who was thinking through matters of freedom and power in explicitly theological terms. Garnet's 1843 "Address to the Slaves of the United States of America," delivered to the National Convention of Colored Citizens in Buffalo, New York, is probably his most well-known antislavery declaration. Many interpret Garnet's message as a call for violent slave rebellion in the vein of Nat Turner, Denmark Vesey, or Madison Washington. This reading is understandable yet nevertheless overly simplistic. In one of the more incisive interpretations of Garnet's address, Eddie Glaude locates the Presbyterian minister in a millenarian tradition of political messianism, "a once-and-for-all struggle, a confrontation that in the end, leads to the transformation of the world."[13] This preparedness for an ultimate struggle, for Glaude, extends from Garnet's "pragmatic view of race shaped by an ironic use of moral reform that took seriously the cycle of existential pain and unrest that penetrated deeply the lives of African Americans, slave or free." In comments directly addressed to the enslaved population of America, Garnet declares:

> The forlorn condition in which you are placed, does not destroy your moral obligation to God. You are not certain of heaven, because you suffer yourselves to remain in a state of slavery, where you cannot obey the commandments of the Sovereign of the universe. . . . Your condition does not absolve you from your moral obligation. The diabolical

injustice by which your liberties are cloven down, NEITHER GOD, NOR ANGELS, OR JUST MEN, COMMAND YOU TO SUFFER FOR A SINGLE MOMENT. THEREFORE IT IS YOUR SOLEMN AND IMPERATIVE DUTY TO USE EVERY MEANS, BOTH MORAL, INTELLECTUAL, AND PHYSICAL THAT PROMISES SUCCESS.[14]

This quote underscores the "ironic use of moral reform" Glaude identifies. Rather than slavery being a moral failure among Christians and slaveholders who defended America's peculiar institution, a commonly held position among many moral reformers and abolitionists, Garnet appealed to the inner moral capacity and agency of the enslaved. In short, if slavery is evil and submission to evil is sinful, then African American submission to slavery is a sin.

For the enslaved to be true to Christianity, they must assume their moral duty and resist sin and evil by any means necessary. Garnet injects this position in the middle of ongoing debates among black intellectuals and abolitionists concerning the appropriate response to slavery. By theologically framing the debate as a moral imperative of the slaves to resist through an exercise of power, Garnet revealed how similar the accommodationist approaches of poet Jupiter Hammon and businessman William Whipper were to the moral reform positions of many abolitionists like William Lloyd Garrison and Frederick Douglass. Both approaches in effect, if not in intent, amount to black acquiescence to slavery, according to Garnet. Regardless of whether one appeals to the enslaved to submit because it is God's will (Hammon and Whipper) or appeals to the faith of slaveholders to manumit out of Christian duty (Garrison and Douglass), Garnet understood the results to be the same. African Americans were left at the moral whims of slaveholders, denied their capacity to live out their Christian duty to resist such a serpentine system, hence rendered morally, spiritually, and socially impotent.

The interesting thing about these very acute readings of Douglass and Garnet is their inattention to religion and gender, respectively. Astute literary theorists such as Eric Sundquist and Jenny Franchot identify rightly the ways Douglass navigates the distance between enslavement and freedom with a masculinist compass. But surely Douglass is also giving voice to the "rational," "literate," and "independent" conceptions of manhood circulating within Afro-Protestant culture. From 1840 to the Civil War, the manhood that was defined as individual enterprise, competitive success, and power over others dominated the literature of the African Methodist Episcopal (AME) Church. Bishop Daniel Payne's resolution to elevate the educational standards toward cultivating a well-educated ministry at the 1844 General Conference mirrors Douglass's instrumentalist Christian outlook.[15] As historian Julius Bailey notes, within the AME Church of this period, the interests of uneducated male ministers and aspiring female preachers coalesced insofar as the former were feminized. An emphasis on a converted heart and charismatic gifts, the argument most evoked by female evangelists, disqualified many male ministers as denominational leaders and "increasingly linked education and manhood to the role of the preacher."[16]

An 1861 editorial "Manliness in Preaching" printed in the AME's *Christian Recorder* provides a prime example. Most likely written by the erudite and conservative-leaning editor Elisha Weaver, the article is consistent with Weaver's Victorian ideals and tendency to advise black families on appropriate social behaviors. In outlining the characteristics of a popular preacher, the author avers "manliness is highly essential" because "men and women love manliness, and get disgusted with effeminacy." Effeminacy is defined, among other things, as "unmanly compromise of truth; by withdrawing its unpalatable aspects from sight; by speaking smooth things; by effeminately overlaying one's style with ornament; by touching the sentiments and kindling superficial sensations." Homiletic manliness, on the other hand, is characterized by its "exhibitions of honest truthfulness, of adherence to principle, of courage," as well as "directness of address" as opposed to "timorous circumlocution."[17]

What's more, Douglass's gendered developmental model of slavery (effeminate and abused) to freedom (manly and empowered) had an ecclesial corollary among prevailing conceptions of Jesus within American Protestant circles. The portrayal of Jesus as an effeminized savior in mid-nineteenth-century American culture is well documented.[18] In both Douglass's oratory and writings, he regularly evokes the image of Esther's abused body as a synecdoche of the horrors of slavery. In Franchot's words, "Her suffering provides him with his credentials as victim—critical to his self-authentication as a fugitive slave orator; her femininity enables him to transcend that very identification—a transcendence critical to his success as the 'Representative Colored Man of the United States.' "[19] Indeed. Yet, this can also be read within a more explicitly theological framework. Douglass puts Esther's body on display as the crucified one, bruised for his iniquities, and by her stripes, he is healed. Esther's whipped body, like the crucified Christ, simultaneously arouses voyeuristic impulses and serves as a call to repentance and protection. Whites are called to repent for their participation in maintaining a slaveholding system. It matters not whether persons cried for Pontius Pilate to free Barabbas rather than Jesus, as did the crowd gathered at the foot of the cross, all are equally culpable. And black men are called to rise to protect the black female body by fighting the unjust evils of slavery that Esther's whipped flesh signifies. Esther, then, calls forth male disciples to take up her cause. She pays the price for Douglass's freedom (and manhood), and it is in and through her that Douglass's redeemed (free) body lives, moves, and has its very being. This is why it is appropriate to conclude that Frederick Douglass's promotion of these particular conceptions and markers of manhood as ultimate values for African Americans placed him alongside rather than at odds with the religious commitments of the premier black denominational leaders of his day.

Eddie Glaude, on the other hand, is deftly attuned to the internalized patterns and theological influences of the political rhetoric of Henry Highland Garnet. Through a reconfiguring of the structures of sin and evil within the Christian tradition, Garnet believes it's appropriate for pious though understandably perturbed people to "force the end" through mass resistance. Glaude is sensitive to the sacred symbols and sounds of black faith communities of the nineteenth century. This makes his inattention to the masculinist dimensions of Garnet's worldview even more puzzling, particularly since it is this very tradition that Glaude argues constitutes the intellectual and ideological archetype of black nationalist discourse, a discourse typically known for its unapologetic androcentrism. Garnet was engaged in more than troubling the theological ground of moral reform that left abolitionists with problematically similar responses of either pious submission and/or moral appeals to white power structures. He was also proffering an image of black masculinity that transcended the identity binary of black men as naturally hyperaggressive and unrestrained on the one hand and as conditioned into docility as a result of a necessary servitude on the other.[20] In other words, savage brutes or servile Sambos were not the only options of manhood available to African American men.

According to historians James Oliver and Lois E. Horton, self-assertion and aggression were key elements of any combination of characteristics constituting American manhood in the nineteenth century.[21] African American men, however, were placed in a double bind. Any display of violence on the part of black men served to reinforce stereotypes circulating within the white imagination, evidence of the need for physical restraint. And, as already mentioned, some interpreted Garrisonian pacifism and moral suasion as too much of a compromise. But in the vein of David Walker, some defended the right for African Americans to demand and/or defend their freedom "like men." Speaking before the African Masonic Hall of Boston in 1833, Walker's close friend Maria W. Stewart encouraged black men to break free from the shackles of cowardice. "For they admire a noble and patriotic spirit in others," she contends, "and should they not admire it in us. If you are men, convince them that you possess the spirit of men; and as your day, so shall your strength be. Have the sons of Africa no souls?"[22]

In 1841, before the American Reform Board of Disfranchised Commissioners Convention, antislavery activist and New York Committee of Vigilance secretary David Ruggles declared, "the age in which we live in [is] pregnant with events which claim our every attention. Our condition is every where [sic] identical. Rise, brethren, rise! Strike for freedom, or die slaves! . . . In our cause mere words are nothing—action is everything."[23]

In his 1843 address, Garnet's appeals to gendered masculine ideals were just as explicit as his overt Christian commitments: "Look around you, and behold the bosoms of your loving wives heaving with untold agonies! Hear the cries of your poor children! Remember the stripes your fathers bore. Think of the torture and disgrace of your poor mothers! Think of your wretched sisters, loving virtue and purity, as they are driven into concubinage and are exposed to the unbridled lusts of incarnate devils!"[24] Garnet is offering *more* than a theological reconceptualization of sin and moral duty, as Glaude argues accurately. Moral agency and resistance to evil are presented as manly attributes. By intertwining the masculinist rhetoric of violent resistance within discourses on Christian piety, Garnet offers a means for African American men to baptize their aggression, hence stripping violent resistance of its negative, brutish connotations when associated with black bodies. In probably the most adept gendered analysis of Henry Highland Garnet to date, rhetorician James Jasinksi concludes, "He [Garnet] imagined a reconstituted African American identity that energized and radicalized the patient suffering servant as it moderated the righteous anger of the avenging messiah. In so doing, he promoted a vision of African American manhood that transcended antebellum America's debilitating feminized child/savage brute dichotomy."[25]

CHAPTER 5

Everybody Knew He Was "That Way"

Chicago's Clarence H. Cobbs, American Religion, and Sexuality During the Post–World War II Period

WALLACE BEST

The announcement came as a surprise to all but those closest to them. In January 1945, the Reverend Clarence H. Cobbs and Jean Starr-Jones gathered "a few intimate friends" in the lavish apartment at 4320 South Michigan Avenue of Marva Louis, former Harlem model and wife of boxing champ Joe Louis, to announce their engagement. The moment the announcement was made, polite congratulations rumbled through the party and, as the *Chicago Defender* reported, Starr-Jones, known for her elegance and light complexion, "beam[ed] with joy" as she happily displayed "an expensive diamond ring."[1] The wedding was to take place in the summer and promised to be the social event of the year.

Weddings were common events in migration-era black Chicago, even among prominent black Chicagoans such as Cobbs and Starr-Jones. But this wedding announcement puzzled many. Not only was the engagement a surprise, but the fiancé and fiancée also seemed an unlikely pair. Cobbs was the pastor of one of the largest and most unusual churches on the South Side, First Church of Deliverance, Spiritual, at 4315 South Wabash Avenue. Starr-Jones was a former vaudeville actress and the socialite widow of one of the city's most notorious African American mobsters, McKissack McHenry ("Mac") Jones. The latter had died in an automobile accident just six months before the engagement.[2] Less a match made in heaven, the engagement between Cobbs and Starr-Jones appeared to be an instance of the church marrying the mob.

Figure 5.1 Engagement photo of Reverend Clarence Cobbs and Jean Starr-Jones taken at the home of Marva Louis and published in the *Chicago Defender* on January 20, 1945.

At the same time, despite the obvious differences in the couple's backgrounds, the pairing was emblematic of the dynamic changes occurring in black Chicago during the Great Migration. A generation prior, the worlds of Cobbs and Starr-Jones would not have ordinarily intersected. If they had, there would have been conflict and clash rather than announcements of marital commitment. Both would have been deemed outside the bounds of "respectable" society. One of the lasting and far-reaching legacies of the migration, however, was the way it disrupted an old order in black Chicago and installed a new one, primarily based on money and power, or capital and social capital, rather than on education, reputation, cultural refinement, and length of time in the city. The purveyors of this new order also rejected the rigid standards and signposts of respectability that had been in force since the late nineteenth century. New standards of respectability kept fewer people out of the realm of the "respectable." In this inclusive new order, not only could the pastor of a Spiritual congregation marry a former mob wife, but the couple could also represent what Davarian Baldwin calls "new visions of respectability."[3]

Beyond the suddenness of the announcement and the seeming oddity of the pairing, there was another reason many black Chicagoans took special note of this engagement. Clarence Cobbs had long been rumored to be *gay*—to employ the mid-twentieth-century sexualized version of the word. Indeed, by the 1940s, most black Chicagoans took Cobbs's homosexuality for granted and as a fact. In the common parlance of the period, everybody knew, and many openly proclaimed that he was "that way." Therefore, the surprise and spectacle of the wedding announcement had as much to do with the perception of Cobbs's homosexuality as it did his reputation as a minister and Starr-Jones's status as the socialite widow of a mob figure. In the eyes of most black Chicagoans, the impending nuptials meant that a prominent male minister, who happened to be "that way," was marrying a woman.

The exact reasons why Cobbs proposed to Starr-Jones were undoubtedly personal and may never be known. The proposal, however, likely had something to do with an elaborate effort to restore his reputation in the aftermath of a 1939 sex scandal. After the *Chicago Defender* published a series of articles in November of that year alluding to Cobbs's alleged sexual indiscretions, the Illinois State's Attorney's office placed Cobbs under surveillance and threatened to bring him in for questioning. The articles did not name the specific allegations but reported that they were of a "scandalous nature" involving an "unsavory incident of serious proportions."[4] During the weeks-long ordeal, Cobbs used his radio broadcast and his pulpit to deny the rumors, asserting that he was a "full man," and long after the event he gave regular "vindication services" aimed at redressing the implied charges of sexual impropriety.[5] His congregation refused to cooperate with the investigation, and Edward M. Sneed, Cook County's first elected African American commissioner, who happened to be a friend of Cobbs, rose to his defense. In December 1939, Cobbs sued the *Chicago Defender* for $250,000. But two years later, citing Proverbs 22 that a "good name" is more valuable than "great riches," he instructed his lawyer, Bernard Allen Fried, to drop the suit. The paper had published an apology for presenting "rumors" as "truth." The apology was not enough, however. In a letter to Mrs. Robert S. Abbott, publisher of the *Chicago Defender* and also a personal friend, Cobbs astutely asserted that "the extent of the damage an article such as the *Chicago Defender* published about me can never fully be determined."[6]

Certainly, the sex scandal played a role in Cobbs's decision, but it was unlikely the sole or even primary factor in his sudden engagement to Jean Starr-Jones. More likely, the decision was rooted in two distinct and highly significant factors. First, the engagement coincided with important shifts in the discourse about sexuality in the United States from the 1930s to the 1950s, particularly in some black churches, and the roles gay persons or people of "nonnormative" sexualities could play in religious life more broadly. Throughout the first half of the twentieth century, several African American male and female ministers and other church workers known or rumored to be gay served uncontested in some of the most vibrant Christian ministries on the South Side of Chicago. The institutional priorities of most churches were seemingly set beyond the simple "toleration" of these ministers to a full acceptance of them as rightful members of the wider religious community. Although this acceptance was conditioned by a carefully mediated social contract, or the social agreement of what Michael Musto calls "the glass closet," it allowed them to live as homosexuals in the Christian ministry within the space of the church.[7] As a space of open secret, nondisclosure, and nonverbal proclamations, "the glass closet" disallowed the fullest articulation of their sexual identity, not to mention sexual practices. Still, it was a site of relative freedom to explore and express a wide range of sexual identities, as well as relational and sexual performances.

This brief era of full acceptance, beginning with the first waves of northward migration, reflected the broader social and sexual trends in Chicago and other urban centers in the United States at the time. Throughout the first three decades of the twentieth century, homosexuals in such places as Chicago and New York coexisted with "normals," as heterosexuals were sometimes called, with relatively little conflict. Moreover, the various "types" or expressions of nonnormative sexualities, including "pansy," "fairy," "butch," and "dyke," were a social reality in modern urban life and an integral part of it, particularly in the realms of entertainment and leisure. Shifts in American sociopolitical priorities, however, along with the growth of religious conservatism, the emerging importance placed on family life, and a growing link between "sex morons" and crime, provided the infrastructure for what came to be known as "the closet."[8] These changes further marginalized homosexuals across the country at every level of society and effectively forged a new era for Chicago's black gay ministers and church workers, forcing them to make new decisions about their lives and the public performances of their sexuality.

The second more likely factor in Cobbs's engagement to Starr-Jones had to do with the notions of sexuality and the metaphysical world as taught by the Spiritual church, the theological and philosophical center of his religious faith. Even though he would mitigate some of his most strident stances in later years, Cobbs's devotion to the Spiritual church and its metaphysical and mystical teachings ran deep, evidenced by his sermons, social activities, and how he conducted his personal life. His reputation as a "mystic" grew from his keen appropriation of the Spiritual church's Theosophical-influenced teaching and his alleged ability to heal, despite counterclaims of his materialism and "worldliness." Indeed, the interstitial, ambiguous, and unfixed quality of Cobbs's life was characteristic of the Spiritual church itself, which allowed for haziness and the undefined in human existence and held that the material world was an imperfect but necessary reflection of the real world. And the real world was spiritual in nature and substance. In the material world, categories of sexuality concretize the real (spiritual) world when in reality, there are no fixed categories of sexuality. In terms of the Spiritual church of Cobbs's day, binaries bore little meaning. Nothing or no one was ever good or bad, homosexual or heterosexual, worldly or otherworldly, black or white. They were both/and, having equal capacities. Far from the sensational oddity that many black Chicagoans took it to be, therefore, the proposed marriage of Clarence Cobbs to Jean Starr-Jones reflected the early Spiritual church's notion that sexuality is not a fixed condition. It is, instead, a material performance in the real world of the spirit and immateriality, which ultimately transcends the body and the temporal. So, while black Chicagoans were likely correct that Clarence Cobbs was "that way," his engagement was not only a response to an illicit sex scandal and the increased pressure of sexual conformity but also a demonstration of his church's conception of the fluidity and instability of sexual categories.

The life and early experiences of Chicago's Clarence Cobbs reveal the critical intersection of religion and sexuality and how religion often has a significant impact on the construction of sexual identity and performance. It shows that the theological and philosophical particulars of his faith assisted him in navigating a rapidly changing sexual culture. Just as importantly, Cobbs's story also elucidates a moment in black Chicago history when African American churches placed primacy on ministerial effectiveness, preaching ability, and pastoral care rather than on clergy members' actual or perceived sexuality. It was a time before the common assumption of the inherent "homophobia" of black churches, when, as bell hooks says, "gay people . . . did not live in separate subcultures."[9] They lived where others lived, including and often very prominently in black churches. Cobbs and a few other black Chicago ministers and church workers known to be "that way" served uncontested in their respective capacities largely because black Chicago churches had not systematized a programmatic or theological prohibition that would prevent them from doing so. Those prohibitions and the accompanying homophobia would emerge with the broad social and political changes that culminated during the 1950s, altering the discourse and the cultural climate surrounding issues of sex and sexuality. Ultimately, the story of Chicago's Clarence Cobbs highlights how broad shifts in American culture have had transformative effects on African American religion, specific religious communities, and the lives and personal choices of individual persons.

"Preacher"

Clarence Henry Cobbs was born in Memphis, Tennessee, in February 1908. The 1930 census reports that at the time, he was head of his South Michigan Avenue household in Chicago, which included his mother, Luella Williams; grandmother, Maggie Drummer; and a single roomer, Oda Taylor. Cobbs's mother had married his father, Frank Cobbs, from Madison, Arkansas, at age seventeen, but the marriage did not last long. During the First World War, she came to Chicago and met and married Willie Williams, after which she called for her mother and son to join her. The marriage to Williams was also short-lived—as the 1930 census classifies her as a "widow."[10] The way Cobbs's family arrived in Chicago places them among the wave of black Southerners who trekked north during the Great Migration beginning at the time of the First World War. The phenomenal demographic shift when millions of African Americans left the South for the promise of better lives in the North led to a radical restructuring of American society. The mass movement had its most profound impact in cities like Chicago, where the black population swelled by hundreds of thousands in a very short time.[11] Having been a member of St. Paul Baptist Church in his native Memphis, Tennessee, Cobbs joined Pilgrim Baptist upon his arrival in Chicago. Pilgrim was an obvious choice not only because of its denominational affiliation but also because it ranked high on a shortlist of black Baptist churches actively engaged in assisting migrants with material as well as spiritual aid. Consequently, by the mid to late 1920s, the membership at Pilgrim exceeded well over two thousand. It was a fitting introduction for the young Tennessean to Chicago's dynamic world of religion and churches.

In May 1929, Cobbs left Pilgrim to establish the First Church of Deliverance, affiliating it with a newly formed denomination, the Metropolitan Spiritual Churches of Christ, Inc. (MSCC). The denomination was an eclectic mix, borrowing freely from several religious traditions within and outside of Christianity, including Eastern Orthodoxy, Catholicism, and voodoo. With a belief system and worship patterns similar to Pentecostalism, Spiritual churches espoused psychic phenomena, acknowledged the "spirit world" and the "Universal Mind," and practiced séances in addition to speaking in tongues and divine healing. They also placed heavy emphasis on sacred objects, sacred garments, incense, and candles.[12] The church's music consisted of a combination of standard English Baptist and Methodist hymns and the newly emerged genre of black gospel. Indeed, First Church of Deliverance grew to prominence partly because of the high quality and innovation of its music, which made it as much a center of entertainment as of worship. As a result, black Chicagoans quickly came to see the congregation as distinct from all others in the city.

Starting as a "storefront" church with just a few members and his assistant pastor, Maggie Thornton, by 1939 First Church of Deliverance had moved into a stunningly refurbished building and boasted a congregation estimated as having between five thousand and fifteen thousand members. For a relatively new church, these were impressive numbers that equaled or excelled those of some of the most established churches in black Chicago, including Cobbs's former church, Pilgrim Baptist. The building had been a hat factory when Cobbs purchased it in 1933, and he hired Walter T. Bailey, the first licensed black architect in Illinois, to assist him with the redesign. Bailey, a graduate of the University of Illinois, whose first major project was the National Pythian Temple in Chicago, designed the church in the Art Moderne style to enhance the congregation's reputation for being "modern" and Cobbs's renown as "forward-thinking." Art Moderne was an unconventional choice for a church building, and First Church of Deliverance became the only church in Chicago with that design.[13]

In 1934, Cobbs launched a weekly radio broadcast on WSBC, where Jack Cooper had become the first full-time African American radio announcer.

In doing so, Cobbs became only the second African American minister in Chicago on the air. Elder Lucy Smith of All Nations Pentecostal Church, located just blocks away from First Church of Deliverance, preceded him by a year and served as his inspiration.[14] By the late 1930s, Cobbs had become renowned for his mysticism and working of "miracles." He had also become known for his flamboyant display during worship services, often changing robes several times during a single service. His preaching was widely regarded as "verbal art," and his ability to captivate radio audiences as well as his congregation with his lively and innovative sermons earned him the simple appellative "preacher," by which he was called for the rest of his life.[15]

First Church's reputation for being modern was well earned. Although Spiritual churches rapidly increased in number throughout the 1920s and 1930s, First Church was the leading and most progressive Spiritual congregation in Chicago at a time of ever-expanding religious diversity. It was the only male-led congregation with a female assistant, making it a forerunner in gender equity in black Chicago pulpits in a denomination where, according to sociologist Hans Baer, "women generally have historically played an influential role."[16] It also brought into the mainstream a form of worship and a set of beliefs previously thought to be anti-Christian. Cobbs maintained his belief in the spirit world for most of his career, declaring, "Spirit is Real. Divine Communication is Real." In 1970 at the forty-fifth annual congress of the MSCC, of which he had become national president in 1942, Cobbs reiterated this point and added that "mediums" are a "connecting link between two forces which may be used for good or evil."[17] In many ways, his belief in mediums connected to the Spiritual church's notion of the "universal mind" and the link between the material and spiritual worlds. Seemingly drawing on New Thought philosophy and the teachings of the Theosophical Society, founded in 1875, early iterations of the Spiritual church asserted the union of all things in their connection to the universal mind. The mind/body connection and the role it played for the church's mediums, as well as a clear articulation of the belief in the universal mind, surfaced in a report on Cobbs and the church conducted by a Works Progress Administration (WPA) worker in the late 1930s. Quoting an unnamed source, the report states that "the material part of man may vanish from sight, the spiritual part and the soul with all its memories, exist forever, just as God and the Universal Mind are eternal."[18]

Despite his espousal of New Thought philosophy and Theosophy, however, Cobbs contended that he was primarily, simply, and devoutly a Christian minister. He routinely affirmed his belief in the basic tenets of Christianity, and his contention that his Christian moral character had been impugned was, in part, the force behind his "vindication services" and his claim to being a "full man" in the aftermath of the sex scandal.[19] Moreover, the theological statements of the Spiritual church varied little from mainstream Christian denominations. Indeed, the Affirmations of Metropolitan Spiritual Churches were based on the Apostles' Creed, acknowledging the denomination's belief in the Bible as "the supreme revelation of God," the Virgin Birth, the Trinity, the deity *and* humanity of Jesus, and the Second Coming.[20] Although the theological statement contained some characteristic ambiguity, including such unconventional Christian notions as the importance of "the mind," the eternality of the human spirit, and converts becoming "immortal" upon their conversion, it was fundamentally a statement of conventional Christian belief.

Clarence Cobbs, however, took a decidedly unconventional and pragmatic approach to Christian ministry, and it was largely for this reason that he was dubbed modern and forward-thinking. He imagined his church as an inclusive space of social and religious service fit to meet the full range of his congregants' needs. Cobbs clarified this point in 1938 to an interviewer who asked him why he had established First Church. "To serve the people, for in serving the people we also serve God; to find heaven here and in the hereafter; to teach love, faith, and devotion to God by service," he declared. "The church was established for all the people from every walk of life," he further claimed, "it is the people's church and its doors stand wide open in invitation to all alike."[21] Cobbs's personal theological approach exhibited the same tension between the conventional and unconventional found in the Spiritual church's affirmations. It also reflected the metaphysical assumptions and anti-dogmatism characteristic of New Thought philosophy and Theosophy. For instance, while the church's official theological statement on "sin" contended that "Jesus Christ is the only Savior from sin; that He died for our sins as a representative, substitutionary, and perfect sacrifice," Cobbs most famously rejected the notion of sin. Rather, he suggested that Christians should embrace those things that have historically been considered sins of the body, such as drinking and premarital sex. These were created for the body's enjoyment, he maintained. Life was to be enjoyed and not approached puritanically.[22] One of his shortest and most famous addresses to his congregation includes traces of this type of thinking.

> There isn't going to be any sermon today. You all have been working too hard raising money for the convalescent home. I want you to do something nice for your own self for a change. Hear me. Go on out and have yourself a good time. The dishes you've been saving for company. Go home and eat off them your own self. Go on out and buy yourself some records. Buy yourself a bag of apples and oranges and every night before you go to sleep eat a piece of fruit and read something good from the Bible. Be nice to yourself. Amen.[23]

In a 1938 interview, he defended his modern approach to Christian ministry and liberal theology, citing the need for religion to match the changing times. "Just as everything gets old fashioned," he contended, "so it is with religion—our father's and mother's ways don't suit us, we want something different."[24]

Poor and working-class black southern migrants comprised the majority membership of First Church of Deliverance, and the congregation was overwhelmingly female. But like many black Chicago churches during the Great Migration, people from all socioeconomic classes and various backgrounds became members or regular attendees. Cobbs was fond of noting that the church had a small number of white members and that the broadcast had countless white listeners. Celebrities visited so often that First Church became known as "the church of the stars." Star parishioners included Duke Ellington, Count Basie, Della Reese, Dinah Washington, Billy Preston, Earl "Fatha" Hines, Red Foxx, and Sammy Davis Jr.[25] Cobbs was adamant, however, about the goal of maintaining egalitarianism and promoting unity among his congregants. During the Great Depression, this conviction prompted him to insist on wearing white during worship services by all members and church workers in particular. Contending that there was no "top echelon or bottom echelon in the Christian society," Cobbs asserted that the wearing of white promoted "togetherness," not "purity," as is commonly maintained. And since most white clothing was cotton and cotton was cheap, it would also provide opportunities for "those who feel they cannot afford to participate in the actives of the church because of their inability to maintain the standards established by the 'so-called' society."[26]

As further evidence of Cobbs's modernity, the music of First Church of Deliverance also radically transformed the *sound* of black gospel when in 1939, his church introduced the Hammond B-3 organ. Thomas Andrew Dorsey may rightfully be considered the "father of black gospel music" and Pilgrim Baptist its "home," but Clarence Cobbs and the First Church of Deliverance played just as significant a role in the history of the tradition.[27] While Dorsey, as the leader of Pilgrim's gospel chorus, was busy writing his blues-inflected gospel tunes, such as "Precious Lord, Take My Hand," and "If You See My Savior," First Church of Deliverance became one of many South Side churches to popularize the new genre with live performances and radio broadcasts. The choir consisted of between one hundred and two hundred voices, and gospel pioneers, such as Sallie Martin and the Barrett Sisters made regular appearances at the church. Into the early 1970s, the church was still having a profound impact on the gospel music world. During that time, Cobbs rearranged the chorus of the classic Herbert W. Brewster gospel song, "How I Got Over," turning it into the church's regular processional and theme song.[28]

In addition to the innovative worship services of First Church, several social and economic outreach efforts also contributed to his reputation for having a "forward-thinking" style of leadership. These included a regular "soup line" during the Depression and the annual distribution of holiday food baskets. He also sat on the executive committee of the Chicago branch of the NAACP, and he was an avid supporter of A. Philip Randolph's effort to secure the passage of the Fair Employment Act, Executive Order 8802, designed to prohibit discrimination in the defense industry and promote equal opportunity in the United States. Cobbs assisted the North American Committee to Aid Spanish Democracy; built a community center, a health care facility, and a $2.5 million convalescent home; and supported a range of black-owned businesses on the South Side.[29] In 1942, Cobbs established a blood bank at Provident Hospital. It was the first African American blood bank in the country in Chicago's oldest African American hospital.[30] He followed that up with a "mobile canteen" designed to bring help and relief to victims and emergency workers.[31] His political connections with the likes of mayors Martin H. Kennelly and Richard J. Daley greatly facilitated Cobbs's leadership ability and the success of his projects.

Despite his many political and social connections, Clarence Cobbs had detractors. The assertion that he made to WPA worker Arthur Weinberg in 1938 that he was "the most disliked preacher" in Chicago was certainly an exaggeration, but there was also some substance to the claim. Although most of the city's black ministers chose not to believe the rumors that circulated about Cobbs in 1939, a few took the opportunity to express their feelings about the popular preacher. William S. Bradden, the pastor of Berean Baptist church, intoned that Cobbs was "a travesty on the sacredness of the Christian Church."[32] In November 1946, Chicagoan Lloyd Davis published a "challenge" in the *Chicago Defender* regarding Cobbs's outreach work. Davis emphatically argues that Cobbs was guilty of neglect in the same areas of service for which he had become known. "He has shown a complete lack of interest in such community issues as better housing facilities, more recreational and social centers for the youth, better schools and cleaner neighborhoods with his own district. He has done very little to help the very people he is supposedly leading." Assailing Cobbs for his "wonderfully expensive radio program," Davis concludes that Cobbs had "completely isolated himself within his own little Utopia."[33] Cobbs struck a few people as haughty, materialistic, disrespectful, and a "slum lord." A former tenant at a building Cobbs owned as a rental property in the 1940s recalled years later that Cobbs was inattentive to the property. He contended that Cobbs's friendship with Mayor Kennelly kept the property from being condemned. Repeated pleas to Cobbs to have the building's amenities fixed, the former tenant claimed, were met with a gruff response. "And that's the way he would talk to you, like you were dirt." Recalling that Cobbs also smoked "a big cigar," drove in a "big limousine," and gambled didn't seem to help matters.[34]

Some Chicagoans likely considered Cobbs a religious charlatan because of his lavish lifestyle and his fundraising techniques. His flamboyance was undoubtedly difficult to miss. He wore fashionable and expensive clothing, threw lavish parties, lived in a twenty-two-room mansion in the Grand Boulevard section of Bronzeville, and regularly took expensive vacations. He raised money for the church's many programs and building projects by selling "blessed flowers," which he promised would bring good fortune to the bearer. As one WPA writer notes, people sought these talismans like "hungry children at a picnic." Cobbs also regularly staged mass candlelight services attended by thousands at which he took in large offerings.[35]

Although a few Chicagoans considered Cobbs a charlatan in the order of New York's George Wilson Becton "of the consecrated dime," typical assessments of him, his leadership style, his church, and his social outreach efforts were overwhelmingly positive. Two months after the publication of

Davis's "challenge," Chicagoan William N. Bowie responded by insisting that Cobbs was "one of the greatest American leaders of this country." For Bowie, Cobbs and First Deliverance had made great improvements to the South Side, evidence that Davis knew "nothing about the man he attempted to evaluate." A few weeks later, Ryllar Jeannette Clayburn, a social worker from Minneapolis, concurred. In her response to Davis, Clayburn underscored the broad reach of Cobbs's radio program, his activity in the NAACP, and his generosity to bereaved families. These, she insists, were "indicative of the fact [that] he (Cobbs) is interested in the welfare of his community."[36]

Bowie and Clayburn did not reference Cobbs's homosexuality; neither did they infer that sexuality would prevent his effectiveness in Christian ministry. As independent Chicago scholar David Jones intimates, Cobbs's reputation as a "mystic" with healing powers may have trumped these considerations.[37] But it is also the case that Cobbs's sexuality would not have been a significant concern among those for or against him, nor would there have been a framework to articulate opposition to him based on his sexuality. Those frameworks of articulation would come later as products of the post–World War II period. The pastor of Chicago's first Spiritual church, a man known to be "that way," left an indelible mark on the city's African American religious culture by his personal and leadership styles, the innovative worship and music of his church, his political connections, and his social programs. Within a few decades after his sojourn from his native Tennessee, "preacher" elicited a wealth of devotion for his contribution to some of the most lasting transformations in black Chicago during the Great Migration.

The Social Agreement of "the Glass Closet"

The devotion Cobbs elicited, however, came with a condition. For all the seeming acceptance of him and other Chicago ministers of nonnormative sexualities, he was compelled to occupy "the glass closet." Although the term *glass closet* came into common parlance in the late 1990s, the concept came into existence in the early twentieth century. It gained special purchase among celebrities in Hollywood during the 1950s. Simply put, the glass closet constitutes a space wherein homosexual men and women can be "out" in some, usually private, areas of their lives but not publicly. This differs in a significant way from the more general notion of "the closet." That more general notion refers to an even more pronounced psychological, emotional, and ideational space wherein homosexuals have felt compelled to mask and/or deny their sexuality in the face of what Steven Seidman has called "heterosexual dominance." The closet is, he further contends, "a life-shaping pattern of homosexual concealment" wherein homosexuals "pass" as straight in all aspects of their lives. It is a means of "adjusting to a society that aggressively enforces heterosexuality as the preferred way of life." Gender theorist Eve Sedgwick calls it "the defining structure of gay oppression in this (the twentieth) century" and "the shaping presence" in the lives of most homosexuals.[38] When the term *glass closet* came into usage in the late 1990s, it more commonly referred to entertainers and politicians known to be gay. Still, in refusing to state their sexuality publicly, they seemingly were employing a level of circumspection and discretion about their private lives. Refusing to declare their sexuality publicly was deemed a decision they had a right to make, particularly since they did not want to be, as Michael Musto puts it, "defined by their sexuality." Actor David Hyde Pierce once quipped, after years of speculation about his sexuality, "My life is an open book, but don't expect me to read it to you."[39]

In Cobbs's case, the glass closet functioned differently in significant ways. It contained the same open secret aspect, but the social contract dictated that people could be honest about their sexual preference *only* as long as they did not espouse a public identity as a homosexual. In this case, the glass closet was an agreement they struck with the church and wider community requiring dissemblance and silence for the freedom to live openly as homosexuals. As Chicago writer and historian Sukie de la Croix claims after numerous interviews with black Chicagoans who knew Cobbs, "Cobbs was gay but never came out," meaning he never publicly declared his homosexuality.[40] Before 1945, however, he seemingly made few attempts to hide or mask his sexuality. Indeed, the social agreement of the glass closet was not a matter of hiding homosexuality or "passing" as heterosexual. It was, rather, a refusal to publicly claim a homosexual identity or indicate that one's same-sex associations grew from or reflected one's sexual orientation. For all the complexities about sexuality and sexual identity he seemingly embraced from the Spiritual church, Cobbs lived as a homosexual man in plain view of the greater Chicago community through a carefully orchestrated series of social codes and a resolute silence about his sexual identity.

Cobbs may have lived in a world of social codes that required silence about his sexuality, but the larger gay world of Chicago was not invisible, particularly from the 1920s to the early 1940s. Indeed, as George Chauncey,

Allen Drexel, Chad Heap, and David Johnson have shown, a visible gay world thrived in Chicago during these years.[41] Cobbs was likely well aware of this world and a participant in it, given that he moved within a circle that included many professed homosexuals. It was also the case that First Church of Deliverance was widely regarded as a "gay church" because it embraced homosexuals during most of Cobbs's pastorate. At least a few gay men found employment on the church's staff, including Lucius Hall, the church's announcer and one of its musicians. Hall, identified as "L" in WPA documents, was considered a "celebrity" and a "diva" because he preferred fur coats. An African American man who frequented the church during the 1940s remembered, "L was really flamboyant and really feminine back in those days."[42] Known as "luscious" because of his remarkably good looks and charisma, Hall was an object of desire for both men and women in black Chicago.[43] Gay men also frequented the nightly broadcast at First Church, often making it a stop on their way to one of several African American gay nightclubs in the area, including the 430 (a.k.a. the "dirty thirty"), the Kitty Kat (where scenes from the 1961 film *A Raisin in the Sun* were shot), and the Parkside. Hall, the same informant recalled, "would be in the Kitty Kat every night after the choir turned out."[44]

The social agreement of the glass closet disallowed a certain level of personal and political expression, but it by no means disallowed the emergence of the distinctive features of a gay community. Throughout the 1920s and 1930s, the signposts of homosexuality were rooted in a set of highly gendered cultural cues, discourses, and mannerisms. In various urban enclaves throughout the United States at the time, but particularly in such places as Chicago, New York, Detroit, and Washington, DC, gay men often walked invisibly among the straight population but were visible to each other. Fastidiousness or flamboyance in dress was often meant (and taken) as a sign of same-sex attraction, including "tight-cuffed trousers" and "half-lengthed flaring top-coats."[45] But the signs could be as subtle as the color of one's tie (red being of particular significance) or the texture of one's shoes (usually suede), or the simple placement of a handkerchief in a suit pocket. This way of dressing was most common among "fairies" or "pansies," "effeminate" gay men who presumably would play the passive role in a male-male sexual encounter. But anyone familiar with the gay world of the 1920s and 1930s, including the more "masculine" counterpart to the "fairy" or "pansy," would have been well aware of its meaning. Since the gay revolution of the late 1960s, any connection between flamboyant dress (or behavior) and homosexuality has been deemed a stereotype. Still, during the interwar period, Cobbs's well-known sense of style and propensity for fancy and expensive clothes was likely an indication of his same-sex attraction and was meant to signal such interest.

Cobbs entered the social agreement of the glass closet early in his ministerial career, having been profoundly influenced by William F. Taylor and Leviticus Boswell. Taylor and Boswell established the MSCC denomination, giving Cobbs his professional start and inspiring his religious eclecticism and mysticism through their commitment to the philosophies of the Spiritual church. Taylor and Boswell also modeled for Cobbs a way to navigate the glass closet's social agreement, which directly impacted many of Cobbs's personal choices about his public presentation. Although they did not publicly identify as homosexual, Taylor and Boswell shared a remarkably close personal bond that was, Boswell claimed, sexual. From the start of their organization, Taylor and Boswell seemingly drew a link between an openness about sex and sexuality and the Spiritual church. Indeed, under Taylor and Boswell's leadership, the MSCC became known as an "umbrella group for gays," not only because the leaders were rumored to be homosexual but also because the organization welcomed gay people into its ranks.[46]

Many things attracted Cobbs to Taylor and Boswell and drew him to the Spiritual church and the MSCC denomination. Like many others, he was impressed with their reputed mysticism, healing powers, and emphasis on the universal mind. Cobbs was also likely drawn to Taylor and Boswell's philosophy of gender and racial "egalitarianism." They committed their church to complete equality for all, creating an ecclesiastical space that was inclusive. They welcomed Cobbs into their fold and authorized him to preach and pastor his own church when he was barely twenty. The fact that the Spiritual church welcomed those with nonnormative sexualities likely played a part as well. Given the bonds and shared codes of those who lived under the social agreement of the glass closet, Cobbs chose to join forces with two men of faith with whom he shared much in common regarding issues of sexuality and sexual identity. Cobbs maintained his close association with Taylor and Boswell until they died in 1942 and 1952, respectfully, both having suffered humiliating downfalls. He was one of only a few friends at Taylor's bedside upon his death in Los Angeles a little over two years after Taylor and Boswell were arrested and brought up on "morals charges" in the spring of 1940 for having "unnatural sex" with two male members of the church.[47]

Mirroring the relationship between Taylor and Boswell, Cobbs maintained a longtime relationship with Richard Edward Bolden, who served as the secretary of First Church of Deliverance from the mid-1930s until he died in 1949. A native of Missouri and a gifted baritone, Bolden had been a secretary at Poro College, the haircare and beauty empire built by Annie Malone in 1902. When Malone moved her business to Chicago in 1930 after a bitter divorce and power struggle for the company, Bolden moved with her. At some point in the mid-1930s, Bolden left Poro to work for Cobbs at First Church. Like Cobbs, Bolden was single, in his midthirties, and lived with his widowed mother.[48] By 1938, the two men had become constant companions and were seemingly inseparable. Everything about their association and activities signaled the nature of their relationship. Bolden was a perennial dinner guest at the many parties Cobbs gave at his mansion. He was, for example, among the "socially prominent Chicagoans" Cobbs had invited to an extravagant Valentine party in honor of Leontyne King of Los Angeles in 1946. "Society has not witnessed in many seasons so lavish an occasion honoring any other visitor," effused the *Chicago Defender*.[49] Although as the church's secretary, he could not be described as "socially prominent," like most people on the guest list, Bolden was usually in attendance at these events. His constant presence marked him as someone of singular importance to the host.

It was the many extended vacations Cobbs and Bolden took together, however, that gave the clearest indication of the nature of their relationship. Beginning in the late 1930s, the two men traveled extensively and often. In 1939, for example, they embarked on a nearly month-long cruise to the West Indies and South America. On the morning of the trip, members of the church, who had raised $322 in a special church service to fund the vacation, met Cobbs, Bolden, and another "close friend" who was "traveling incognito" at the train station for a "surprise bon voyage send off."[50] They traveled by train to New York City, where they were to board a cruise ship. WPA worker Arthur Weinberg matter-of-factly noted the vacation in his report: "Rev. Cobbs is taking a twenty-six day cruise on the ocean and is being accompanied by the secretary of the church, R. Edward Bolden." Many of the vacations coincided with Bolden's and Cobbs's birthdays, February 4 and 28, respectively. In January 1943, for example, they arrived in Los Angeles for a "month's vacation in the Southland." Cobbs had many friends in the "Angel City," the *Pittsburgh Courier* noted.[51]

In adherence to the logic and the code of the social agreement of the glass closet, the relationship between Cobbs and Bolden was never subjected to public scrutiny, even though it was well known. The members of First Church were certainly aware of it, as were most Chicagoans familiar with the church. With the intimacies of their relationship kept private and no proclamation of a homosexual identity, Cobbs and Bolden could move about their world as a same-gender couple and two of the highest officers in one of the most prominent black churches in Chicago. And their bond was an exceptionally close one. Cobbs was said to have been "personally devastated" when Bolden died in 1949 and staged for him one of the most elaborate funerals in the history of First Church. For many years after the death of Bolden, the "beloved church secretary," Cobbs found ways to honor his memory. As late as 1958, he was still instructing the church to decorate a "memorial table" for Bolden at the church's annual Mother's Day Tea.[52]

From the Social Agreement of the Glass Closet to the Closet

By the end of 1945, Chicagoans were still waiting for the promised wedding between Cobbs and Starr-Jones. Although the couple was seen together from time to time, they made no mention of their nuptials and attempted to avoid all questions about it and any further publicity. Cornered by reporters at Harlem's Hotel Theresa in December of that year, Cobbs quickly ushered Jones out of sight, pleading, "No pictures, for heaven's sake. No pictures." In response to the spectacle, gossip columnist Dan Burley teased, "They were supposed to be married at one time, you know."[53] Indeed, the fact that Cobbs and Starr-Jones had not followed through with their engagement became fodder for more speculation about the true (or false) nature of their relationship and seemingly provided further confirmation of Cobbs's homosexuality.

The reasons why the wedding did not take place are not clear. The engagement dissolved just as mysteriously as Cobbs's little-known and brief first engagement to violinist Victoria Rice of Los Angeles in 1943.[54] The couple seemed to be on good terms and was often seen together as they had been in Harlem. And in 1946, Starr-Jones was still to be found among the guests at Cobbs's parties. Cobbs's same-gender attraction would not have kept him from marrying Starr-Jones. His seeming belief in the instability of sexual categories as taught by the Spiritual church and further evidenced by his first engagement suggests that he would have deemed such a union well within the realm of possibility. Ultimately, the issue is not so much that Cobbs and Starr-Jones never followed through with their marriage—it is why Cobbs felt compelled to become engaged at that time in the first place. The scandal most likely played a role, as did his notions of sexuality and sexual identity. But broad cultural shifts taking place in the United States regarding marriage, the family, sex, sexuality, and homosexuality, in particular, played just as significant a part in the decision. Put simply, American society was undergoing rapid change in the mid-1940s, and those changes made the social agreement of the glass closet untenable as it gave way to tighter strictures of "the closet." Most likely, Cobbs's engagement to Jean Starr-Jones also signaled his attempt to mask his homosexuality under the growing pressure to conform to the sexual status quo of the mid-1940s and 1950s. Indeed, during and after World War II in America, same-gender attraction became a reason to marry, not a reason to avoid it.

World War II and the era of the 1950s generated some of the most far-reaching cultural changes the United States had ever witnessed. The middle of the twentieth century left marks on the culture that continued to reverberate socially and politically into the twenty-first century. The war and its aftermath comprised the centerpiece of these changes for the way they reshaped marriage, gender roles, and family life. And these changes, in turn, generated new thinking about sex, sexuality, and homosexuality. Marriage had been going through significant changes in the United States since the late nineteenth century when there was a move away from marriage as a legal arrangement that had as much to do with property and protection as love and affection. The dawn of the era of "companionate marriage" in the early part of the twentieth century opened space for the decision to get married based on emotional attachments, which gave as much liberty to women in the decision as it did men.[55] Companionate marriage, however, also made marriage a personal matter and created legitimate space for the decision to remain unmarried. Marriage rates dropped to their lowest rates in a generation. By the late 1920s and 1930s, during the Depression, men and women of all races and class levels, particularly those in urban areas, remained unmarried and exerted greater freedom to express themselves sexually outside the bonds of marriage and the perceived entrapments of domesticity. The war complicated matters by generating a stark gender imbalance, reducing the available stock of marriageable men. It also brought more women into a workforce dominated by men, who were now on the battlefront on distant shores. The iconic image of Rosie the Riveter was not only an expression of cultural pride during a time of war, but it also signaled the era of independent, single American women who were entering the workforce and making their way in the world without the presence of men or the "benefit" of marriage.

By the early 1940s, however, many Americans began expressing discomfort with the large numbers of single people in the United States, equating singleness with potential immorality and instability. This became even more pronounced during the "profamily" decade of the 1950s, a "profamily period if there ever was one," Stephanie Coontz contends.[56] Even during the 1930s, some observers had begun to attribute the perceived moral laxness of the time to singleness. The situational condition of large groups of men living together in encampments during the Depression led to immorality and threatened family stability, they maintained. "Unattached persons," as Margot Canady asserts, were viewed as particularly prone to homosexual encounters. In these encampments, "the normal longing of these individuals for intimate companionship with the opposite sex [was] thwarted or turned to illicit channels."[57] The pressure to marry during the 1940s and 1950s grew from anxieties about singleness and from a newfound primacy put on family life. Throughout the late 1940s into the 1950s, singleness was shunned, as marriage was equated with happiness and stability. A 1955 study found that "less than 10 percent of Americans believed that an unmarried person could be happy," and a popular advice book proclaimed, "the family is the center of your living." "If it isn't," the book warned, "you've gone [far] astray."[58] Americans responded dramatically. Marriage rates increased, and the median age of marriage fell. Birth rates increased, inaugurating the baby boom in America. Divorce rates decreased. As the heterosexual couple took primacy and became the American ideal in the 1940s and 1950s, "the proportion of never-married persons declined by as much as it had during the entire previous half century."[59]

The preeminence of the heterosexual couple as the American ideal began in part with the New Deal's economic privileging of marriage; a greater intrusion into private, intimate matters during the war; and the fear that homosexuality was not only destabilizing but also seditious and "pathological." Before the 1940s, government intrusion into private life was fairly limited and noninvasive. Certain questions about intimate matters posed by the federal government were deemed out-of-bounds and improper. Beginning in 1940, however, for the first time in the nation's history, the U.S. military asked potential recruits about their sex lives. Psychological screeners began asking versions of the question, "Do you like girls?" A negative answer to the question could render one "unfit for service." As John D'Emilio asserts, "In an era when silence most typically characterized society's approach to same-sex eroticism, the military medical examination was a significant exception. For gay and nongay men alike, it represented the first and perhaps the only time that they faced such inquiries in a public setting."[60] The question proved traumatic for gay and nongay men alike and shaped their military experience around carefully crafted perceptions of straightness. It reinforced the notion that heterosexuality was normal and for the greater good, contributing to a virulent antihomosexual climate in the military.

The medicalization of homosexuality had begun in the late nineteenth century, but in the 1940s, it escalated, serving as the engine driving the emerging antihomosexual climate. The question posed to potential recruits by psychiatric screeners during World War II gave evidence of the growing influence of psychiatry in the armed services, which had taken, in Neil Miller's words, "an extremely negative stance toward homosexuality."[61] For the first time, there emerged in the military a prohibition on homosexual *persons* rather than homosexual *acts*. But the reach extended into the general society as well. As a consequence, homosexuality shifted from the realm of illegality and vice to pathology. This move went far in the way to build the infrastructure of the closet. After the state began to regulate the intimate affairs of American citizens with the sanction of the mental health community, "the government mobilized its considerable resources and authority to crack down on homosexuals." This was precisely the moment, as Steven Seidman has argued, that "the closet became the defining reality of gay life in America."[62]

By World War II, the medicalization of homosexuality joined law and religion as one of the most potent forces that influenced attitudes toward homosexual persons and acts. The law classified homosexuality as a crime, religion rendered it a "sin," and the medical profession began to consider it a disorder. Indeed, as John D'Emilio argues, "Medical views bore a complex relation to the older perspectives of religion and law." In his view, "they reinforced the cultural matrix that condemned and punished persons who engaged in homosexual activity."[63] Although some medical or psychological theories of homosexuality as a disease of the mind had been circulating before the midcentury; it was not until the early 1940s that the medical model of homosexuality began to circulate gradually among medical circles. It began, curiously, with several disciples and followers of Sigmund Freud. Although Freud himself had proffered the notion of "universal bisexuality," one of his chief disciples, Sandor Rado, rejected that possibility in favor of a view that homosexuality constituted a fear of the opposite sex and that heterosexuality was innate to everyone.[64] The implication of what came to be called the "Rado View" was that heterosexuality was normative, and homosexuality was the expression of a troubled mind. By the late 1940s and early 1950s, the view became dogma, despite countervailing studies such as the ones conducted by sexologist Alfred Kinsey.[65]

The idea that homosexuality was "sick" fit nicely within a wartime and postwar culture that was in no mood for nonconformity and was desirous of confirming the conservative values of home, family, and church. The trauma of the war and the uncertainty in its aftermath generated within American society an unprecedented push for cultural conformity and national unity. As the country attempted to reimagine itself politically and spiritually, most trends regarding expanding gender roles and liberal ideas about sexuality prevalent in the early part of the twentieth century were called into question.[66] Scholars have long noted the emergence or resurgence of conservative religion in the postwar era when God and country became issues of pride and allegiance. The phrase "under God" was added to the Pledge of Allegiance, "In God We Trust" was imprinted on U.S. currency, and churches set records for attendance. By the 1950s, expectations for the nation's leaders had been ratcheted up to include "spiritual" and political leadership. Ways of life that countered this new America were deemed suspect, subversive, and un-American. "Dissent and nonconventional lifestyles," remarks Steven Seidman, "were associated with political subversion."[67]

These factors, the emphasis on family life, the construction of the heterosexual couple as the American ideal, the government intrusion into soldiers' sexual lives, and the medicalization of homosexuality led to one conclusion: it was wrong, bad, and even dangerous to be homosexual. The American cultural climate had become decidedly antihomosexual, and the previous social agreements of the glass closet began to fade. In its stead rose the closet as a way of reinforcing the normalcy of heterosexuality and the abnormality of homosexuality. For some who chose to occupy the closet, this meant "passing" in a heterosexual marriage; for others, it meant developing various means of hiding same-sex attraction. Ironically, this antihomosexual climate coincided with increased gay visibility, particularly in urban areas, as gay men and lesbians continued to develop communities signified by new organizations, publications, and social establishments.[68] The climate also shaped the notion of gay identity and provided the means activists would employ in the gay liberation movement of the 1960s. Until that time, however, America's heterosexual dominance resulted in gay oppression, reinforced by law, religion, and the medical profession.

By the end of the 1940s, Jean Starr-Jones was out of Clarence Cobbs's life. With the death of R. Edward Bolden in 1949, Cobbs moved from the social agreement of "the glass closet" to "the closet." He remained single and unaccompanied until he died in 1979. The social agreement of the glass closet had suited him, but the absence of any details about his personal life beyond the late 1940s strongly suggests a change in his approach. It could also register the extent to which he felt the loss of Bolden. But the man that everybody knew was "that way" became the man about whom few people knew any details at all, particularly personal details. It is not that Cobbs disappeared from public view, ceased his work, or changed his leadership style. On the contrary, his postwar activities seemed to escalate, garnering him even more praise from the wider Chicago community. To honor him for over forty years of service to the greater Chicago area, for example, in 1971, the "Citizens Foundation to Bring Us Together" named Cobbs "Black Minister of the Year." The ceremony that marked his fiftieth year in ministry included telegrams from Mayor Jane Byrne, Governor James R. Thompson, and President Jimmy Carter. Rev. Jesse Jackson spoke at the event, calling Cobbs his "spiritual father."

To a large extent, however, Clarence Cobbs became a different person publicly in the post–World War II years. Although he maintained his dapper image, having regularly won recognition for being one of the "best dressed" men in Chicago, he moved away from what Cayton and Drake called the "sporting life" that once characterized him. Cobbs became more conservative politically, socially, and religiously. He called for significant changes in the Spiritual church, insisting on conformity with mainstream black churches in Chicago. In 1968, for example, he requested that all Catholic iconography be removed from every church within the Spiritual church denomination, including his own First Church of Deliverance.[69] Séances and "mediums" had been falling out of favor within the Spiritual churches for many years. Cobbs actively discouraged them in the late 1950s, as he became much more of a conventional gospel preacher.

Cobbs's move from the social agreement of the glass closet to the closet was his response to a rapidly changing world in the post-World War II era. And the broad cultural changes not only influenced his personal choices and those of many others, but they also radically transformed the gay world of black Chicago of which he had been a part. A proliferation of gay bars and nightclubs throughout the late 1950s through the 1970s occurred on Chicago's South Side, including the Mark IV, the Grapevine, Maxine's, the Boulevard Room, the Jeffrey Pub, and the Cellar. This proliferation, however, did not signal the kind of visibility and acceptance that had characterized the community in the 1920s and 1930s. Rather, the number of gay bars on the South Side meant that the community was becoming more restricted, more homogeneous, and less free. The previous generation of bars and nightclubs had a large gay clientele but catered to a vast cross-section of black and white Chicagoans, gay and straight. However, the post-World War II bars were almost exclusively African American, and for the first time, catered either predominately to gay men or lesbians, due to what a former bar patron described as "the alienation between gay men and lesbians."[70]

The general climate for homosexuals in the United States declined during these years. In black Chicago, that declension took the form of tensions within the community and greater scrutiny from without. Testimonials about the period contend, "If you minded your own business, you had no problems." But this uneasy calm required a type of self-policing, was very fragile and was predicated on notions of the inherent immorality of gay people. As one former bar patron intoned, "People tolerated us, and I think people stayed within their own community. They had their bars and they say, ok, let them have their little fun. As long as they don't molest the children or the dogs."[71] In other instances, Chicago's South Side community of black gay men and lesbians were subject to outright hostility, lived under the constant threat of arrest, and suffered intense scrutiny from civic authorities. In early March 1968, the Chicago police raided Maxine's and arrested everyone, charging them with being "inmates of a disorderly house." Men who dressed in drag and the South Side's many "female impersonators" were particularly prone to arrest. Ebony Carr, who worked both as a drag performer and a male nurse during the 1960s, recalled, "Back in those days it was a heavy scrutiny being gay and being a male nurse, and once they find out you're a transvestite or something like that, that made it even worse." Carr was arrested and harassed twice, and it was only because the performer complied with the city's ordinance that a man must have "at least two parts of male clothing on" at all times that he was able to beat the charges. Jane Byrne ordered police to close "the Alley" after witnessing the popular gathering spot off Fifty-First Street during her term as mayor of Chicago. Known for its live music and cocktail parties, the Alley, located in a garage in an actual alley, had come under constant police surveillance in the late 1970s. Byrne reportedly said, "I have to have this closed down."[72]

Tristan Cabello is certainly right to claim that the emergence of the civil rights movement and the ascendancy of middle-class values of "respectability" among Chicago African Americans during the 1950s ended the "laissez-faire attitude toward gays." But to fully understand the issues that "push[ed] the black gay world into the closet and out of the mainstream of black cultural life," as Marybeth Hamilton argues, we must also look to the changed discourse and cultural climate surrounding issues of sex and sexuality during the post–World War II period. These dramatic shifts directly impacted American society as a whole and African American religious cultures in particular. Indeed, one consequence of the shift has been the rise and continuation of robust homophobia in many African American religious communities. As scholars Kelly Brown Douglas and Horace Griffin show, black religious communities tend to be excessively homophobic and antigay in rhetoric and practice. As Griffin contends, "There are few arenas where the dread and condemnation of homosexuality is more noticeable than in black church settings."[73] In 2006, two bishops of the historic African Methodist Episcopal Zion Church (AMEZ) publicly denounced homosexuality, stating that the church was "diametrically opposed" to it and that if left unchecked homosexuality would "destroy us all." In recent years, high-profile ministers such as megachurch pastor Bishop T. D. Jakes and Rev. Bernice King (daughter of Martin Luther King Jr.) have been on the forefront of antigay bigotry and employed it in the service of some of the most hotly contested contemporary debates. Jakes has claimed he would never hire a gay person, has opposed gay marriage, and called homosexuality "brokenness." King has emphatically asserted that "deep in her sanctified soul," she knows her father "did not take a bullet for same-sex unions."[74]

The story of Chicago's Clarence Cobbs is so vitally important for the way it provides a historical context for the views of the two AMEZ bishops, T. D. Jakes and Bernice King. Since Cobbs, as a homosexual, served uncontested and unchallenged in his ministerial role in one of the most acclaimed churches in black Chicago before the mid-1940s, it would suggest that the homophobia found in many black churches is a post-World War II development. Indeed, Cobbs's life bridged two historically significant periods in the United States. The consequences of the important shifts in the aftermath of the war regarding sex, sexuality, family life, and cultural conformity can be traced out in his life and the lives of many other gay and lesbian black Chicagoans. His story shows that broad cultural shifts have a direct impact on specific communities as well as individual lives. As imperfect as it was, the social agreement of the glass closet under which he lived was a time when gay American citizens were more fully integrated into American society, and gay ministers and church workers were accepted as full members of their communities.

CHAPTER 6

Interrogating the Passionate and the Pious

Televangelism and Black Women's Sexuality

MONIQUE MOULTRIE

Beyoncé croons, "If you liked it then you shoulda put a ring on it" in the chorus from "Single Ladies."[1] As *Rolling Stone's* best single of 2008 and a recipient of three Grammy awards, this song arguably became a female anthem. It speaks to the pursuit of marriage for single women and the need to be in a relationship with someone. This song fits into a popular and religious culture that promotes marriage as the ultimate ideal despite the reality that, just like Beyoncé sang, many women will go home as single ladies.

For black churchwomen inundated with such religious and secular messages, this song could also reflect their lives. Yet when I did a focus group with young black women at my local Baptist congregation, I was shocked at their interpretation of Beyoncé's song. They saw in the lyrics not a reiteration of marriage but rather the promotion of healthy sexuality—that a man should put a ring on it (a condom) before trying to connect with them sexually. They understood the church's religious restrictions on premarital sex but were also aware that they should be responsible if (and when) they were sexually active. Stunned by such disparate views, I recognized the need for a new type of sexual ethics that deals with the plethora of messages about sexuality that complicate black women's lives. This is especially true of black women supporters of televangelists and faith-based sexuality ministries. Thus, this chapter explores how the religious messages emanating from televangelists and faith-based sexuality ministries inform and influence black women's sexual decision making. I will utilize the methodologies of womanist sexual ethics and poststructural cultural studies to argue that black women are negotiated readers of these religious messages and need a more robust sexual ethics for their complex sexual lives. As a womanist cultural critic, I am concerned with the lived realities of black women, and I desire to promote a womanist sexual ethics that deconstructs the sources of religious messages restricting their sexuality by offering beneficial practices for black churches.

Black Female Televangelists and Faith-Based Sexuality Ministries

Interrogating religious messages given to black churchwomen is a topic of great import given the extensive increase in faith-based sexuality ministries in recent years. These ministries include Christian televangelists, Christian women's and singles conferences, and Christian media—for example, videos, audio, and live streaming. It is rare to see analyses of these mediums in any discipline, but research is desperately required. These ministries have turned into a "multi-million dollar industry—with books, classes, Internet and gospel radio dating services . . . and conferences." For example, Christian Mingle boasted 16 million members in 2016 and earned over $115 million in revenue that year.[2] Recent movies in the industry, like the 2014 romantic comedy *Christian Mingle*, tend to focus on the experiences of white single women. Still, an equally expansive market attempts to help black women understand their sexuality *and* spiritual walk with God. Recent scholarship on televangelism typically ignores the messages that animate this religious marketplace and focuses on advocates of the prosperity gospel.[3] Yet faith-based sexuality ministries are often as lucrative a market as those promoting prosperity. Additionally, these messages and ministries must be investigated because of their collective effect on women's lives. Anthropologist Marla Frederick astutely notes that black women make decisions about their sexual practices based at least in part upon their adherence to television messages.[4] Often, these messages correspond to those they receive in church (especially since many church leaders are seeking to emulate the formula of televangelism). Yet, these alternative religious spaces offer an abundance of ways to market that same message. A pastor's sermon may be forgotten after Sunday service, but televangelists operating faith-based sexuality ministries are in constant communication with their supporters via email, social media, text messages, journals, meditations, and television. This stream of media provides a vast market to interrogate. However, this article focuses specifically on two black female televangelists—Prophetess Juanita Bynum and Evangelist Ty Adams.

I am highlighting black female televangelists because the current research on black televangelists focuses solely on males. While not disregarding the work of Shayne Lee, Jonathan Lee Walton, Marie Dallam, and Marla Frederick, studying black female televangelists whose niche is singles sexuality elucidate unique data for understanding black churchwomen's sexual decision making. For instance, in ethicist Jonathan Lee Walton's work on black male televangelists, he reads them as part of the dominant televangelism culture while retaining remnants of black religiosity. He portrays these black male televangelists as "both uniquely 'ours' and 'theirs.'"[5] I agree and read black female televangelists through a similar lens. They have emulated the best of capitalist televangelism (as perfected by white televangelists) even as they have portrayed the sensibilities of black religiosity. However, they must also be read through the lens of their gender, making them equal parts dominant ideology, black religion, and black female. This is an important distinction because black female televangelists are usually seen as emulating a prominent male televangelist, such as Bishop T. D. Jakes. But there is something uniquely "ours" in referencing the particular experience of black women and girls in their rhetoric and movements.

The black female televangelist's body disrupts how an audience receives her message because, as a female, she usually has to fight to claim biblical authority. As a racial and gendered minority, she has to fight to make her message reach beyond the black community to other ethnicities. Yet, when she does open doors, she has an outsider/insider relationship that gives her the ability to say and do things that male televangelists are hindered from doing. For example, when a female televangelist addresses issues related to women's sexuality, she can critique women in a way that would seem uncomfortable if the message came from a man. Given the tendency of televangelists' audiences to be female, the messages of a female televangelist are particularly persuasive.

Producing the Prophetess

This is especially true of Prophetess Juanita Bynum, arguably the progenitor of the modern movement on singles sexuality. Before Bynum, there was a successful history of evangelical sex manuals dating from the 1970s. Yet, these manuals and other Christian sex advice media primarily related to married couples. When Bynum entered the scene in the late 1990s, her take on singles sexuality carried on the line of singles discussions that had been going in churches but with a twist. She began with an acknowledgment of her sexual desire and daily struggle to remain celibate—a truthfulness not present in other material. The previous Christian singles market had focused on spiritual topics like living in God's will, but it rarely addressed bodily needs. To be clear, she still advocated for sex within marriage, but she did not act as if sex was something that should not even be thought of until marriage. This more honest discussion of sex made Bynum's entry into the market a welcome change.

An additional rationale for Bynum's popularity is that the cultural milieu of the time was one where black women seemed relegated to perpetual singleness. This lament inspired novels like Terry McMillan's *Waiting to Exhale* and Pearl Cleage's *What Seems Like Crazy on an Ordinary Day*, as well as dozens of articles in *Ebony* and *Essence* that reiterated a dire statistic that, in the late 1990s, nearly a fifth of all black women had never been married.[6] Bynum's context rehearsed the mantra that "all the good men are taken," emphasizing that black women were too independent for marriage. Thus, when Bynum preached about her struggles with singleness in a room full of black women and stated that she was telling "our" story, they trusted that she had found a solution to their problem.

This solution came through in Juanita Bynum's stirring sermon-turned-video, *No More Sheets*. In the video, which was taped during T. D. Jakes's 1997 singles conference in Dallas, Texas, she revealed her sexual past as she used four sheets to demonstrate how every man she'd slept with walked away, leaving her in "spiritual bondage."[7] Preached before an audience of more than ten thousand predominately black listeners, her sermon went on to sell more than a million copies. As she spoke to the black women in attendance and those who listened live in their own homes, she relived her past—which resonated with so many of her audience's experiences.

Raised Pentecostal, Bynum had waited until marriage to express her sexuality—only to watch her marriage dissolve after a year and a half. After divorcing, she had a series of sexual relationships that she believes led to a mental breakdown. When discussing her sexual escapades in the sermon, her constant refrain is, "Can we talk?"—a significant statement given how taboo sex is in black churches. At one point, she exclaims, "If the church don't get real with the people of God . . . we're gonna lose a whole lot of folks . . . [and] how can you help somebody if you don't tell anybody where you been?"[8] Her biographical sermons and books reiterate that she has been where her listeners are. They also pose a solution—the only way out is for women to leave premarital and postmarital sexual relationships behind and embrace covenant relationships with God instead. While Bynum is ultimately advocating for the ideal of celibacy until marriage, she also refrains from condemning less-than-ideal behavior. If someone slips and finds herself "in the sheets" again, instead of castigation and public shame, she receives the opportunity to rededicate her life to prayer and God. Bynum's sermon offers a "sisterfriend" feel as she weeps in front of the camera. Her words and actions suggest that she is merely telling listeners something for their own good as opposed to giving them a mandate.

Reading Bynum as Text

Perhaps it is this camaraderie that helped make her ministry so successful. This solidarity is an example of the poststructuralist philosopher Louis Althusser's concept of interpellation. In cultural studies, interpellation is the moment the subject realizes that a particular message is for her. This recognition comes from signs carried in her language that represent who she thinks she is. When she responds to a particular hail, she recognizes and accepts a certain social position and ideology that is already present within the hail. In the case of Bynum's messages, black women are hailed because they recognize themselves in the messages she is relating about herself. Just as with advertising, these women see themselves as her target group, or they believe that she is speaking prophetically just to them. This is part of the genius of interpellation in that it makes subjects think that the message they receive is real. Althusser explains that a subject's particular response to a hail can be an act of "ideological misrecognition" if she believes that she alone is the special person that is being hailed.[9] This misrecognition allows the subject to properly receive the message that the sender wants her to receive. In the case of Bynum, despite her message offering nothing more than prayer to quench the passions burning in single black women, her style is received as so honestly refreshing that one can temporarily forget that sex is now forbidden. With this rhetoric and her goal of helping the listener become more intimate with God and not just another person, Bynum's message speaks volumes.

This does not mean that there can be no criticisms of her message. She preaches that women should obey scripture completely, submitting to the teachings of the church and male leadership while they wait on "God's man" to arrive in God's time. For as much as the sermon is about finding a woman's purpose in God, it's also reaffirming an exclusively heteronormative vision of sex within marriage. As highlighted in her story of marital abuse, which by her admission she endured from the man that God prepared for her because she was obedient, her messages have resulted in physical and emotional ramifications for her own body with clear implications for her worldwide audiences.

Bynum's frank but disapproving discussion of masturbation is also questionable as a healthy sexual ethic. Positing that masturbation is the "bait that Satan uses to become a master of you," she considers self-pleasuring as a manifestation of a "spirit of perversion" and admits that she would rather come to the altar to repent from having sex, as it is at least the more enjoyable of the two sinful options.[10] Yet, her understanding of spiritual perversion is perhaps most damaging in her depiction of gays and lesbians. Bynum's reliance on Paul's letter to the Romans results in her belief that gays and lesbians dishonor their bodies through unnatural sexual relations. For lesbian sisters, her message becomes one of shame, stigma, and sexual sin.

Despite these harsh messages, black women have made Bynum's ministries successful because they believe her solution is suited just for them. These women share a history and experience of being labeled as sexually loose, but she offers them a way to be loosed! Viewed as a group, they are simultaneously ashamed and holy, with their status dependent on their context in the conference. Yet, with Bynum's advice, they can go from being ashamed and ignored singles to being empowered and committed singles. Although all Bynum offers them are steps to celibacy, as a group, their self-understanding is transformed from being passionate and pious to being saved, single, and satisfied.

Successor Evangelist Ty Adams

A successor to Bynum's mantle in the singles' circuit is Evangelist Ty Adams. Her book *Single, Saved, and Having Sex* (2005) was an *Essence* magazine bestseller and one of Amazon's Top 100 Sellers. While Adams does not have the celebrity preacher status that Bynum claims, her message has been widely popular, and Evangelist Adams is much more graphic than Prophetess

Bynum in her depictions of sex. She duplicates the same style of self-disclosure as she reveals her life of what she calls sexual sin, which included premarital relationships and homosexual relations. Following Bynum's model of sexual testimony, Adams succeeds in filling in the gaps that are left when traditional black churches remain silent on issues of sexuality. As Marla Frederick asserts, one of the promises of television ministries is that they deal with controversial topics and they are seen as eager to address the "personal concerns of their constituencies."[11] Adams claims the authority to tackle sexual sin because she admits her own mistakes while offering a potential solution. For instance, she reiterates that God created sex and that it is meant to be both passionate and pleasurable. She lambasts her same-sex desire, all the while never denying how it took her years of personal struggle to move beyond the pleasures of lesbian sex. While, like Bynum, she solely advocates heterosexual marital unions, Adams vividly describes the pleasures of homosexual sex. However, this candor does not negate the damage she does when she begins to advise on sexual practices.

For Adams, premarital sexual sin includes homosexuality, pornography, foreplay, masturbation, oral and anal sex, penetration of any kind, and even tongue kissing.[12] Although Bynum dared to discuss masturbation, her successor takes things a step further by suggesting that masturbation is either a spirit of molestation or a gateway to same-sex desire, as it still consists of a woman engaging in sex acts with a woman (in this case, herself).[13] Due to the hypersexualization of black women and the linkage in Christian church doctrine and practice of sexual pleasure with sin, it is rare to hear messages about the sexual pleasure found in same-sex relationships, masturbation, or oral and anal sex. Adams acknowledges the shock effect of her message as she discusses premarital oral and anal sex while, by her count, "there are a lot of undercover Christians literally under the covers," and "we've been sugarcoating this for far too long."[14] Duplicating Bynum's format, she succeeds in getting stagnant Christians to discuss sex and sexuality. By offering her sexual past and feelings of shame as an example of how unlawful sex "severs your union with the Lord"—and left her with her panties and her self-respect on the floor—she models for her audiences a sexual honesty that she encourages them to inhabit.[15]

Adams's book was a bestseller because it offered an information-starved generation clear-cut "facts." The simplicity of her message resonated with her audience as she packaged a clear, declarative statement about sex and sexuality that directly addresses single black women. The message the book delivers leaves much to be desired, but it is upfront and frank, a tone Adams continues in the 2016 sequel *Single, Saved, and Having Sex 2: A 30-Day Guide to Celibacy*. The appealing factor for ministries like Bynum's and Adams's is that they do not decry natural sexual urges or the real sexual pleasure that women feel. They offer solutions that mirror the abstinence message that single black women receive in their churches, but that conventional message has the bonus of coming from someone who is likewise struggling to remain celibate while honestly acknowledging sexual desire.

Unfortunately, the solutions proposed by Adams leave a shadow of disdain on single Christians who choose to engage in sexual relationships. Adams chastises them for being overcome by temptation and suggests that they should use "celibate Jesus" as their example. She purposely seeks to shame women into realizing that sex outside of marriage leads to hellfire because she sees such sexual expression as a conscious choice to move away from God. While this condemnation inflicts psychological damage, perhaps an even more pernicious abuse occurs as Adams counsels single black women to forgo contraception. She questions why single Christian women would carry condoms or birth control as she asserts: "You are planning to fail. You cannot plan to overcome and fail at the same time. You cannot have a "just in case I fall" plan. If you are taking birth control pills or carrying condoms, the first thing you need to do is throw them away. You cannot grab a hold to a future of celibacy with a grip on your sinful past."[16]

However, what happens with women who do "fall" after she has told them to throw away their condoms and birth control pills? What are the solutions for those who fail to uphold Adams's idealized standards?

Negotiated Readers

Bynum and Adams offer women ideal solutions to their sexual struggles by sharing their sexual testimonies as a means for leading women into a godly direction.[17] Both of these televangelist authors have gained popularity and relative wealth because black women accept their messages. However, this presumed solidarity does not mean that black women passively accept everything that is preached to them. On the contrary, viewers rarely accept everything that a televangelist says. Instead, they pick and choose from media ministries, just as they typically pick and choose what to follow from the Bible. In the case of televangelism, cultural critic Bobby Alexander asserts that viewers "bring their own perceptions and understandings of conservative Christianity to their viewing," and they make their "own independent judgments about what is presented, evaluating the message in light of their own faith or opinions."[18] This selective interpretation is known in cultural studies as performing a negotiated reading.

Black feminist cultural critic Jacqueline Bobo argues that as a whole, black women have learned to sift through messages, accepting what is beneficial and blocking out the rest. In her study of black women as cultural readers of the book and movie *The Color Purple*, she determines that when a person comes to view and interpret a text, "she/he does not leave his/her histories, whether social, cultural, economic, racial, or sexual, at the door."[19] Using this framework as a means of womanist cultural analysis recognizes the importance of analyzing televangelists' messages without jettisoning the spirituality that black women bring to their viewing practices. This requires interrogation of black women as negotiated readers of living "texts" like Prophetess Bynum and Evangelist Adams.

As negotiated readers, black women may not adhere to everything that Bynum and Adams say, but they may leave unquestioned these television preachers' emphasis on the pursuit of marriage as the ultimate end. In their discussions of sexuality, they accept the dominance of heterosexuality, gender norms within traditional marriage, and marriage as a means to the American dream. However, despite this collusion, black women followers of televangelists are not cultural dupes. Instead, they make their meanings by wrestling with the polysemous messages provided. For example, many accept the emphasis on marriage because it resonates with their desires, but they simultaneously resist certain expectations like total celibacy until marriage. While celibacy is a choice, it ceases to be a free decision when it is seemingly the only option available. These women personally wrestle with the advice that comes from competing religious frames of reference. Their churches advocate abstinence only and do not talk about what to do with sexual urges, while the televangelists advocate abstinence but offer repentance should viewers fall into sexual sin. Thus, it is not as simple as viewers and listeners doing what they are told. Instead, they struggle and negotiate with these living texts in their daily lives.

As a womanist cultural critic, I also read black women as negotiating their own meanings as they pursue sexual pleasure or find a variety of ways to secure the intimacy that they desire. In fact, in Marla Frederick's *Between Sundays*, she interviewed black churchwomen in rural North Carolina and discovered that these women and their churches were experts in redefining relationships outside of marriage as acceptable. The women knew that marriage was considered the ideal, but the ideal often did not match the reality of their situations. In these instances, churchwomen like Ms. Sylvia acknowledge that "it is definitely sinful to be involved sexually at this stage of the game [but] . . . everybody needs to be loved, to be cared for." Her desire to be loved and cared for allows her to enter what she would consider "less biblically ideal, yet nurturing relationships."[20] Women like Ms. Sylvia are constantly negotiating their desire for intimacy with the abstinence messages they receive from churches and televangelists. In doing so, they embody a womanist sexual ethics that is based on mutuality, pleasure, intimacy, and agency.

Constructing a New Womanist Sexual Ethics

This womanist sexual ethics seriously considers the complexities of black churchwomen's sexual lives and posits that their sexual decisions must be healthy and feasible. This often requires a negotiation between traditional sexual tropes that demand total celibacy and a type of sexual restraint where they remain celibate except under the "right" circumstances. A womanist sexual ethics that speaks practically to the needs of black churchwomen acknowledges that they are caught between church proscriptions that ban their sexual desire and living a dual lifestyle that is sexually risky. For these single black churchwomen, a womanist sexual ethics offers a lens to critically analyze the religious messages that they are receiving from televangelists like Bynum and Adams. Instead of demanding celibacy, this sexual ethics makes space for a responsible sexual agency that takes on a variety of forms.

The first step in this new model is a similar move to the messages promulgated in the preachings of Bynum and Adams. A womanist sexual ethics that adequately addresses the realities of black churchwomen must address sexual pleasure in the same ways that these televangelists advocate (or at least acknowledge) the pleasures of sexual expression. It must also acknowledge black women's truth-telling. As a cultural theorist, Tricia Rose notes in her landmark book on black women's sexuality, "Sexual stories about black women are all around us, but they almost always rely on key myths, while few stories told by black women about their own sexual lives are available."[21] Thus, a new womanist sexual ethics must reflect black women's competing sexual realities and provide space for those who honestly admit that they are both (sexually) passionate and (spiritually) pious.

The next step in a new womanist sexual ethics is a revamping of biblical interpretation. Arguably, when women have a more liberal biblical interpretation, they tend to be more at ease when their sexual practices don't adhere to the idealized norm of heterosexual marriage.[22] Such a perspective affirms interpretations such as the one provided by womanist Hebrew Bible scholar Renita Weems, who contends that the Song of Solomon was "eight chapters teeming with lust, love, sex, and passion in the middle of the Bible—and not once does the heroine or her beloved talk about marriage."[23] Rather than read this narrative as an allegory about God and Israel, Weems ponders what it might mean for churches to explore the sexuality that is so positively expressed in this book. This alternative interpretation makes space for women to reinterpret biblical meanings for themselves, recognizing that regulations meant for the early church may be inappropriate for a twenty-first-century, contemporary context. Utilizing a more liberal interpretation acknowledges that biblical restrictions on premarital sex often involve a totalizing view of sexuality that is lust-based and not expressed in loving, monogamous relationships. A more modern reading could be that those participating in healthy sexual relationships are participating in God's plan for sex and sexuality to be sacred and intimate.

Thus, a womanist sexual ethics posits that healthy intimate relationships can exist without leading to or requiring marriage, and that marriage is not the only indicator of relational success. Accepting this reality would represent a significant change to the standing sexual politics of black churches. In this vein, Christian ethicist Traci West posits that ministers in the church could use their power to "lift up the complexity of human sexual desire that God has created and the extraordinary, unlimited opportunities to explore the depths of that gift in covenantal relationships with each other."[24] A womanist sexual ethics would encourage black churches to reaffirm that marriage is but one means of securing intimacy. This would also involve celebrating all forms of healthy sexual expression, which include lesbian relationships and covenantal yet nonmarital heterosexual relations. To be clear, black churches are often more accepting of such relationships than they typically acknowledge, as the actions and behaviors of members (and clergy) are often more radical than what is publicly named as church values. For instance, in Robert Franklin's study at the Hampton University Ministers Conference, Franklin surveyed six hundred black ministers and found that 85.3 percent preached against premarital sex, yet 86.8 percent would dedicate a baby born out of wedlock.[25] Congregations often engage in a dangerous game of "don't ask, don't tell" around sexual relationships, which results in contradictory messages like Adams denouncing her lesbian lovers while simultaneously exalting the pleasures of lesbian sex. Given the confusing sexual messages present in both black churches and televangelist ministries, womanist cultural analysts must take on ethicist Katie Cannon's charge to "make available to the contemporary church community counter-hegemonic strategies that debunk and unmask normalizing structures of compulsive heterosexual acceptability."[26] This will certainly require a shifting of paradigms in many religious communities. However, it is a necessary step if black churches are truly to address the lived experiences of members or make a claim to be justice-oriented.

Sexual justice demands willing clergy and congregations who are resistant to standards that do not lead to the personal and communal flourishing of the individuals and communities they serve. It also requires that black women who are followers of televangelists, faith-based ministries, and congregations that do not properly prepare them for their sexual realities be free to make sexual decisions that are in their own best interests. By resisting messages that teach that the "sinful" body does not have to be valued, black women can disrupt a theologically reinforced connection of low self-esteem and unsafe sexual practices that can result in dire physical consequences like increasing HIV infections.

Ultimately, one of the goals of my womanist sexual ethics is to foster a more practical application of Christian faith, one in which black churchwomen are empowered by their religious communities to make better (and more healthy) sexual decisions. Yet, these decisions do not have to reiterate the heteronormativity present in black churches. Instead, these women's decisions can embody a new path that leads to sexual agency, pleasure, and love in a variety of forms. However, this new sexual ethic ought to involve the whole black community including the black religious, social, and academic spheres. The damage done by churches, televangelists, and other forms of religious media cannot be undone without an integrated analysis that provides space for a new sexual ethics. Thus, this womanist sexual ethics requires developing public forums that combat the religious messages circulating through various platforms, such as in broadcasting, magazines, as well as on television, in movies, and on social media. Media and cultural studies are the last frontiers that public intellectuals and especially theologians and ethicists must address regarding black women's sexuality. Womanist discourses on sexuality reach smaller audiences while the wider public is being inundated with messages from Prophetess Bynum, Evangelist Adams, and others. I offer my constructive womanist sexual ethics as both a prophecy and a promise to the next generation of black churchwomen who seek to live both passionately and piously before God.

PART FOUR
Identity and Inclusion in Black Churches

CHAPTER 7

The Self-Interested Politics of Collective Religious Transformation

Issues of Family Definition and LGBT Inclusion in Black Churches

MELYNDA J. PRICE

I am a scholar of religion, politics, and law. It may surprise many to know that this requires very little investigation of the debates within religious circles or the religious claims made by politico-religious actors once they enter the political process. We allow respondents to self-identify. We then take their articulations of what their faith requires at face value. As a discipline, political science is interested in the nexus between religious and other identities and political engagement and/or attitudes. How people come to their religious identity has been even less of a question, particularly if they are African American—a community for whom religiosity has been regarded as a given. But the subject of this writing is of greater interest to me than simply scholarly curiosity.

I, like many African Americans, am from a devoutly religious family headed by a single mother. Today, I consider myself to be an ethnic Christian in that my understanding of my blackness is very much interwoven with Christianity in ways that I cannot disentangle. I have tried. My family has evolved from poor to solidly middle class, from a storefront church of sixty people to a megachurch of more than fifteen thousand, and from Baptist to United Methodist. Where in my childhood, issues of sexuality—outside of necessary reproductive information to prevent unwanted and untimely pregnancy—went unaddressed, we became a family that has worked hard to expand our practices of love and support to countereducate our children against homophobia and create a safe space for my sister, niece, and their same-sex partners. So my contribution to this discussion will draw primarily from what I see as gaps in my disciplines' studies of these issues, from my own anecdotal experiences, and of witnessing attempts to find inclusive space within traditionally black religious space.

I have to begin with the admission that, although there has been extensive research on black churches and the influence of religion on African American political participation, attitudes, and policy preferences, there is a limited amount of research on those who hold overlapping political identities, like members of the black LGBT community. Beyond the important work of Cathy Cohen, there has been minimal research in black politics on the relationship between African Americans and the LGBT community more broadly defined. As a legal scholar, I think that the legal challenges that affect the black LGBT community have also been given short shrift largely due to the perception that within the hierarchy of important questions—a hierarchy constructed by scholars themselves—they do not rank as high or can be collapsed into other questions. Questions on the impact of intersectional legal binds of black LGBT individuals are obscured by both scholars of queer legal theory and race theorists except for the work mostly put forward by scholars who themselves are members of both minority communities.[1]

There are three kinds of questions at work in the larger topic of this volume, as I understand it. The first pertains to the relationship between LGBT members of the black community and black churches. The second concerns the relationship between black churches and the LGBT community writ large, in which some members of black churches have also found spiritual and political community. The third examines what lessons can be learned from existing literature and our collective experiences about the possibility of finding common ground.

Political science research on black religious institutions and black LGBT persons, though limited, can offer the first steps into the investigation of how to bring the above questions together and to even improve the relationship between both groups.[2] For the second question, of the relationship between black churches and the larger LGBT community, the research on black churches and the LGBT community (broadly defined) has yet to be taken up as it should. Political science offers us little in understanding that relationship, and there is little foundation for speculation on how to move forward. However, my aim here is to glean prescriptive lessons on how to foment greater LGBT inclusion within black religious communities by culling from political science research, placing the observations in the context of the broader literature, and raising a few additional questions for further consideration. I note here that the implications of the research I discuss mean not just inclusion in black religious institutions but also raise the need for greater access to black political power and the addition of key issues on black political agendas.

The overarching theory of black political participation and behavior in the post–civil rights period can be summed up in the theory of "linked fate"—or the predominant belief by blacks that their lot is cast collectively with other blacks. The idea has been routinely measured in multiple waves of the national black election surveys that ask respondents whether they believe that what happens to other blacks influences what happens to them. As far back as the 1984 National Black Election Study (NBES), approximately 75 percent of African Americans had a strong identification with other blacks. In that survey, "Only two blacks out of the sample of 1,150 voluntarily told interviewers that they never think about their race."[3] Additionally, in 1996 nearly 86 percent of black respondents in the NBES believed they shared a common fate with other blacks.[4] Linked fate is a highly predictive measure of black political behavior. While such sentiments help to facilitate collective action, the intensity and durability of linked fate sentiments have also been a problematic aspect of black politics.

Recent research on contemporary black politics argues that the focus on linked fate obscures real political differences within the black community. The concept of linked fate falters in exactly the areas where this project is concerned.[5] If the discussion is about consensus issues (e.g., support for increased government support of opportunity programs or health care), then most African Americans view their prospects as linked to the entire black community. But on issues where there is internal disagreement—for example, the status of black gays and lesbians, or gays and lesbians generally—linked fate does little to bind those on the margins to the political processes at the center of the black community.

In *The Boundaries of Blackness*, her work on black politics, the AIDS epidemic, and how attitudes toward sexuality rendered the black political process ineffective in fighting that epidemic, Cathy Cohen argues that more cross-cutting issues that obscure internal tensions and cleavages dominate and define the black political agenda, which then fails to address the concerns of subgroups (i.e., black LGBTQ people) that are the least empowered.[6] In the face of these cleavages, traditional political processes within the

African American community, in Cohen's words, "break down." These subgroups, Cohen argues, are subject to secondary marginalization. Like others in their group, they are marginalized by the dominant society because of their group membership. They are then marginalized further by the group itself for acting outside of its internal norms.

Cohen is analyzing the failure of the African American community to lobby on behalf of those with AIDS/HIV. But underneath the political failure to address this epidemic is a highly religious community that has silenced or condemned black gays and lesbians because of their perceived "moral culpability" in contracting HIV. The addition of other groups disproportionately affected by the disease, like intravenous drug users, was "inevitable" because they too were somehow morally responsible for their condition. As more blacks became infected and died, black leaders and institutions failed to appreciate the severity of the disease's impact on the community. The unwillingness of many black leaders and institutions to take a more inclusive approach and to stop silencing individuals—some of who had been sitting in the same pews and Sunday school classes—helped to create a context in which the spread of disease was inevitable. Religion—the black church, specifically—was extremely important in the process of further marginalizing LGBT members of the African American community. Cohen's assessment of the black church's response is most accurately described by the title of the chapter in which it is discussed, "Willing to Serve, but Not to Lead." Ultimately, Black churches' readiness to condemn black gays and lesbians slowed the community's response to the AIDS epidemic—particularly when compared to other health, social, and political fights in which it had been on the front lines.

Cohen's discussion of the secondary marginal position of black gays and lesbians is telling in understanding how we articulate prescriptive thoughts on how to study and repair the relationship between this segment of the black community and black churches. It is to some degree a call to "cast down your bucket where you are"—to paraphrase Booker T. Washington—and highlight the common concerns of the black church and the black LGBT community.[7] The process of secondary marginalization takes place when the marginal community polices its boundaries. Individuals who step outside of the "norms of 'acceptable blackness' "—because of their sexual identification, for instance—are denied access to the dominant resources, but they are also separated from indigenous leaders and sources of advocacy.[8] The issue of resources is not a small one when considering the power and resources of black churches. It is not only that black churches—together—comprise a religious body, but they are also—together—a uniquely political one. Historically, the black church is the wealthiest, most independent, and self-sustaining institution in the black community. The operation of public opinion within this critical institution has a powerful impact. Linked fate could be viewed as a strong organizing principle or a community-level avoidance technique to suppress substantial conflicts. However, linked fate also functions constructively in the role of advocate—a role that black religious institutions have played well historically—where bridges can be built. As Cohen suggests, black churches are willing to serve, but the question is how to transform the crisis response into real leadership on questions of inclusion as they relate to sexual difference within black communities.

This may mean that projects of inclusion have to be intentional in those black churches that are targeted for coalition building. Because of the importance of black churches in the freedom movements of the 1960s, many social scientists assumed that high levels of religiosity—as measured by church attendance, the importance of faith in one's life, and views on certain policies like prayer in school (all measures on which African American score higher than the general population)—were positively correlated with political engagement.[9] I foreground political engagement as a political scientist, of course. But, more personally, I do so because I feel that there is a greater prospect for forward movement if African Americans are educated about specific *political* connections between both black churches and black LGBT persons. So, for example, we know from 1996 NBES data that 60 percent of black Americans favor laws to protect homosexuals against job discrimination.[10] Recent research also shows that discrimination against gays and lesbians, as well as transgender persons, is more legible to black Americans than whites.[11] Successive waves of the same survey have found that black Americans were also the most likely to "*oppose* allowing small business owners to refuse to provide products or services to gay or lesbian people, if doing so would violate their religious beliefs."[12]

Presumably, these African Americans are also highly religious. So, if they can see overlapping interests concerning job discrimination then maybe there are other areas where there is common ground. Increased engagement between black churches and evangelicals has certainly led to the support and success of electoral and legal exclusion. One only has to look at the work of operatives by the George W. Bush 2000 and 2004 campaigns. Led largely by Karl Rove, the Bush campaign was able to siphon off votes from the Democratic Party by placing provisions against same-sex marriage on state ballots in key states.[13] Because of the strategic use of black churches as tools of exclusion and earlier scholarship on political engagement in black churches, I argue that any efforts at greater LGBT inclusion in black churches require a very intentional selection process to begin with religious institutions that are engaged in other kinds of social justice and anti-discrimination activism. Part of the political mythology of the "Black Church" is its singular stalwart stance against external forces of racism. Black churches have indeed been sheltering spaces for black people in difficult times, but they are not a monolithic institution.

Research by the political scientist Allison Calhoun-Brown suggests that the connection between political engagement and black churches depends greatly on the particular ideological perspective of the congregation.[14] She finds statistical support for the hypothesis that attending a "political church" is more important than simply attending church because political churches can move beyond affective feelings toward providing the organizational resources for which black churches are famous to "impact the motivations and consciousness of individuals as well."[15] This finding strongly suggests the importance of focusing programmatic and research efforts around the greater inclusion of LGBT persons in those spaces where congregations are already engaged in social justice work in other spheres. They are likely the ripest for change and most likely able and willing to be leaders among their peers.

The issue of political advocacy is also complicated by an increased market for the political endorsement of black religious leaders. These leaders may see themselves as detached politically from their congregants or as individual political entrepreneurs who operate as spokespersons for their religious commitments rather than the collective agenda of their congregants. This, at times, can lead to a kind of political schizophrenia, but it may also be reflective of a sea change in the role of black clergy as political and ideological leaders within their congregations. This is a question I have been contemplating for some time since the pastor of the church my family attends has taken just such a fractured public position. I spent my formative religious years in this church with this pastor whose spiritual guidance and intellectual competence provided a respite for my family and me. It still provides as such for my family. He prayed at the inauguration of George W. Bush, officiated the wedding of the president's daughter, and was an outspoken supporter of Barack Obama. Only after coverage by the press, and a subsequent request from the Obama campaign, did the church remove a link on its website to an organization that purported to cure participants of homosexuality. In the protracted debate over whether the United Methodist Church would change its official policy toward homosexuality, this church that had nurtured my family for decades made public that it would separate from the denomination if the rules were amended to allow full participation of sexual minorities.[16] This highly visible bipartisan posture, which is tethered to a conservative stance on sexuality, requires a fair amount of political and spiritual juggling for my family. However, one of the most interesting things uncovered in the fallout of these events was that many of the parishioners verbalized what may have been true all along: that their pastor's political views did not dictate their political behavior. Even so, the pastor's activism makes the question of what constitutes a political church an important one, particularly concerning gender identity and sexual orientation issues. Distinguishing political churches in the context of modern racial and religious politics—with a backdrop of debates about same-sex marriage—from those that have no consistent political bent seems like a worthwhile endeavor in and of itself.

Another trajectory that would be interesting to explore follows the migratory paths of black gays and lesbians within and across black religious institutions. How do attitudes within black religious institutions influence that movement? Who is where at what time? Are there maximum and minimum membership thresholds at which black LGBT persons cannot sustain even limited contact with black churches? When black LGBT church members leave black institutions, where do they go? Whom do they take with them? My family has proven that we come to all things, including spirituality, as a unit. Whither thou goest—particularly my mother—we all follow. Do institutions like the Metropolitan Community Churches and other LGBT religious institutions do a better job of fulfilling the spiritual and, of interest to me, the political interests of black LGBT persons? There is a need for basic data about who the LGBT individuals are in black churches—the positions they hold, their levels of participation, and so on—and what the other congregants believe about the LGBT members in their midst. What are the public secrets of these congregations? At what levels are LGBT members tolerated as long as they remain silent and invisible? Does the slow evolution of ideas in black religious institutions lead to greater invisibility among black LGBT persons than their nonblack counterparts who may not hold familial, cultural, and political ties to institutions that force such choices? What kinds of bargains have already been struck in black churches, and is it possible to use those bargains as a starting place for renegotiation? Or do they need to be scrapped entirely for real progress to be made?

We also need some substantial reframing and outreach that highlights the overlapping interests between the LGBT community and black churches—both broadly defined—over the issue of family. I think one of the reasons my family did not break down into an afterschool special when first my niece (at seventeen) and my sister (in her late thirties) "came out" is because we had already recovered from the attempts to chip away at our belief that we were a family—in every sense of the word. Growing up in the South, black churches are filled with paper fans emblazoned with the image of a heteronormative black family ideal—mother, father, son, and daughter. This was not my family—and ours is not an exceptional story in this regard.

My mother, an oncology nurse who discusses with pride her work in the first hospital in Houston to treat AIDS patients before the disease had a name, had been sensitized to the concerns of gays and lesbians for a decade or more before she would need this knowledge in her personal life. My mother never let us believe that our family formation was anything less worthy than what we saw enshrined on the heteronormative fans provided by our local funeral home. This is not just important for my immediate family. To allow the religious right and conservative forces within the black community to use weapons of shame against another group would be to sanction the continued denigration of my family and, frankly, the reality of black family life in general. Numbers have been floated that as many as 70 percent of black women are unmarried, and black women are twice as likely to never marry as their white counterparts.[17] The statistics on marriage do not alter the reality that they will likely give birth to children and may go through periods of long-term cohabitation. Almost as much as marriage for the LGBT community needs redefinition, the black community—both gay straight and all other people on the sexuality spectrum—needs to challenge any attempt to define nonheteronormative families as less than.[18]

Additionally, it is important to make clear that taking leadership on LGBT issues does not and should not require loyalty contests. As long as the blackness of black gays and lesbians—and subsequently their membership in black institutions and the black community—is contested in internal dialogues among black religious institutions and their leaders, we will be stalled. What is left undone in the mire of moral judgment is the hard work of finding common ground for our filial, religious, and political kin to have at least as much power as the rest of the black community. The great news is that politics does not have to engage people on moral judgments but can be highly successful in engaging them with appeals to their basic self-interest. By pointing out the ways that discrimination against LGBT persons is part and parcel of discriminatory structures that support racial oppression, we allow non-LGBT African Americans to act in their self-interest for the greater good of all marginalized groups and begin building the foundation for solidarity and inclusion. The unfinished business of challenging heteronormative family ideals, securing housing and employment, and going about the business of human living free of discrimination continue to be the struggles of our communities. Insofar as this volume is concerned with how we might create greater inclusion in black churches, one might assume that pathways to reaching those goals are also spiritual. I argue that by emphasizing those issues that are common to individuals within these communities, we can begin the process of building spaces for collective transformation.

In conclusion, we need to reeducate older blacks and educate younger blacks on the political and physical consequences of "other"-ing. The main focus of my research is on the death penalty in Texas, where my family has lived in relatively the same place for eight generations. In earlier periods, white citizens tolerated the twin systems of execution and lynching there—just as citizens across racial categories now tolerate legal forms of violence. This is driven by the willingness to engage in the practice of exclusion. Once separated from the larger community, it leaves those who are the "others" open to aggression from the majority. Inclusion as an antiviolence measure, as a Christian precept of loving thy neighbor, has to be something to which even the most conservative black religious institutions can commit. Not perpetrating violence—whether spiritual, physical, political, and/or verbal—against LGBT persons within or outside of black religious communities seems to me to be the minimal standard. If the oppression of gays and lesbians is sufficiently linked to how "other"-ing has led to violence historically against black women and men due to their racial identity, this can be a powerful basis for coalition building.

CHAPTER 8

Intersectional Invisibility and the Experience of Ontological Exclusion

The Case of Black Gay Christians

VALERIE PURDIE GREENAWAY, RICHARD EIBACH,
AND NICK CAMP

As noted in the introduction to this volume, in the run-up to the November 2008 presidential election, a series of news articles drew attention to a curious situation in California. Analysts predicted that the same black voters who would turn out in record numbers to support Democratic candidate Barack Obama would confirm the passage of Proposition 8, a conservative state ballot initiative overturning a state supreme court ruling mandating full legal recognition of same-sex marriages in California. The predictions rested on the dual assumptions that black voters tended to be more religious and more homophobic than white voters and that gay voters were more likely to be white and nonreligious than straight voters. The assumptions were bolstered by media observations that "gays [and] blacks are divided on Prop. 8."[1] Journalists and pundits treated racial and sexual identity as multiple points on a single spectrum, claiming that Proposition 8 "placed two pillars of the Democratic coalition—minorities and gays—at opposite ends of an emotional issue."[2] In this way, religion, race, and sexual orientation became conflated in the public discourse in such a way that one would think that all blacks were straight and Christian, and that all gays were nonreligious and white.

Of course, the existence of individuals who are black *and* gay *and* Christian exposes the fallacy of assuming that racial, sexual, and religious identities do not overlap.[3] The media attention around Proposition 8 revealed that knowledge of one of these identities (e.g., sexual orientation) does not necessarily tell us about the others (e.g., race, religion), although we often act as though this is the case. The result of this compartmentalized thinking is that we draw mental boundaries in ways that make the "prototypical" combination of identities—black = straight + religious, or gay = white + nonreligious— more prominent at the cost of other intersections of identities. We call this phenomenon intersectional invisibility.

Intersectional invisibility refers to the general failure of people to fully recognize individuals with intersecting identities as members of their constituent groups.[4] People who have multiple subordinate group identities (e.g., black gay and lesbian Christians) tend to be defined as nonprototypical members of each of the groups to which they belong. Because these individuals do not fit the prototype of each of their respective identity groups, and because Christianity attunes people to *prototypical* or *seemingly normative* aspects of personhood more than nonprototypical aspects, both the black church and the LGBTQ community may cause people with multiple subordinate group identities to be marginalized compared to more prototypical members of their constituent groups.[5]

Renowned scholars across multiple disciplines have written about intersectionality and the politics of recognition,[6] marginalization of gay people within black churches (i.e., Joseph Beam, Essex Hemphill, Kendall Thomas), and lack of progressive theologies around masculinity, sexuality, and eroticism (i.e., Kellie Brown Douglas, Michael Eric Dyson, Cornel West). Each of these disciplines relies on impressive methodologies—close readings of Scripture, autobiographies, and historical and legal analysis, for instance—to illuminate marginalization within black churches and the need for widespread change. Given the consistency of their "take-home message," it is tempting to conclude that black churches and black gay Christians' different perspectives are somehow irreconcilable—that they reflect divisions of interest, politics, and experience that are too deep to overcome in the foreseeable future. Thus, one might question what social psychologists offer in debates about the affairs of black churches and sexuality, a topic of which we tend to be either woefully uninformed or silent bystanders.

In this chapter, we illuminate the ways that social ontologies and prototypes operate in normative ways consistent with how our brains categorize others and outside of people's everyday consciousness to render black gay Christians invisible in both the black church and the LGBTQ community. This perspective critically advances conversations about sexual identity and the black church in three ways. First, a social psychological analysis sharpens definitions of marginalization and stigma by demonstrating the effects of invisibility on basic psychological processes such as *attention* (e.g., people either ignore or overly draw attention to black gay Christians), *memory* (e.g., people misremember information stated by black gay Christians, crediting it to straight black Christians), and *decision making* (e.g., people prefer prototypically straight black Christians to represent the black church publicly, discriminating against their gay counterparts). Second, a social psychological framework on intersectional invisibility draws attention to the marginalization of black gay Christians in both the black church *and* the LGBT community *at the same time*, an insight required to transform current social ontologies and definitions of prototypicality. Third, a social psychological analysis points toward novel interventions that may substantially lessen the experience of invisibility, interventions we review at the close of this chapter.

The quagmire of Proposition 8, the dismantling of Don't Ask, Don't Tell policies toward gay people in the military, and the legalization of same-sex marriage all draw attention to the urgency of interrogating sexual identity and the black church at this historical moment. Since 2015, same-sex marriage has been legal in every state, but it has not yet achieved full acceptance in the black church and large white denominations fracturing over the same questions. It is most curious and unusual that gay marriage is rarely discussed as a spiritual affair, only a legal affair related to partner benefits and the right to live together. But many gay people, especially black gay Christians, desire the union of spirituality and legal rights, placing the wage over bodies and souls front and center in black churches. As another example, adoption of children on the part of interracial or black same-sex couples has dramatically increased, expanding the definitions of "the Black Family."[7] Finally, the dismantling of Don't Ask, Don't Tell will assuredly increase the number of black gay and lesbian soldiers returning from military service in need of material resources and spiritual healing. Marriage, family, battles for political recognition, and healing of souls are domains where black churches are traditionally at their strongest. But the mere placement of the words *gay* or *lesbian* in front of each of those domains—*gay* marriage, *gay* black families, *gay* soldiers, *gay* souls, and so on—has crippled many black churches into silence and inaction.

In this chapter, we first review how theory and research on intersectional invisibility can help to explain why black gay men and lesbians are vulnerable to being inadequately recognized as members of their ethnic and sexual orientation communities. Next, we review theory and research on the psychological consequences that people experience when their sense of social belonging is threatened in this way. Finally, we discuss possible forms of activism and community outreach that could affirm black gay people's membership in the black and gay communities and potentially heal some of the damage that ideologies of exclusion have inflicted on their sense of belonging. In particular, we examine how ideologies of exclusion are often transmitted by messages and practices that are prevalent within black churches, and we suggest strategies that black gay Christians might use to reaffirm their feelings of belonging to their racial heritage, sexual identity, and religious communities.

Black Gay People's Intersectional Invisibility Within the Black Religious Community

The decision to come out of the closet is made difficult for many black gay people because it threatens to jeopardize their relationship with the black Protestant church, which is as important a source of spiritual sustenance and social integration for many black gay people as it is for many black heterosexuals.[8] Because intolerance of homosexuality is still prevalent within black churches, many black gay men and lesbians feel that if they publicly affirm their homosexuality, they risk exclusion from the nurturing resources of the church. For many of them, estrangement from the church may be a cost that is too much to bear, leading many black gay individuals to attend nonetheless. In their ethnographic study of black gay men living in Harlem, William G. Hawkeswood and Alex. W. Costley found that many of the participants looked to the black church as a place to fulfill their need for belonging. As one of the participants explained, "The most important black institution to me is the church. I don't care which church. But you better be in the church. That's such an important part of black life. It's your whole bein'. Without the church, you ain't shit!"[9]

However, black gay men and lesbians often encounter heterocentric definitions of black Christian identity within the black church that can seriously jeopardize their feelings of belonging within that setting. While there are spaces in the church, such as the choir, where gay orientation may be tolerated so long as it is not expressed too overtly, these positions hold, in the words of Reverend Irene Monroe, who is lesbian, "prestige but no power to cause . . . a paradigm shift or systemic change within the body of the entire church."[10] Gay church-goers thus must decide whether they will participate in this constrained sphere or risk church sanctions. As Cathy Cohen writes, "Nowhere in this choice does the idea of inclusion as fully recognized and empowered members exist. . . . Their gay identity places them outside the indigenously constructed boundaries of both Christianity and blackness as defined by the church."[11]

A consequence of this uneasy arrangement is that the church remains silent on issues that have particular relevance for their gay and lesbian parishioners. For example, in Washington, DC, where black gay men made up the largest group of people with AIDS in the early 1990s, church leaders were hesitant to publicly address the issue. One minister, when asked whether the black church was doing enough to address the AIDS epidemic, responded that the church "should not be expected to be the Messiah in relation to those issues."[12] Where gay members have experienced the support of the church, this access has often come at the expense of recognition of their sexual identities. Cohen writes:

> Gay men are to be loved and taken care of when they are sick, but their loving relationships are not to be recognized nor respected. Most individuals affected by [AIDS] can tell at least one story of going to a funeral of a gay man who died from AIDS and never hearing the acronym mentioned. Family members and ministers are all too willing to grieve the loss of a son or church member, without acknowledging the total identity of that loved one. Lost to AIDS is not only the son so dearly missed but the totality of his life, which included lovers and gay friends who also grieve for their loss.[13]

These exclusionary messages and practices ultimately drive some black gay men and lesbians away from the church. Summarizing the experiences of many of the black gay men in their study, Hawkeswood and Costley write:

> Suffice it to say, the Christian churches' teachings against homosexuality have proved problematic for many gay men and have no doubt played a role in the significant level of lapsed or relaxed participation of gay black men. . . . Seventeen of my informants no longer associate with a church or religion. Seven current Baptists and two current Catholics do not attend church. One current Methodist and one

current Baptist were both formerly Catholics, and two Buddhists were formerly a Methodist and a Baptist. The latter still sings in a Baptist choir on Sundays. Many of those informants who no longer attend church, or who have changed church or religion, will cite church teachings as a reason for their absence or conversion.[14]

Black progressive intellectuals both within and outside the church have argued that the strained relationship between the black church and its gay parishioners stems from ideological issues such as interpretations of Scripture, the value placed on masculinity in black culture, or social beliefs about the origins of sexuality. We as psychologists know that intentional beliefs are only the tip of the iceberg; study after study has shown that processes outside of a person's conscious awareness, including unconscious stereotyping and cognitive processes of categorization, play a strong but unseen role in bias and exclusion.[15] We believe that independent of conscious interpretation, we categorize people into groups in a predictable way. Specifically, individuals who stand at the intersection of multiple subordinated identities (e.g., gay *and* black, female *and* gay) are seen as nonprototypical members of either group, a feature which leads them to be passed over in discussions of either constituent group. After explaining this theory in greater detail, we will show how our theory helps to explain ways in which black gay Christians are left out of the church, as well as social psychological outcomes of these exclusions, and possible interventions.

Intersectional Invisibility

Cultures are partially defined by their social ontologies, the possibilities for personhood that they create and recognize.[16] In contemporary North American culture, three defining dimensions of personhood are an individual's race/ethnicity, gender, and sexual orientation. Any person is supposed to have some kind of racial/ethnic identity, some kind of gender identity, and some kind of sexual orientation identity, with a limited set of culturally recognized options for each of these identity dimensions. These dimensions of personhood are officially supposed to be independent of one another, such that a person's ethnic identity or gender identity does not determine that person's sexual orientation and vice versa. Knowing a person's race or gender, for example, should not give us any insight into what their sexual orientation might be. However, in practice, people do not treat these dimensions as though they were orthogonal. Rather, for each of these identities, certain members of identity groups receive privileged cultural recognition when it comes to defining the standard representation of that identity; this privileged "default" role of certain groups in defining identity norms renders relatively invisible others who technically share that identity. We define *ontological exclusion* as the privileging of some people's experience over others when it comes to defining identity groups, a process that necessarily makes some members "defaults" and some members invisible.

The process of ontological exclusion is not random but is rather shaped by various ideologies, both explicit and implicit. For instance, describing exclusionary definitions of personhood within the black community, Cathy Cohen writes of "the ability of patriarchy and sexism, homophobia and heterosexism, as well as classism to define the experiences and concerns of certain [members of the black community], primarily middle-class, heterosexual men, as representatives and markers of the progress or threat experienced by the entire community."[17] Androcentrism, ethnocentrism, and heterocentrism are three such prevalent cultural ideologies that function to ontologically exclude certain individuals from fully recognized personhood. Androcentrism defines the standard person as male (thereby excluding women from fully recognized personhood), ethnocentrism defines the standard person as white (thereby excluding racial and ethnic minorities from fully recognized personhood), and heterocentrism defines the standard person as heterosexual (thereby excluding gay and lesbian individuals from fully recognized personhood). Sometimes these exclusionary definitions of personhood are explicit—black slaves, for example, were intentionally defined as white men's property in antebellum America, thus excluding them from legal personhood. However, exclusionary definitions of personhood can also be more implicit, as when workplace policies that are allegedly designed to fit all workers match the experiences of white men much better than they match those of white women or black people of either gender.[18]

Our research investigates how the intersecting influences of ideologies such as androcentrism, heterocentrism, and ethnocentrism can cause individuals with certain configurations of identities to be particularly vulnerable to experiencing ontological exclusion, a phenomenon we call intersectional invisibility. Any person who is ontologically excluded across at least two of his or her identity groups is at risk. For example, the intersectional invisibility model predicts that black women will be vulnerable to being perceived as both atypical women and atypical black people due to ethnocentric definitions of femininity and androcentric definitions of black identity. It is this invisibility that Sojourner Truth appears to have been protesting when she defiantly asked, "Ain't I a woman?"

Our theory of intersectional invisibility extends to people with more than two subordinated identities. Black lesbians, for example, experience not just these ethnocentric definitions of femininity but also androcentric definitions of black identity and heterocentric definitions of gay identity. Because they are not included in the "default" of *any* group, they thus find themselves excluded from fully recognized personhood within *all three groups*: the black community, the gay community, and the feminist community. These experiences of ontological exclusion may be psychologically painful as Adrienne Rich writes, "When those who have the power to name and to socially construct reality choose not to see you or hear you . . . there is a moment of psychic disequilibrium, as if you looked into a mirror and saw nothing."[19]

If members of multiple nontypical groups are truly rendered invisible, we would expect these intersectional members to be absent in the representations of each identity group. We decided to test this hypothesis by looking at common depictions of race and gender identity: magazine covers. Specifically, we examined photographic depictions of women and ethnic minorities on magazine covers over eighty-five years to study the intersectional invisibility that black women face due to the combined effects of ethnocentric definitions of femininity and androcentric definitions of black identity. Our theory predicted that, due to ethnocentric definitions of femininity, women portrayed on magazine covers would be disproportionately white. Indeed, we found that the represented proportion of white to black women exceeded the actual proportion of white to black women in the U.S. Census. Similarly, the represented proportion of male to female black people on the magazine covers surpassed the actual proportion of black men to black women in the U.S. population, consistent with our hypothesis that androcentric definitions of race would lead to black female underrepresentation. In popular representations of both women and blacks, we found that persons with intersectional identities were less likely to be represented than their nonintersectional counterparts. Having found that individuals with multiple subordinated identities were overlooked in media representations of each group, our next step was determining whether intersectional identities were overlooked in people's mental representations as well.

To answer this question, we asked participants to interpret trends among different groups. This kind of thinking should be familiar to anyone who has opened a newspaper or read an article online. Imagine, for example, that you are reading an article about a candidate in an upcoming election that states that he is supported by 70 percent of female voters and 50 percent of male voters. What portion of the general population supports the candidate? Assuming roughly equal numbers of male and female voters, the reasonable answer would be midway between the two given proportions, or 60 percent. Importantly, it shouldn't matter whether 70 percent of female voters and 50 percent of male voters support the candidate, or the split is 50 percent of male voters and 70 percent of female voters. The trend for the overarching group would be the same.

In our study, we asked participants to do this very task. We showed them graphs depicting "changes in quality of life over time" among intersectional (black women) and nonintersectional (black men or white women) groups. In actuality, these graphs did not portray real trends; rather, we drew the graphs ourselves. While both intersectional and nonintersectional graphs depicted the same general trajectory, we manipulated whether the trend was stronger in intersectional or nonintersectional groups. After showing them the graphs for the intersectional and nonintersectional groups, we asked participants to draw a graph summarizing the trend for the overarching group (that is, for women or blacks). All participants saw the same trends, with only the labels for the intersectional and nonintersectional groups varying from person to person. Remember, common sense would predict that the aggregate graphs we asked participants to draw would be the same regardless of which graph had which label, just as it shouldn't matter in our previous example whether 70 percent of men or women supported the candidate. What we found went against common sense and in favor of our hypothesis: people consistently weighted their guesses toward whichever trend was labeled with the nonintersectional group. In other words, when the graph labeled "white women" or "black men" appeared to be increasing steeply, participants drew graphs for women and blacks more steeply; when these graphs increased only slightly, our subjects made more modest estimates.

Together, these studies point to something beyond conscious, explicit discrimination. Our participants were not trying to put down black women by underestimating their contribution to the overarching categories of black men or white women. Likewise, magazine editors had no ax to grind in keeping intersectionals off the covers. Rather, these results suggest that the very way we process information leads us to focus on the prototypical at the cost of the intersectional on both an individual and an institutional level.

Black Gay People's Intersectional Invisibility Within the Black and Gay Communities

Heterocentric definitions of black identity and ethnocentric definitions of gay identity are not only conveyed by discourses and practices prevalent in the broader culture; these exclusionary practices and discourses are reproduced within the black and gay communities as well. Indeed, it may be the heterocentric and ethnocentric definitions of identity within these specific identity communities that most seriously threaten black gay and lesbian individuals' feelings of belonging. An intersectional perspective demonstrates the importance of recognizing the various ways that the experiences of black gay people might systematically differ from those of both black heterosexuals and white gay people. It also illuminates how individuals at this juncture of these racial and sexual identities are poorly represented in each community.

Ethnocentric definitions of gay identity can cause black gay and lesbian individuals to feel estranged from the gay community. Just as mainstream colorblind ideology assumes whiteness when claiming to focus on individual characteristics, the gay rights movement sets whiteness as the default when it attempts to focus on "just gay" issues without acknowledging race. This colorblindness is evident in such strategies as analogizing white gay leaders with black civil rights leaders. As Allan Bérubé observes, "If the gay civil rights movement is already part of the ongoing struggle for the dignity of all people . . . then there is no need for gay equivalents of Dr. King, racial segregation, or the civil rights movement. If the gay movement is not already part of the civil rights movement, then what is it?"[20] The result of conceptualizing the gay community as differing from "normal" white America only on sexual orientation is a movement in which gay people of color are invisible.

On a personal level, by their positioning at the intersection of the heterocentrism of the black community and the ethnocentrism of the white-dominated gay community, the decision about whether to "come out of the closet" and publicly affirm their sexual orientation is potentially more difficult for black gay people than it is for white gay people. The dominant narratives of the coming out experience have been ethnocentrically defined around the experience of white gay people as a movement from a community in which one is rejected—one's heterosexual community of origin—into a community in which one is accepted—the gay community. However, because white privilege still dominates within the gay community, for many gay people of color, coming out is not a straightforward movement from a less accepting to a more accepting community. In an analysis of the coming out experience that is remarkably sensitive to the intersectional social location of black gay people, Seidman writes:

> White privilege in the gay world means that blacks manage their homosexuality somewhat differently than whites. Whites may come out to an unfriendly world of kin and friends, but they anticipate easy integration into a gay world that will affirm their sense of self and offer an alternative type of community. By contrast, if blacks exit from the closet they expect a struggle for acceptance not only in the straight but also in the gay world. To state the contrast sharply, whites expect a trade-off when they come out: estrangement from the straight world in exchange for social integration and acceptance in the gay community. Blacks do not expect such compensation for their anticipated disapproval and diminished status in the straight world. Given their more ambivalent relationship to the gay community, blacks may be more likely to manage their homosexuality within the framework of the closet.[21]

Cohen describes how heterocentric definitions of black identity undermine black gay and lesbian individuals' feelings of inclusion within the black community when she observes, "A gay sexual identity has been seen in black communities as mitigating one's racial identity and deflating one's community standing."[22] Seidman further identifies the greater financial and social interdependence black people have with their heterosexual community of origin as another factor black gay men face in the decision to come out, which plays less of a role among gay white men.[23] He writes:

> Maintaining strong ties with kin and a race-based community is a cornerstone of black identity in a way that is obviously not true for whites. If whites grow up with a sense of racial entitlement and a feeling that it is their America, many blacks experience and

expect an inhospitable reception in the larger society. Experience and kin have taught them that their personal and social well-being depends on maintaining solidarity with a black community. . . . And if the individual turns out to be gay, the black community has often demanded that this identity be kept private as a condition of acceptance.[24]

The result of contending with ethnocentrism within the gay community and heterosexism within the black community is that gay black individuals are rendered invisible to both worlds. Summarizing this intersectional perspective on the decision to come out of the closet, Seidman writes that for black gay men and lesbians, coming out "threatens social isolation from both the straight and gay worlds. It risks being cast adrift in a society that does not recognize or value being black and gay; it jeopardizes a secure sense of belonging and protection (physical and economic) in exchange for an outsider status."[25]

Consequences of Intersectional Invisibility for the Individual: Threatened Belonging

It is hard to feel like you belong to a group when you are invisible to it; intersectionals, in general, are doubly estranged from the gay and black communities. Black gay Christians are rendered invisible from gay and black communities and the black church. This is troubling because social psychological theory and research have identified belonging as a fundamental human need and a universal motive.[26] People who chronically experience social exclusion and diminished belonging are vulnerable to several detrimental psychological and physical outcomes.

Belonging is such an essential psychological need that people may be motivated to manage their identity expression to protect their feelings of belonging to important communities. Specifically, black gay and lesbian individuals may attempt to downplay their racial identity when interacting with other members of the gay community to avoid jeopardizing their sense of belonging to the gay community. By the same token, they may conceal or downplay their sexual identity when interacting with other members of the black community to avoid jeopardizing their sense of belonging there as well.[27] Audre Lorde describes how she experienced pressures to compartmentalize her various marginalized identities in different settings of her life when she writes, "As a Black lesbian feminist . . . I find I am constantly being encouraged to pluck out some one aspect of myself and present this as the meaningful whole, eclipsing or denying the other parts of self." Such identity compartmentalization can be psychologically costly, as Lorde acknowledges, noting, "This is a destructive and fragmenting way to live. My fullest concentration of energy is available to me only when I integrate all the parts of who I am openly, allowing power from particular sources of my living to flow back and forth freely through all my different selves, without the restrictions of an externally imposed definition."[28]

Our recent research documents that identity compartmentalization can have lasting effects on the organization of a person's self-concept—their self-knowledge or sense of who they are in the world—and their psychological well-being. Specifically, we find that people who suppress an identity in one setting that they express more openly in other settings develop strongly differentiated self-concepts associated with these respective settings and that this intense differentiation of setting-specific self-concepts leads them to experience psychological distress.[29] Thus, while identity compartmentalization may be a convenient strategy for immediately coping with the marginalization of different components of one's identity across different settings, this strategy comes with measurable long-term costs. Specifically, the price of a more secure sense of belonging may be diminished identity integration. In short, when black gay and lesbian individuals are rendered invisible, they must choose between feelings of estrangement or compartmentalizing the self; this is truly a lose-lose situation, as both options have negative psychological consequences.

In addition to being a psychologically costly strategy for managing the belonging needs for people with intersectionally marginalized identities, compartmentalization is also problematic on political grounds because it involves the individual accommodating his or her identity expression to an oppressive social environment. Reforming the black and gay communities or the black church from within to make them more inclusive of black gay men and lesbians would represent a more politically progressive strategy for fulfilling these individuals' need to belong. In the next section, we suggest how findings from recent psychological studies might be used to design interventions to enhance black gay men's and lesbians' feelings of belonging to their ethnic and sexual identity communities.

Consequences of Intersectional Invisibility for the Black Church: Poor Health and Empty Pews

Social psychological research finds that individuals who have social identities that have traditionally been the basis for exclusion from a given setting are often highly attuned to cues that might indicate whether their identity is currently accepted within that setting. When they do not see others who share their social identity visibly represented and they do not receive unambiguous messages that their social identity is valued by others within that setting, they are vulnerable to feeling a low sense of belonging, which leads them to mistrust others within that setting.[30] This effect of threatened belonging on trust is particularly noteworthy because trust is an important source of social capital that motivates constructive, collaborative action within groups. Individuals who lack trust in others are less likely to initiate or join activities that promote the common interests of the group, and they are less likely to take the kinds of risks that could lead to social innovations. Thus, the very conditions that threaten a person's feelings of belonging within a community are likely to undermine that person's social agency for promoting the kinds of changes that could promote greater inclusiveness for themselves and others who share their threatened social identity.

Given that the presence of others who share their identity is an important cue that individuals with a devalued identity often pay attention to when gauging their sense of belonging in a setting,[31] the black community and the gay community might be able to cultivate greater feelings of belonging on the part of black gay men and lesbians by enhancing the visibility of other gay black people within those communities. Every black gay man or lesbian who publicly comes out of the closet and remains actively involved with the black and gay communities has the potential to help create a more hospitable climate for other black gay people. It may be particularly identity-affirming to see other gay black people assuming leadership roles within both the black and the gay community.

Advocacy organizations within both the black community and the gay community may thus strive to foster greater inclusivity and promote greater feelings of belonging by making greater efforts to recruit black gay men and lesbians into visible leadership roles. However, policies of inclusion need to be designed and implemented with care to avoid the impression that organizations are practicing tokenism. Members of disadvantaged groups are not only sensitive to information about their numerical representation in leadership roles and decision-making bodies within community organizations, but they also pay careful attention to information about the authenticity of leaders and decision makers who are supposed to represent them. If representatives are not selected by the people whom they supposedly represent (or if those representatives do not actively cultivate solidarity with the constituents they are supposed to represent), then they will likely be perceived as tokens. Tokenism is hardly an effective policy for promoting feelings of belonging and indeed it could backfire by further highlighting problems of belonging.

The 2000 Millennium March on Washington (MMOW) offers an instructive example of how a poorly designed inclusion policy can backfire and create an impression of tokenism.[32] Previous Washington marches organized by gay and lesbian groups were criticized for lack of inclusiveness because their planning committees predominantly consisted of white gay men. To correct this problem, the planning committee for the 2000 march made sure that half of its members were people of color. However, critics pointed out that rather than being nominated by grassroots organizations representing gay and lesbian people of color, these committee members were nominated and selected by other committee members. These concerns were expressed by one black lesbian critic who said, "If I continue to hear about the 50 percent of persons of color on the MMOW board, I'm going to scream. With all due respect, there is a qualitative difference between being a person of color and representing a person-of-color constituency." Thus, the MMOW board members' status as authentic representatives of gay and lesbian communities of color was put in doubt, which may have undermined the organizers' goal of promoting a more inclusive event. Indeed, one observer estimated that only about 1 percent of those attending the march were people of color.[33]

Another strategy for increasing black gay men's and lesbians' feelings of belonging to their racial, sexual, and religious communities is to create safe spaces in which all of these identities can be freely expressed and affirmed. Churches that adopt a policy of tolerance toward same-sex sexuality and full inclusion of gay and lesbian members may offer a particularly affirming space for black lesbians and gay men to experience an integrated expression of their racial, sexual, and religious identities. For example, Mignon Moore describes the identity affirmation that black gay men and lesbians experienced from a spiritual center that combined elements of traditional African American Christian worship, New Age spirituality, and progay messages.[34]

However, while the increasing availability of churches and other religious organizations that openly welcome gay men and lesbians as members may expand the options for identity expression for black gay men and lesbians, it is important to recognize that there may be important barriers to pursuing these options. Demographic studies of religious behavior indicate that black Americans may face greater barriers to switching religious affiliations than white Americans. Indeed, black Americans are about half as likely as white Americans to switch away from their parents' religion.[35] Fidelity to one's parents' religion may be higher among black believers in part because religion is more closely tied to one's ethnic identity for black Americans than it is for white Americans. Thus, advocating switching to a more gay-affirming church as a solution to escape homophobic discourses and practices in traditional churches may be premised on an ethnocentric assumption about the ease of switching religious affiliations.

Churches that openly welcome gay and lesbian congregants tend to be unorthodox in many other elements of their doctrine and worship practices, which may constitute another barrier to recruiting black gay men and lesbians to these churches. Compared to white religious believers, even white evangelical Protestants, black Protestants tend to be more orthodox and traditional in their beliefs and practices.[36] Thus, black gay Protestants may find that churches that are more tolerant of their same-sex sexuality do not satisfyingly embody other important elements of their religious faith. Given the barriers to switching congregations that many black gay people of faith may experience, it will be important for gay and lesbian activists not only to develop and promote new gay-affirming religious options but also to pursue gay-affirming reforms within existing black religious congregations, whether that means expanding the sphere of acceptance beyond the choir to church leadership positions, or, in the words of Rev. Edwin Sanders II, creating " warmth and connection . . . a comfort zone in which [congregants will] eventually deal with the issues that might be their point of difference."[37]

In a 1987 interview with the historian George Chauncey, Bayard Rustin described how the experience of being both a racial minority and a sexual minority affected his civil rights activism. Published under the title "Time on Two Crosses," the interview powerfully referenced the dual pain of both racism and homophobia.[38] Rustin's example reminds us that black and gay identities intersect in the lives of individuals who are members of both communities. They may be victims of racial oppression within the gay community and homophobia within the black community in addition to enduring both forms of prejudice within the broader society. The symbol of the cross to represent Rustin's experiences of both racism and homophobia may be particularly useful for illuminating intersections of the black and gay communities because for the Christian believer the cross is a reminder that all people are ultimately linked with each other in the singular event of Christ's redemptive suffering. Thus, just as the symbolism of Christianity can often be used to sow divisions within communities, it also has enormous potential to help heal those divisions.

PART FIVE

Theological and Pastoral Visions of an Inclusive Black Church

CHAPTER 9

Gay *Is* the New Black, Theologically Speaking

MONICA A. COLEMAN

This essay examines how four theological categories—creation, theological anthropology, sin, and ecclesiology—intersect with contemporary issues around sexuality and sexual ethics, with particular attention to homosexuality. I will illustrate that despite the historical and sociological differences between black and GLBTQ communities in America, there are similarities in the theological arguments made in perpetuating their oppression and exclusion. This essay advocates and relies upon two theoretical positions: (1) that race and sexuality are socially constructed (rather than ontological); and (2) that sexual ethics should focus on the content of relationships (rather than form). Finally, I will offer three concrete recommendations for how black churches wrestling with sexual politics can proceed.

The Problem with "Gay Is the New Black"

December 2004: Rev. Eddie Long, the pastor of the largest black church in greater Atlanta, Georgia (with twenty-five thousand members), led a march calling for various social and political stances—including a state constitutional ban on same-sex marriage.[1] With almost ten thousand participants, the march began at the birthplace of Martin Luther King Jr. and was co-led by Rev. Bernice King, Martin Luther King's youngest child. Eddie Long named the march "Reigniting the Legacy" as a direct reference to his belief that his social and political positions aligned with Martin Luther King's vision. Other civil rights leaders such as King's widow, Coretta Scott King, Congressman John Lewis of Georgia, and Julian Bond, then chair of the NAACP, supported same-sex marriages. This is one example of how prominent black Christians have differed on issues of sexual politics and how they have diverged in their understandings of the legacy of the black freedom/civil rights movement of the 1960s.

November 2008: The week after the historic election in which Barack Obama was elected as the first black president of the United States, the *Advocate*, a national magazine billing itself as "the world's leading gay news source," printed a lead article that referred to how the same voting day that elected Obama also saw four different states pass legislation against same-sex marriage, same-sex couple adoptions, and/or same-sex domestic partnerships and unions. When the magazine hit the newsstands, the cover featured the following words in large yellow letters on a black background: "GAY IS THE NEW BLACK: The Last Great Civil Rights Struggle."

The phrase, "the new black," simultaneously refers to the renewed popularity of a classic concept and the oppressed group in a contemporary period. Both notions collide in the expression, "gay is the new black." Every year the fashion world identifies "the new black." This naming refers to the fact that clothing in the color black functions as a classic wardrobe staple. Thus, in some years, "gray is the new black," and in other years, "brown is the new black."[2] While the color black remains an important staple in the fashion world, blackness in a racial sense has been thought to signify a state of oppression. In contemporary theology, the late James H. Cone articulated blackness as an ontological category that connotes the experience of oppression that black people in America have faced. Cone's link between blackness and oppression emerged from the context of the civil rights and Black Power movements of the 1960s. For Cone, "black" transcended physiological traits and referred to both one's experience of oppression and one's desire to resist that oppression in the social and political realms.[3] This designation elevated "black," and the category of race, as the most significant arena of oppression (as compared to gender, class, etc.).

James Cone's discussion of "black" as an ontological category has come under significant critique. The most poignant critique was leveled by African American philosopher Victor Anderson, who notes that identifying "black" with a state of oppression negates the reality that many aspects of life in the black community are positive, life-giving, and lived outside of the gaze of white racism.[4] Outside of theology, "black" is seen as an ontological concept through the category of biology. Connecting blackness to brown skin allows many individuals to claim that one cannot choose to identify as black; rather, it is an inescapable state of being. Much of this concept is tied to the "one-drop rule" instituted during U.S. slavery that held that if a person had any known ancestor of black African descent, he or she would be categorized as "black." This was primarily an economic distinction designed to grow the slave labor force during forced and voluntary racial mixing. Thus, individuals may range from a fairly light beige color to a very dark brown color and still identify as "black." Although this could undermine the physiological character of ontological blackness, it usually serves to reinforce the biological—and thus ontological—connection to a black identification. Such understandings of blackness complicate the nomenclature of "black."

As media sources and members and advocates of gay, lesbian, bisexual, transgender, and queer (GLBTQ) communities articulate the position of GLBTQ persons in society as "the new black," they enter a minefield of racial signifying. When one says that "gay is the new black," it refers to the way that many media entertainment outlets feature television shows and advertising campaigns that feature GLBTQ protagonists and advocacy. One strong example of this is the television show *Queer Eye for the Straight Guy* that debuted on the Bravo television network in 2003. On this show, five openly gay men representing the fields of interior design, fashion, personal grooming, culture, and culinary arts, conduct a several-day makeover of a straight man. In its third season, the series became simply *Queer Eye*, so that makeovers could be done for individuals whatever their gender or sexual orientation. While the original series ended in 2007, the video streaming service Netflix did a popular reboot of the series in 2018 that produced and sired four new seasons by mid-2019. Both iterations of *Queer Eye* won Emmy and GLAAD Media awards.

GLBTQ persons are also "the new black" in the sense that the issues of same-sex marriage and GLBTQ-related hate crimes often are framed as issues of civil rights. Since "civil rights" generally is taken to refer to both a legal designation and the black freedom struggle of the 1960s, invoking the language of "civil rights" signifies an association with the historical experiences of African Americans. The voting rights and anti-Jim Crow campaigns of the African American civil rights movement and the state-by-state voting campaigns on same-sex marriage and GLBTQ-related hate crimes evoked some of the same legal and political issues. They both involved the role of state rights, federal protection of citizens, and equal rights. Both cases ultimately required federal intervention for resolution. In 1965, President Lyndon Johnson signed the Voting Rights Act outlawing discriminatory voting practices. In 2015, the Supreme court ruled that state bans on same-sex marriage are unconstitutional in *Obergefell v. Hodges*.

Amid such linguistic framing, some individuals and communities vehemently oppose comparing the experiences of GLBTQ and black persons. Although issues around gender identity and sexual preference and orientation have received more media attention in recent years, the actual experiences of GLBTQ persons often contradict the notion that "gay" has the level of acceptance and vogue that the color black does within the fashion industry. GLBTQ-related hate crimes, the disproportionate rate at which GLBTQ teens are displaced from their homes and attempt (and commit) suicide suggest that GLBTQ identification is not popular or accepted even after the achievement of marriage equality.

Suggesting that the experiences of GLBTQ individuals and African Americans are analogous also has its shortcomings. In the most generous understanding of such a comparison, there are two significant limitations. First, referring to GLBTQ persons as "the new black" ignores the fact that there are African Americans who identify as GLBTQ. The term "the new black" can easily offer a public portrayal of a white GLBTQ community juxtaposed against a heterosexual African American community. Second, the experiences of oppression and the quest for equality among (primarily white) GLBTQ persons and African Americans have manifested themselves differently in the history and politics of the United States. Thus one can make the argument that "gay is *not* the new black" on social and historical grounds.

Despite the differences between GLBTQ communities and African Americans, the challenges in labeling race as the primary referent for the bases of oppression, and the question of whether one is persuaded that "gay is the new black," the theological rhetoric used against both marginalized groups (GLBTQ and African Americans) has conflated and collapsed them as the same. That is, there is a history of Christian theological arguments that have and continue to elucidate why both GLBTQ individuals and persons of African descent are unacceptable in God's eyes and Christian communities. Since these arguments are similar, or even corollary, gay *is* the new black, theologically speaking.

Creation, Anthropology, Sin, and Ecclesiology

There are four major issues of Christian systematic theology that arise in the conversation about GLBTQ persons in Christian churches. The first issue is one of creation. In conversations about creation, theology asks questions such as: How does God create us? When? And out of what material, if any? For what purpose are we created? What are our relationships to other people and other aspects of creation?

Another closely related issue is that of theological anthropology: What does it mean to be made in the image of God? Who is made in the image of God? Is there a difference between being made in the image of God and the likeness of God? Is part of our physicality, mentality, and sexuality included and encoded in this idea of being made in God's image or likeness? And again, what is our God-ordained mission on earth?

GLBTQ issues also raise the question of sin. How is sin defined? By intention? By actions like practices or behaviors? Is sin an individual condition or a social one? Is there such a thing as original sin? If so, how did it happen, and what are its effects and consequences? Is it a propensity toward violence or a kind of fallenness? Are our sins punished? If so, by whom, and how? And is there any relief from sin?

Fourth, our understandings of ecclesiology or the doctrine of the church are raised in GLBTQ discussions. What does it mean to be a church? What is the role of the church to its constituents and the world? Who is included in the church? Do all people in the church have a right to leadership/ordination? What rituals do churches perform and why? Are all people welcome to participate in those rituals or only certain members?

While other areas of systematic theological study may be relevant, these four are illustrative of the comparison at hand. This section will examine conservative positions on GLBTQ issues from a Christian perspective and correlate them with a theological question.

Under the rubric of creation, two primary issues emerge. First, some conservatives have been heard to argue that "God made Adam and Eve, not Adam and Steve." The underlying theological question here is: Does God create humanity in male and female genders to send a message about how families should be structured? A second trope is, "Two men or two women can't make a baby, so God didn't mean for that to happen." The underlying theological question: Are human beings and our sexualities designed for the sole purpose of procreation?

"It's just not natural." As an issue of theological anthropology, the statement asks whether human beings are created to be heterosexual beings, to the extent that any deviation from that norm is a perversion of how God creates us. There is at least one other statement about how God creates humanity within conservative understandings of GLBTQ positionality in Christianity. "People choose to act that way" assumes that sexual desire, preference, and orientation are free choices. In the same vein, "I don't approve of the homosexual lifestyle" presupposes that a homosexual identity is chosen, and raises a question about whether our sexualities are defined by our behaviors or our desires.

In the category of hamartiology (sin), the following statements are expressions of a conservative (nonaffirming) perspective: "Well, you know he was molested as a child and that's why he thinks he's gay now," and "AIDS is God's curse on gays and lesbians." These statements ask whether a non-heterosexual orientation is a result of someone else's sin and whether God issues out punishment for the sin of non-heterosexual behavior, respectively.

Finally, "Hate the sin and love the sinner" asks questions of ecclesiology: Are churches truly inclusive if they declare that they can love someone while repudiating an integral part of who someone is? Likewise, marriages and same-sex unions also reveal questions about the sacramental dimension of churches. When an individual is told, "You will lose your ordination if you officiate at the blessing of a same-sex union," it confines church rituals and sacraments only to people of a certain sexual orientation. The declaration that "we will not ordain practicing homosexuals" correlates to theological questions about whether church leadership is restricted to a particular section of the church population determined by sexual orientation and behavior.[5]

These same statements and theological questions correlate to historical understandings of the social and theological equality of African Americans from a Christian perspective. Here are some from U.S. history:

- "Blacks make better slaves." This suggests that God created humanity in different races to send a message about who should serve whom.
- "The Aryan race is superior" implies that God desires particular qualities for humanity that one race naturally possesses and other races simply do not, or to which they can only aspire.
- "No matter the racial identification of one's parents, if one is black, then the child is black" and "You know, so-and-so is light enough to pass." Is race transmitted through blood, phenotype, or cultural affiliation?

- "So-and-so acts white" assumes there are forms of behavior, speech, and phenotype that typify one race or another.
- "Blacks have the Curse of Ham." The notion of blackness as a curse views black people as an aberration from what God intended for the creation of humanity and therefore as not fully human.
- "Blackness is a generational curse that stems from Ham to all other black people." This imagines a God whose punishment of one individual for sin can transfer to that individual's biological and spiritual descendants.
- "Blacks must sit in the balcony and pray there." Are churches truly inclusive if they declare that they can love someone while asking them to observe different practices than a privileged group?
- "I won't take communion administered by a black preacher." Individuals who believe this are proposing that church rituals and sacraments are only valid when performed by people of a certain race.
- "Black clergy in predominantly white denominations get the smallest churches in the most rural locales." This restricts church leadership to certain sections of the church population based on race.

The conservative Christian positions that deny equal worth and treatment to GLBTQ persons and African Americans stem from nearly identical theological questions. In his book, *Their Own Receive Them Not: African American Lesbians and Gays in Black Churches*, Horace Griffin asks what it means when African American Christians who, based on race, have had these theological arguments lobbied against them and been denied full inclusion in church and society but then make the same theological arguments based on sexuality and sexual orientation to deny a segment of their community such inclusion.[6] Griffin refers to how many African Americans accept and advocate for the theological inferiority of homosexuals while rejecting the analogous theological arguments against the inferiority of blacks.

While one could identify black churches with conservative positions on sexual orientation as maintaining theological hypocrisy, Griffin finds hope in the Christian theological correlation between GLBTQ and African American communities. Griffin believes that if African Americans have applied a liberative theological interpretation to scripture and Christian traditions in terms of the full humanity of African Americans, then they have the tools to do the same along lines of sexuality and sexual orientation.

The challenge is this: Many African Americans feel that race is an inescapable ontological category, while sexuality or sexual orientation is a choice.

As noted earlier in the essay, blackness, and race in general, is not well-grounded in biology. The "one-drop rule" in the United States that categorized individuals as black and white could, in other societies (i.e., Brazil) be categorized as one of thirty racial identifications that correlated more specifically to phenotypical characteristics, color, and class. With the legality of racial mixing in the United States, increasingly individuals identify as multi- and biracial as they feel a biological and cultural connection to family members and communities who identify differently in relationship to available racial categories. When understood in this rubric, race exists along a spectrum of phenotypes with racial designation shaped more based on experience and cultural identification than an unchosen biological feature. Gender and sexuality are often understood in the same way. Critical race theory, gender studies, and queer studies have long noted that biology does not always divide (with chromosomes and genitalia) into two simple categories of male and female. Even if it did, the characteristics constituting feminine and masculine are shaped by society, or even the subcultures within a society. Thus, sexual preference, orientation, gender, and race are constructed more by the history and contemporary mores of society than by biological necessity. In the face of such knowledge, there is still a common conception that race is biological and sexual orientation is chosen. Such an understanding permits and justifies the application of different hermeneutical approaches to race and sexuality and supports theological heterosexism in African American churches.

The consequences of this are grave. Horace Griffin highlights the typical kinds of responses that many African American lesbians and gays experience within black churches under several kinds of passing. They range from an internalized self-hatred and rejection to various levels of closeting and acceptance of partial inclusion in the life of the church. This cultivates secrecy, shame, and partial alienation so that GLBTQ Christians bring only part of their lives into their church spaces while witnessing and even participating in the full inclusion of their heterosexual brothers and sisters. Thus, just as in the tradition of lighter-skinned blacks passing into white society, passing comes at a high price—the most theologically relevant being the failure to live into one's full and authentic self. At its worst, the ecclesial and familial rejection of GLBTQ persons contributes to the homelessness and suicide rates of GLBTQ youth. Allow me to give just a couple of numbers here: A 2017 report indicates that GLBTQ youth had a 120 percent higher risk of being homeless compared to youth who identify as heterosexual and cisgender.[7] In the United States, suicide is the second leading cause of death among young people between age ten and twenty-four. A 2016 student indicates that GLB youth are almost five times as likely to have attempted suicide compared to their heterosexual counterparts.[8] By 2015, 40 percent of transgender adults indicated that they attempted suicide at one point in their lives.[9] While theological conservatism is not the sole cause for the homeless and suicide rates among GLBTQ youth, I believe it is a significant contributing factor. This is particularly true in African American churches that have a long history of functioning as institutions of spiritual, political, social, economic, and emotional support. When such resources are denied to African American GLBTQ persons, theologically supported heterosexism in African American churches can have life-and-death consequences.

Three Theological Recommendations

So what could help? Although Griffin suggests various pastoral approaches to incorporate African American lesbians and gays in black churches, his methodological approach suggests an additional strategy. By disclosing great gays and lesbians of African American society—such as James Baldwin, George Washington Carver, James Cleveland, and Barbara Jordan—African American churches may be more likely to welcome African American lesbians and gays. Roger Sneed questions this historical retrieval approach as flawed for reasons of accuracy and effectiveness.[10] Along with Sneed, this essay argues that a theological—or even philosophical—approach may be better suited.

First, black Christian communities need to deconstruct the idea that race is ontological while sexual orientation is a matter of choice. Church leaders must learn and teach that race, gender, sex, and sexuality are not best discussed in dualist terms, nor as biological necessities. Rather, they are both social constructions whose consequences have real effects but do not have a grounding in biology. Dwight Hopkins's *Being Human*, Emilie Townes's *Womanist Ethics and the Cultural Production of Evil*, Victor Anderson's *Creative Exchange*, and Brian Bantum's *Redeeming Mulatto* are poignant works by black religious scholars with excellent sections on how this applies to race.[11] This will affect how we understand creation and theological anthropology. One can take the stance that sexual orientation is as biologically determined as race and consider both as a priori categories of God's good creation.

This essay argues for a more radical position that God did not biologically *make* us into a particular race, gender, or sexual orientation. Our likeness to God is thus more spiritual than physical or sociological. We assume these categories in our social inheritance and then work within them concerning our environments.

Second, church leaders must also redefine sin. Liberation theology discusses sin as the oppression of other people or aspects of creation. Such a definition leads to a position wherein the exclusion of any person, especially GLBTQ persons, is a sin against those persons—a sin committed by the larger community. Likewise, activists who speak out in faith communities against sexual violence emphasize that sexual violence is a crime and activity based on power, not on sexuality, and that it does not *make* a person straight or gay.[12] Thus, we must stop assuming that all sexual violence occurs in heterosexual formats. This is particularly pertinent given the incarceration rates of African American men and women. That is, the same-gender sexual behavior that occurs in prison is often more about power and hierarchy than about preference or orientation.

Third, church leaders also need to talk about sex, sexuality, and sexual behavior in ways that focus more on the content of relationships than the form of the relationships. Thus, an ethic and practice of care, intimacy, mutuality, love, and communication become more important than the gender identities of who is involved in these relationships. Such theological anthropology makes clear how much human freedom is involved in choosing the character of relationships—even while we can see how easy it is to hurt, disrespect, and offend our fellow human beings.

Three Congregational Recommendations

In *Trans-Gendered: Theology, Ministry and Communities of Faith*, Justin Edward Tanis describes the decision to live openly as a transgender person as a vocational calling.[13] Black churches could expand conversations of vocation and calling beyond the call to ordained ministry and into the calling to live as God has made us—authentically, abundantly, and in ways that creatively transform the world around us. Doing so would challenge existing ecclesiologies. That is, what constitutes church is less a discussion of the qualities or decisions one must make to be considered inside the community or about how God is conveyed in the sacraments of the church. With this expanded ecclesiology, the church is measured by the authentic and communal interaction of the members.

How might this be lived out in church communities?

First, committed church leaders could, for example, take the radical step toward committing themselves to an extensive sermon series teaching about sexuality and Christianity. In the late 1990s, the late Fred Price—best known for his proclamation of the "Prosperity Gospel"—preached on race every Sunday for close to two years. Of course, there are consequences to this approach, which is not popular and can have negative financial results for a church. Yet this commitment to inquiry, growth, and justice may also enliven the community and stimulate new membership.

Second, black churches might also make a theological statement. Here is an example from one particular church that is a part of the Reconciling Ministries Network within the United Methodist Church. The Reconciling Ministries Network is constituted by United Methodists of all sexual orientations and gender identities that are committed to transforming the "church and world into the full expression of Christ's inclusive love," even while the larger denomination does not.[14] This church had a float in the annual Pride parade with the word *human* painted in large letters.[15] Church members rode the float and made a powerful theological statement as they cried out: "God loves everyone."

Finally, African American GLBTQ persons and those who stand in solidarity with them may follow in the African American church liberation tradition that refuses to be mistreated and used by white churches for their gifts, graces, and tithes while being treated as second-class church citizens. GLBTQ Christians and advocates may *not* decide to fight from within (as many African American women have done concerning their apartheid situation of theology and power). GLBTQ Christians may leave African American churches and begin their own faith communities—as many have already done.[16] This is a viable option in good keeping with African American church traditions.

Theological Hope

The aforementioned options illustrate that theology, too, is constructed. That is, theology is sourced by various understandings of Scripture, reason, tradition, experience, and culture. Individuals and communities construct theology per normative ideals of what is acceptable. The variety within Christian theology is a reminder that theology is not a given. Like race and sexuality, theology is not ontological; it is constructed in an environment that interacts with numerous other influences.

The constructed nature of race, sexuality, and theology illustrates a creative tension. Theology can be a means through which equality and acceptance are denied, but it can also be a means through which equality and acceptance are asserted. The similarities between the theological arguments against the full equality of GLBTQ persons and the full equality of African Americans can challenge the prevailing sexual politics of black churches.

In such a challenge, one may resist some of the comparisons between GLBTQ experiences and African American experiences encapsulated in the expression, "gay is the new black." Neither African Americans and GLBTQ persons are so trendy and acceptable that hate crimes and social discrimination have ceased to be significant problems. African Americans and GLBTQ persons have distinct experiences of oppression, intersectionality with gender and class, and relationships to legal civil rights issues. At times these experiences overlap; at other times they diverge. There is understandable resistance to identifying racial blackness as the primary referent for experiences of oppression and thus "gay as the new black." Yet how theological argumentation for and against the social and spiritual equality of GLBTQ individuals and African Americans are analogous may well lead one to say that "gay is the new black, theologically speaking."

If Griffin is correct, such a designation indicates that the same African American faith communities that employed sophisticated hermeneutical tools to their experiences of racial oppression in Christianity may bring the same kinds of analysis and protest in terms of sexual politics.

CHAPTER 10

Flesh That Needs to be Loved

Wounded Black Bodies and Preachin' in the Spirit

LUKE A. POWERY

In the beginning was the Word . . . and the Word became flesh and lived among us.

—JOHN 1:1, 14

It is our body that actually lives our life.

—LORNA MARSHALL, *THE BODY SPEAKS*

This is flesh I'm talking about here. Flesh that needs to be loved.

—BABY SUGGS, *BELOVED*

To be human is to have a body and (em)body forth life. Cheryl Townsend Gilkes says, "All human experience is embodied experience."[1] The body is always with us, "*is* us."[2] Yet, there is a "somatic dis-ease" within black religion and life, implying a dis-ease with the whole black self.[3] This cultural hesitancy to engage the body is reflected within African American homiletics. Though one Euro-American scholar defines homiletics as "theology processed through the body,"[4] and another calls it "enfleshed speech,"[5] the fleshly physical nature of preaching is still viewed with much suspicion and remains rather silent in African American homiletical theory even though "danced religion"—that is, embodied worship—has been noted to be the epitome of worship in traditional black settings.[6] In preaching theories developed by African Americans, the black body is almost fully absent, but in the practice of preaching in many black churches, the body is on full display, present. Because of this absent presence, absent in theory but present in practice, revealing a gap between theory and practice, one may assume that African American preaching is essentially a disembodied venture.

Yet, this is far from the truth. There is much hooping, shouting, dancing, jumping, and gyrating that occurs in the pulpit even as the black body of the preacher is rarely discussed in preaching texts written by African Americans. There is a somatic silence in African American homiletical literature, a lack of love for black flesh—an analytical obscuring of the physical black preaching body.[7] The body is written off as insignificant; thus, hardly any words are written about it. The body is made invisible through silence only to "allow the black body a shadowless participation in the dominant cultural body" of homiletics.[8]

This chapter aims to rewrite the homiletical script for the black body by giving voice to that which has been silenced in black homiletics and asserting the significance of the body for black preaching as an initial attempt toward a constructive dialogue about sexual politics in black churches, especially as it relates to the pulpit ministry. Preaching involves some-body and this is true for every-body, even though as Anthony Pinn asserts, "Black theology is often a theology of *no-body*, a system of theological expression without an organized (re)presentation of the body as body."[9] What follows is a corrective to the field of African American homiletics that is apparently "materially empty."[10] The first section will explore possible reasons for the silence of the black body in African American homiletical discourse, particularly due to the treatment and view of the body in the history of slavery and Christianity. The second section will explain how, through the lens of the Spirit, the black body is critical for the practice of preaching as the conduit of the divine. The third section will discuss what this exploration of the black homiletical body might mean for fostering healthy conversations about different kinds of preaching bodies in black churches; it will do so by using the preaching of Baby Suggs in the clearing, in Toni Morrison's *Beloved*. Through this exploration of the black homiletical body, it will become clear that an open discussion about the black body in preaching, making it visible and audible in homiletical discourse, may pave a healing path to honor all black bodies that have been wounded and dishonored.

(Black) Body as Theological Possibility: Some-bodies

Incarnation

Despite the hurtful legacy of Christianity that denigrates the body's potential, at the heart of Christian revelation, and thus preaching, is the incarnation of the divine into a human physical body. When John writes, "the Word became flesh and lived among us" (Jn 1:14), he reveals how the divine embraces the body by the divine Word becoming a human body, living as any human being. The Incarnation claims "that God trusted flesh and blood to bring divine love to earth."[11] The incarnate Word is the embodied communication of the divine to humanity. When the Logos, the Word, becomes flesh, then it comes to life in our world. But without movement in a body, the word, preaching, is not alive. For African American homiletics, the incarnate Word paves the way toward an incarnational ethic of proclamation through which black bodies are some-bodies and reclaimed as beautiful.

There is dis-ease with black bodies, yet the black Christian preaching tradition still affirms that Jesus is the "divine housed in a body like ours."[12] The black body has been wounded and broken and considered a no-body historically. Yet, the highlighting of the suffering and wounded black body is an avenue to uncover "the [incarnated] suffering body at the heart of Christian belief."[13] If the cross is considered to be the heart of preaching, then at the heart of preaching is a broken body. The theological memory of black Christianity interweaves the cultural trauma of broken black bodies with the tortured and broken body of Christ. For African Americans, "Jesus' death by crucifixion is a prototype of African Americans' death by circumscription."[14] Traditionally, African Americans have identified the story of Jesus's suffering as their story of suffering to such an extent that theologians like James Cone speak of the relationship between the cross and the lynching tree, calling Christ a "lynched black body."[15] Real fleshy dark bodies are hung out to dry and die on wooden trees. The heart of the black word, preaching, is the body, a tortured body that gains much focus in the spiritual and sermonic tradition of African Americans with songs like "Were You There When They Crucified My Lord?" and sermons like "The Crucifixion" that proclaim:

> Jesus, my darling Jesus,
> Groaning as the blood came spurting from his wound.[16]

Whether wounded or whole, "the incarnation of Jesus is proof of the importance of the body as a means of grace."[17] This incarnation graces the black body as some-body.

Spirit and Material (Black) Body

The incarnation of God in the flesh, even as a wounded broken body, is a happening of the Spirit.[18] The Spirit initiates enfleshment, which is particularly important for black congregations because one of the gifts of black people is the "gift of the Spirit."[19] The Spirit embraces the black material body because the divine Spirit plunges us deeper into our physical selves. Thus, bodies are temples of the Spirit (1 Cor. 6:19), housing the divine presence within black flesh. This means that embodiment is significant for spiritual practice. The Spirit honors the body to such an extent that "the sacraments state that the word of God wants to enter our bodies, that is, our lives, and that for anyone in-dwelt by the Spirit the road of the God of Jesus Christ necessarily uses the human road."[20] The "human road" of the black homiletical body is a path for sacramental activity because "that which is most spiritual thus comes only through the mediation of that which is most corporeal."[21] The spiritual embraces the material, making the black body "a site and mediation of divine revelation" in preaching.[22] The materiality of the Spirit's work through black bodies is affirmed by Robert Hood who argues that the Spirit is an "untidy, dynamic, and ecstatic power" in black American religion and within the larger context of African religion, in which immaterial, incorporeal spirits take on human shape.[23] This shape is in the form of a black (wounded, broken) body that reveals signs of being possessed by the divine.

Throughout history, there have been many "signs" of black bodies being indwelled by the Spirit due to the somatic sensibility of black religiosity. The pneumatic has always converged with the somatic in black religion. I elaborate on this connection elsewhere,[24] but what is critical is that the black body is a site of the Spirit's manifestation. Joseph Murphy notes, "The spirit of the Black Church is the ceremonial experience of God's ultimate freedom in the body of the congregation. In word, song, music, and movement, the spirit is brought down to become incarnated in the very bodies of the devotees."[25] The bodily manifestations of the Spirit have not only been called "the frenzy" historically but also the "regular" shout or "getting happy"[26] and other ecstatic expressions of the body. The enslaved had a proclivity for "bodily exercises"—movements influenced by the African heritage of dance.[27] This is not surprising because "the strongest of African residua are expressed through the body."[28] The choreography of the body in worship settings is what led C. Eric Lincoln and Lawrence H. Mamiya to call the Black Church the "first theater in the black community."[29]

Through pneumatic possession, wounded and broken black bodies move toward healing and the reclamation of their humanity. Black people, considered objects under the regime of chattel slavery, reclaim their black flesh through the materiality of the Spirit. "In American slave religion, the slaves . . . take their bodies back,"[30] gaining control over their own body to "signify or twist social control."[31] Moreover, the brutalized black body, despite the attempt of white erasure, was affirmed by God as sacred in the act of worship. Any sign of the Spirit in the body exemplified "the sign of special favor from the spirit."[32] Because of this, the same black body that was viewed as ugly and only useful for labor "was transformed into a ritual device through which the glory of God and the beauty of human movement were celebrated."[33] Bodies that were wrecked under slavery and oppression were now "redeemed" through bodily rituals.[34] Through the Spirit, the black body becomes a "sacred text,"[35] speaking of the horror of being deemed a no-body and through divine possession being recreated as some-body who can proclaim a word from the Lord.

A Preaching Black Body

The black body as a sacred "nontraditional text" is a some-body that is also a sermonic text, preaching words of hope and life in the Spirit.[36] "In the Spirit" is significant because as revealed earlier the Spirit utilizes the flesh, which means preaching in the Spirit does not escape the body but inhabits it more fully. Pneumatology implies embodiment even in preaching. Historically, the old-time folk preacher did not acknowledge his craft but "the power of the spirit which struck him and 'set him on fire'" in his bodily delivery of the word.[37] James Forbes affirms this when he calls preaching a "living, breathing, flesh-and-blood expression of the theology of the Holy Spirit."[38] Preaching in the Spirit is "flesh-and-blood," suggesting that the black homiletical body plays a significant role in the preaching event because proclamation in the Spirit is not just sonic but somatic. The expression of somatic pneumatology continues in the black homiletical body, even if wounded. The black body is the site of the preaching event, speaking "a world without uttering a single word."[39]

Though the body has been denigrated, the Spirit deems it of great worth for spirituality because "every spiritual practice begins with the body."[40] The ministry of preaching is no different. Preaching is part of the larger liturgy and in the liturgy, the body is less an object than it is an event.[41] One could view the black body as the event of preaching, not only because it is a ritual space but also because "a weak delivery can overshadow all the preliminaries."[42] A bad delivery can destroy a sermon. Nonverbal body talk "assists in or impedes the preacher in persuading the listeners."[43] Black homiletical bodies influence the reception of the sermon and are critical to the oral-aural enterprise, especially if what Elochukwu Uzukwu says is true: "While it is likely in Africa to have motions of the body unaccompanied by speech, it is less likely to speak without body movement."[44] The black body is inextricably intertwined with the spoken word such that preaching is impossible with no-body but necessarily involves some-body. To say "black preaching" implies black some-bodies. In preaching, as in any public discourse, the body is inescapable. Without the body, there is no preaching. There cannot be no-bodies in preaching because "there is a scandalous fleshiness to preaching, and while sermons may be 'pure' theology all the way through Saturday night, on Sunday morning they are inescapably embodied and, thus, rhetorical."[45] The rhetoric of black preaching is substantially a rhetoric of the black body that turns the ink of a sermon manuscript into the flesh and blood of a real human person in motion.

Without full embodiment of the sermon, sermons will flunk. One homiletician remarked about his own experience and said, "I believe my sermon fell flat that Sunday morning at a Pennsylvania college because I was not sufficiently there as a *body*, responding in the flesh to the glory of a new morning."[46] Other scholars realize the significance of the body in performance and declare "the *word* exists only as it comes alive in our flesh."[47] Despite the absence of the black body in homiletical literature, African American preachers have historically and intuitively utilized their bodies in glaring ways during preaching. The embodied nature of black preaching causes historian Albert Raboteau to speak of the chanted sermon in the following way: "It is not, then, merely the word as spoken—much less as read—but the word as *performed* that must be taken into account if the sermon is to be adequately understood."[48] The "dramatic delivery," the embodiment, of slave preachers was eye-catching.[49] The embodied performance of black preachers has been a distinct feature of African American preaching. The black body has gained attention, but this is not surprising, especially in light of the insights of communication theory.[50]

For instance, the folk chanting preacher is described as one who "takes on a musical tone, which indicates a concomitant rise in emotional pitch. The preacher's voice changes: the timbre becomes harsh, almost hoarse. His vocal cords are constricted; his breathing is labored. All the while he moves, gestures, dances, *speaking with body* as well as voice."[51] James Weldon Johnson tells of a sermonic scene in Kansas City that prompted his 1927 collection of poems, *God's Trombones*. His description is centered on the embodiment of the preacher as well:

> He strode the pulpit up and down in what was actually a very rhythmic dance, and he brought into the play the full gamut of his wonderful voice, a voice—what shall I say?—not of an organ or a trumpet, but rather of a trombone, the instrument possessing above all others the power to express the wide and varied range of emotions encompassed by the human voice—and with greater amplitude. He intoned, he moaned, he pleaded—he blared, he crashed, he thundered. I sat fascinated; and more, I was, perhaps against my will, deeply moved; the emotional effect upon me was irresistible.[52]

How the preaching body moved, and the sounds that came forth from the preacher's body are the heart of this preaching event. This is not to say that it is *all* of the preaching moment; but it is a vital part and, thus, should be explored (rather than ignored) in African American homiletics. The body, though wounded and broken, is a wonderful fleshy conduit of divine power, grace, and love. In his classic 1903 book, *The Souls of Black Folk*, W. E. B. DuBois gazes on a preacher at a southern revival and notes, "The black and massive form of the preacher swayed and quivered as the words crowded to his lips and flew at us in singular eloquence."[53] The form of the preacher's body is part of the sermon's form because it is "through the body—we communicate to those who hear *and behold* our proclamation."[54]

This beholding suggests that black preaching is not just word but also deed. The body speaks in ways that verbal speech cannot articulate. It is the "core" of human communication,[55] making the black body the heart of black preaching. Some may critique this perspective and say the black body is gazed upon as an object in preaching, when in fact the black body is itself *the* subject, reclaiming subjectivity and humanity, despite a brutal history. Through a divine presence, these homiletical bodies become sacramental, resisting the past and present dehumanization of their bodies as no-bodies.

The divine embrace of the black homiletical body, as such, has the potential of moving black churches towards a posture of honoring every black body.

(Black) Body as Practical Progress: Baby Suggs and Every-Body

To draw out the implications of the previous exploration of the black body in preaching for a conversation about sexual politics in black churches, I will utilize a sermon from Toni Morrison's *Beloved* to assert an explicit and implicit embodied message about the black body. An "unchurched preacher," Baby Suggs preaches to a collective black body in "the Clearing," despite the violence of slavery having "busted her legs, back, head, eyes, hands, kidneys, womb and tongue." She declares from her "heart" (and I quote at length):

"Here," she said, "in this here place, we flesh; flesh that weeps, laughs; flesh that dances on bare feet in grass. Love it. Love it hard. Yonder they do not love your flesh. They despise it. They don't love your eyes; they'd just as soon pick em out. No more do they love the skin on your back. Yonder they flay it. And O my people they do not love your hands. Those they only use, tie, bind, chop off and leave empty. Love your hands! Love them. Raise them up and kiss them. Touch others with them, pat them together, stroke them on your face 'cause they don't love that either. You got to love it, you! And no, they ain't in love with your mouth. Yonder, out there, they will see it broken and break it again. What you say out of it they will not heed. What you scream from it they do not hear. What you put into it to nourish your body they will snatch away and give you leavins instead. No, they don't love your mouth. You got to love it. This is flesh I'm talking about here. Flesh that needs to be loved. Feet that need to rest and to dance; backs that need support; shoulders that need arms, strong arms I'm telling you. And O my people, out yonder, hear me, they do not love your neck unnoosed and straight. So love your neck; put a hand on it, grace it, stroke it and hold it up. And all your inside parts that they'd just as soon slop for hogs, you got to love them. The dark, dark liver—love it, love it, and the beat and beating heart, love that too. More than eyes or feet. More than lungs that have yet to draw free air. More than your life-holding womb and your life-giving parts, hear me now, love your heart. For this is the prize." Saying no more, she stood up then and danced with her twisted hip the rest of what her heart had to say while others opened their mouths and gave her the music. Long notes held until the four-part harmony was perfect enough for their deeply loved flesh.[56]

Baby Suggs is a woman preacher who is wounded—"busted," as the novel describes her—yet she preaches. Not only is her explicit sermonic theme an exhortation to the communities to love their black bodies—"love it, love it" she preaches—but she even dances forth her message with her black body without saying a word. Her body brings the sermon to completion, as she "danced with her twisted hip the rest of what her heart had to say." In doing so, she reveals how the wounded black body is still some-body, despite what those "out yonder" might have to say. Implicitly, Baby Suggs uses her black homiletical body to reinforce, to embody, her sermon to love the flesh. She exhorts her black congregation to love their physical bodies, to honor their bodies, though others may desire to dishonor them.

Based on what I have argued earlier, it should come as no surprise that this sermonic scene has been called a "liturgy of Spirit" because it is a literary example of the relationship between the Spirit and flesh or body in preaching.[57] The pneumatic implies the somatic, a love of the black body, whether made explicit or not. In this case, the embrace of the black body, the call to love it, is an embrace of the Spirit because material bodies suggest a pneumatic presence. The embrace of the Spirit's presence through an embrace of the black body is an embrace of incarnational homiletics, specifically made up of black bodies. To acknowledge the Spirit leads one to honor the black body, to love the flesh. This black flesh has worth as demonstrated in this sermonic message, spoken and enacted. Through Baby Suggs's embodied sermon, in word and deed, this liturgy of the Spirit displays black bodies as vessels to be honored. They "are worthy of care and blessing and ought never to be degraded or exploited," Stephanie Paulsell argues; and "It is through our bodies that we participate in God's activity in the world."[58] Similarly, Baby Suggs's exhortation to love each of one's different body parts suggests her acknowledgment of divine connection with black bodies. This sermonic scene resists the usual rules of dehumanization and the assembled black bodies "are momentarily mitigated by the Holy Spirit's presence and establishment of *communitas*—a space in which external dilemmas are held at bay and harmony is the rule."[59]

Literally, the harmonization of community is presented in this preaching moment as the collective black body that completes the sermon. When Baby Suggs speaks through her hip what is on her heart, Morrison writes, "others opened their mouths and gave her the music. Long notes held until the four-part harmony was perfect enough for their deeply loved flesh." The black collective body harmonizes as a way toward healing amid of the community's shared brokenness. The collective body finishes the sermon, preaching along with Baby Suggs. Their harmony is a re-sounding way to beat back the powers of slavery that attempt to destroy them. The musicality of the sermonic harmony suggests the blessing and incorporation of all of the black bodies present in the Clearing. No body is left out but every body is included. The Spirit is not just poured out on Baby Suggs, but on all flesh, all bodies, democratizing the preaching moment. This particular liturgy of the Spirit points to the presence of a Spirit who creates a collective black body. "Through the animation of the Spirit we are knitted and joined together," M. Shawn Copeland explains.[60] The harmony of the communal black body is an artful manner of depicting how this specific community had been "knitted" together to honor their collective black flesh. In the face of the harsh realities and legacies of slavery and Christian theologies that devalue the body, this sermonic scene honors black bodies, all of them, and attempts through preaching to provide protection and care for them. The homiletical moment, then, is a communal effort to affirm different kinds of bodies because each body is a member of the whole body and thus is essential to the entire black body in preaching.

Knowing the importance of collectivity in African American preaching, even as demonstrated in this literary example, suggests that "our fragile bodies require communal attention, and so honoring the body is a shared practice, one that requires the participation of all."[61] Through this literary scene of preaching, all bodies are deemed good and thus need to be loved; and this is the responsibility of the whole black body. The embrace of the collective black body as the site of harmonization in the sermonic moment challenges churches to embrace different bodies in preaching. In and through the sermonic moment, all bodies are welcomed into the black community. If not, harmony is not achieved, and an unresolved dissonance persists. There are many different bodies, including wounded and broken ones; yet they, too, participate fully in the performance of the word.

Because of the Spirit's work revealed through Baby Suggs, the entire black body, individually and corporately, is affirmed and honored. In the case of *Beloved*, bodies wounded due to slavery's torturous violence are not isolated or unvaluable in the preaching moment. As noted, for Baby Suggs, the highlighted preacher, slavery had "busted her legs, back, head, eyes, hands, kidneys, womb and tongue," and left her with a "twisted hip." She was wounded due to slavery, just like millions of black ancestors in history. Yet, she also performed the Word with her wounded and broken body. Members of the community gathered in "the Clearing" had also been wounded and scarred, which is why Baby Suggs exhorts them to love their flesh. Those over yonder want to pick their eyes out, flay their skin, chop off their hands, and noose their necks, she recounts. Her sermon, through the naming of the community's embodied truth, is a form of resistance to the wretched pattern of oppression that they have experienced. She tells them to love themselves because they have been hated and are wounded. Yet even still they, as a collective body, preach with song and dance in the sermonic climax. Their wounds do not get in the way of proclamation. Baby Suggs honors the body as a method to keep these "wounded bodies visible not as objects but as persons made in God's image."[62] Making wounded black bodies visible and audible by giving voice to them through literature, in preaching, heightens our awareness of those who are metaphorically or materially wounded today, specifically as it relates to gender and sexuality.

The wounded preaching body leads one to talk about those who are wounded by hatred for various reasons and implies that the black body, though wounded, is significant. In preaching it is even sacramental, leading one to honor the black wounded body. If "our bodies are prophets," as one scholar notes, then these wounded preaching bodies resist demonization and dehumanization.[63] They preach, "I am somebody," even if wounded and called no-body. The wounds are not erased, but instead, they aid the proclamation of a gory gospel at the heart of which is the broken body of God. The wounded black body critiques a society that would hate it, calling the world to love it and love the God who made it. It preaches an embodied word that challenges others to honor all suffering bodies. The importance of the black body in preaching, as I hope this essay has shown, calls us to honor wounded bodies, historical and contemporary. This includes women's bodies and other bodies who are denied access to pulpits and endure different standards to preach. The ambiguous legacy of the body in Christianity has led to "a destructive fear of women and suspicion of the goodness of sexuality."[64] However, the embrace of the Spirit of the black body in preaching suggests a more constructive approach to different (socially wounded) bodies in the pulpit.

Baby Suggs, the headlining preacher, is not only wounded from a sinister system of racial slavery but also because she is a woman. Morrison's words reveal that black women's bodies can proclaim life-giving words too. Suggs does not have to be a man, sound like a man, or act like a man. She can talk with her hips and have that be acceptable. In offering a liturgy of the Spirit that is poured out on the collective body, the entire black flesh, Morrison offers a subtle critique of sexism because the Spirit rests with women, men, and children. The Spirit is indiscriminate and nudges this particular black community to love each of their body parts and every single body. The Spirit's embrace of every black body (including, and perhaps especially, women's bodies) in preaching, challenges contemporary black churches that hinder women from preaching or are lukewarm toward the practice, to reevaluate their theoretical and practical posture. A woman's body is not to be objectified in or out of the pulpit. As a preacher, a woman's body becomes a subject and a sacred text, as in the case of Baby Suggs. A woman's homiletical subjectivity should be encouraged because this is the path toward ecclesial change. Grandiose ideas about women preaching are insufficient without implementing change in black churches by creating safe spaces for women to fully embody the word through preaching. "It is only when the intellectual understanding is fused with a new somatic repertoire that the culture is transformed."[65] Women need to preach, being heard and seen, in order to change the somatic memory of a congregation and to "rewrite the script that the body has memorized,"[66]—whether it is the internalized struggle of women who are called to preach or the overt, external resistance of a community. Nonetheless, the bodily witnesses of African American women, the walking wounded, represent a potential preaching cohort despite the hurtful legacies that have been mentioned. As Wallace Best asserts, "Perhaps the embodiment that black women evoke necessarily projects our attention back to the incarnational aspect of the Christian faith, leading black churches and the wider black community to new understandings of the sanctity of sexuality and the paradoxes of gender."[67]

The incarnation embraces flesh, sanctifying it wholly; thus, even those who have been wounded because of their sensuality and sexuality are potential preachers. The work of the Spirit does not segregate a person into compartments. Rather, the Spirit moves holistically. When a black body enters the pulpit, that whole person is present, not just a so-called idealized spiritual being. A human person is an "embodied spirit,"[68] which means that the body with all of its pleasure and pain cannot be divided from the spirit. The "rejection of the sex(ual) self [cannot] result in greater spiritual knowledge and experience" because "neither female nor male ministers jettison their sexualities when they occupy sacred space in their sacerdotal roles."[69] Traditionally, the sensual, sexual body was not considered as valuable as the spiritual, but what Baby Suggs stresses is that preaching involves even our most sensual sexual selves. This is made fairly explicit in her sermon as she emphasizes that listeners should, "love [their flesh] hard." She encourages them to kiss their hands, touch others with them, stroke their necks, love their inside parts, and love their "life-holding womb and . . . life-giving parts." Finally, Baby Suggs preaches that they should love their hearts. This literary sermon points to the intimate, erotic, sensual, and physical aspects of humanity, demonstrating a convergence between preaching and "love" in all of its dimensions. There is no fear of the body in this sermonic moment. There is an affirmation of the body in all of its variety and difference, in all of its blackness and woundedness. The black body is embraced in this liturgy of the Spirit holistically. But this should not be perplexing, as Lee Butler argues:

> Is the spirit willing and the flesh weak? I do not think that is the lesson we learn from the passion of the Christ child. The message that comes to us from the empty tomb is the spirit is willing and the flesh is too! Without embodiment, why should we have hope in the rapture or dream of walking around Heaven? If the spirit is willing the flesh must be equally willing. What does it mean to be a "living soul" if not the integration of spirit and body? Maintaining a hierarchal split between spirit and body diminishes our humanity and denies the gospel of the abundant life.[70]

To preach the gospel necessitates a whole human person—spiritual and physical, the spirit and the body. Only a whole person can truly preach. The example of Baby Suggs makes this clear, explicitly and implicitly. If preaching is disembodied, then the phenomenon of preaching cannot truly occur. If preaching is disembodied, we do not have to take the body seriously; thus gender, sexuality, and sensuality are insignificant and the difference that bodies make does not matter. However, when we preach in the Spirit, we bring our whole selves into the pulpit, including the black body in all of its pain and pleasure. The Spirit embraces some-body in preaching, resisting the tendency of the church to reinscribe the creation of black no-bodies.

Conclusion

This essay has attempted to give voice to the black body in preaching, an entity that has largely been silent in African American homiletics, and by doing so assert its significance not only for proclamation but also for the initiation of a constructive conversation about sexual politics in black churches. The somatic paucity in black homiletical literature contributes to the atrophy of a vital conversation about different kinds of black bodies, differences within the collective black body, and their place in the ministry of preaching. The legacies of slavery and Christianity may have devalued the body, but a constructive theological approach to the black homiletical body, particularly through the lens of a material-working Spirit, reveals its essential sacramental presence in preaching and its overall value as God's good creation. Thus, black bodies previously considered no-bodies are revalued and honored as some-bodies, especially those socially wounded and broken by the prevailing logic of gender or sexuality within black churches and American culture. Baby Suggs foregrounds the body, making a conversation about bodies the subject and sacred text of black preaching. Through her liturgy of Spirit, all black flesh is loved. The Christian church may have "lost confidence in the body," but the Spirit never has.[71] An anointed Jesus gave his wounded body for all bodies because "his ministry was about encountering those whose flesh was discounted by the world in which they lived."[72] He loved all of human (black) flesh, and it is about time that the black church does the same.

CHAPTER 11

Aiding and Abetting New Life

"Sex-Talk" in the Pulpit, Pew, and Public Square

BRAD R. BRAXTON

> Christianity is about forming a people who take seriously resurrection in their everyday lives, and move their bodies and lives into places where their embodied power can make a difference. . . . Whenever the power of death cannot silence the power of life, I believe we are standing in the presence of resurrection.
> —CHRISTINE MARIE SMITH, *PREACHING JUSTICE: ETHNIC AND CULTURAL PERSPECTIVES*

African American churches have been incubators of life in deadly circumstances. However, concerning sexuality, many African American churches create hostile environments, especially for lesbian, gay, bisexual, and transgender (LGBT) persons. Congregational leaders, scholars, and activists must encourage these congregations to stop unholy "character assassinations" and aid and abet new life among sexually diverse people.

While increased theoretical sophistication in discussions of sexuality is beneficial, *practical* implementation is necessary to achieve two objectives in African American congregations and the larger society: (1) healthier conversations about sexuality and (2) greater affirmation for LGBT persons. Thus, *practical theology* provides the methodological framework for this chapter. The word *practical* is often misconstrued to mean "simplistic" or "uncritical." Practical theology seeks to correct this misunderstanding.

Practical theology is concerned with the profound cultural knowledge and moral wisdom contained in and conveyed by practices. The theologian Dorothy Bass remarks, "Focusing on practices invites theological reflection on the ordinary, concrete activities of actual people. . . . Focusing on practices demands attentiveness to specific people, doing specific things together within a specific frame of shared meaning."[1]

Grounding its theories in everyday life, practical theology considers our experiences of love and lovemaking as vital locales for learning about ourselves and God. As a *fleshly* approach attentive to the activities of our bodies, practical theology is well suited to foster progressive and welcoming environments for constructive "sex-talk." To return to Bass's statement, this chapter will consider specific people (African American Christians) doing specific things (religious practices such as pastoral care, preaching, and worship) within a specific frame of shared meaning (the beliefs that persons are created in God's image and that God desires peace and abundant life for individuals and communities).

Practical theology also investigates the relationship between religious practices inside faith communities and other practices in the public square. The theologians Kathleen Cahalan and James Nieman insist, "Practical theology, though oriented toward discipleship and ministry in faithful communities, always looks outward to explore its mission in the world. . . . The field therefore seeks to connect with wider publics especially in order to focus on practices where there may be shared interest."[2] Thus, the chapter concludes by examining how faith communities can embody important values that foster healthy dialogue in the public square and moral discernment about significant contemporary issues.

An Inclusive Gospel

The kin-dom of God—God's beloved community where social differences no longer divide and access to God's abundance is equal—was the primary theme of Jesus's ministry.[3] Jesus desired loving communities that would serve as a foretaste of the coming commonwealth of God. When Christians exclude people based on social identity, we defame the character of Jesus whose primary impulse was inclusion. The theologian and preacher Peter Gomes observes:

> If Jesus Christ is the center of the biblical witness . . . how do we reconcile his expansive and inclusive behavior as recorded in scripture with what has so often been the constricted and exclusive practice of the church? . . . Jesus' generosity and hospitality got him into terrible trouble. . . . Nowhere in scripture do we find the mantra "Love the sinner and hate the sin"; history has shown that it is the "sinner" rather than the sin that is usually ostracized, criticized, and even crucified.[4]

Christians should model reconciling, inclusive love. Jesus describes the gospel this way: "The thief comes only to steal and kill and destroy. I came that they may have life, and have it abundantly" (John 10:10). Abundant life is the heart of the gospel. However, by promoting patriarchal perspectives on gender and puritanical perspectives on sexuality, some African American congregations steal the peace, kill the joy, and destroy the hope of many women, LGBT persons, and people advocating for their empowerment. Congregations should aid and abet God's bestowal of life upon all who seek better ways to become better people for the sake of a better world.

Jesus encouraged his followers to go into the "streets and lanes of the town" with an inclusive invitation to God's party so that God's house would be filled (Luke 14:15–24). In the spirit of Jesus's teaching, congregations should be "holy house parties" where hospitality is abundant and the sacredness of diverse forms of covenant love and sanctified sexuality are celebrated. As a heterosexual ally with LGBT persons, I raise this question: How do we take an inclusive gospel to the streets?

Pastoral Theology: Taking It to the Streets

My pastoral experiences reveal the importance of harmony between means and ends. If the goal is to sponsor *real* change in congregations, we must "keep it real" as it relates to our means. We must avoid the confusing language and irrelevant theorizing that frustrate genuine transformation in the grassroots and on concrete streets—which is to say, in churches and congregations. The pastor and ethicist Samuel Proctor remarks:

> Theology never comes alive in abstract debate. It is best understood when it is lived. A good pastor will take the time to show the people how life should be lived. . . . The pastor recognizes that life must be lived in very pedestrian ways and that people who are lacking in sophistication need teaching at the street level. Not everyone needs such help, but the pastor must always be ready to give it.[5]

Reaching African American congregations at the "street level" with progressive understandings of sexuality will require (1) relevant styles of communication (i.e., keeping it real) and (2) emphasizing the importance of relationships (i.e., keeping it relational). A discussion of each point follows.

Keeping It Real

Many forms of African American communication involve "body talk." The homiletician Teresa Fry Brown highlights the prevalence of African American "sisterspeak," which is "informal, no-pretense, at-home, dangling-participles, double-negative, tell-it-like-it-is, intense-body-language speech."[6] These forms of communication also are found among many African American "brothers." The stereotype of embodied African American communication—head-swerving, hand-moving, body-swaying—is anchored in some truth. The anthropologist and author Zora Neale Hurston refers to these dramatic, fleshly (even sexualized) forms of communication as the "characteristics of Negro expression":

> Every phase of Negro life is highly dramatized. . . . Everything is acted out. . . . Frequently the Negro, even with detached words in his vocabulary . . . must add action to it to make it do. . . . A Negro girl strolls past the corner lounger. Her whole body . . . posing. A slight shoulder movement that calls attention to her bust. . . . She is acting out "I'm a darned sweet woman and you know it." These little plays by strolling players are acted out daily in a dozen streets in a thousand cities, and no one ever mistakes the meaning.[7]

"Body talk" is a major strand of African American cultural DNA. The contemporary theological task is to demonstrate how sexuality and the inclusion of LGBT persons in African American congregations are also forms of "body talk." Bodies are on the line here: lesbian, gay, bisexual, transgender, and heterosexual bodies—all constituting the body of Christ. If scholars retreat, in the name of academic respectability, into disembodied, abstract language typical of much elite, intellectual discourse, we might fail to connect with the very bodies in the pews and on the streets we want to heal and convert through a gospel of radical inclusion.

The homiletician Martha Simmons insists that if religious leaders are going to take an inclusive gospel to the streets, they must mix "James Brown" with "James Cone."[8] James Cone is the revered father of black liberation theology. Yet, to fully activate an inclusive gospel of liberation, we need a communication style that takes cues from James Brown, the godfather of soul, whose unshackled bodily movements convey freedom and truth at a level deeper than what is often considered pure rationality. The transformation of sexual attitudes and values requires more than scholarly argumentation. Practical teaching methods that illustrate deep truths will also be necessary.

Despite the risk of too much self-disclosure, an example of "keeping it real" is instructive. I served for five years as the senior pastor of Douglas Memorial Community Church, a socially engaged African American congregation in Baltimore, Maryland. Once during a sermon series on relationships, I preached a sermon titled "Sanctified Sexuality." The pastoral aims were to depict sex and sexuality, with candor, as our sacred desire for emotional and physical intimacy and to promote approaches to sexual expression that glorify God and edify the community.

The sermon could have begun with a dry rehearsal of theories about sexuality, but a sermon about sexuality, to my mind, also needed "sex appeal." So, my wife had a small, cordless microphone attached to her dress as she sat in the congregation. The sermon began with the two of us reading passionately to each other erotic love poetry from the biblical book the Songs of Songs. While we were spatially distant from one another, our voices caressed and revealed to congregants that on other occasions more than just our voices had caressed.

Eavesdropping on this erotic dialogue, one female parishioner started fanning herself with the worship bulletin. Perhaps she was having a "hot flash" recalling a "hot time" from yesteryear or maybe yesterday. Preaching openly about sex and sexuality will bring a range of emotions to the fore, and it will no doubt make some churchgoers (and readers) uncomfortable. Yet, like good foreplay, this dramatic sermon introduction opened minds and lubricated hearts so that people could interact more intimately with their sexual existence in the context of church.

Keeping It Relational

"Street level" teaching will also emphasize the development of godly relationships amid social diversity. To enlist an analogy, streets are sites of "intersections," and intersections imply plurality—the convergence of diverse people, experiences, and ideas. Street-level theology should facilitate people's ability to safely navigate cultural and theological intersections without committing vehicular homicide. When people recklessly converge at intersections, destruction and death result. However, when intersections are negotiated with care and work constructively, they facilitate travel and allow people going the wrong way to find new directions.

Enabling constructive encounters with diversity is a primary pastoral task of congregations. Pastoral care ultimately is the responsibility of an entire congregation and not a duty to be fulfilled exclusively by clergy.[9] Clergy facilitate the ministry of care through example and instruction. However, presenting God's multidimensional truth and multifaceted love requires a multiplicity of voices. Apart from diversity, the pursuit of truth becomes an idolatrous affair of a community worshipping its limited perspectives, and the practice of love becomes egotistical self-adoration. By welcoming diversity in the embodied presence of others—in this case, LGBT persons—congregations enhance their capacity to offer and exemplify truth and love.

The door leading to godly truth often swings on the hinges of social diversity. Even the Bible was the result of complex debates spanning thousands of years and involving many languages, diverse cultures, and a host of political decisions about which books to admit and omit. The plurality of voices in scripture reveals a clear biblical message: sacred truth demands diverse perspectives. The pastoral theologian Emmanuel Lartey celebrates diversity's role in truth-making: "Truth, knowledge, and justice are not attained in solitary thought. . . . Truth involves . . . a basic act such as engaging in dialogue with the Other. . . . To practice truth is to welcome the Other."[10]

Similarly, the pastoral task of "making love" requires an affirmation of diversity. The phrase "making love" should not be reduced exclusively to erotic activity. Making love is the mission of the church. The Apostle Paul's beautiful love hymn reminds the church of its love-making mandate: "If I speak in the tongues of mortals and of angels, but do not have love, I am a noisy gong or a clanging cymbal. . . . Love is patient; love is kind. . . . Love never ends" (1 Corinthians 13:1, 4, 8). This hymn entices believers to embrace a practice of genuine love—the compassionate concern for others that transcends sheer self-interest and removes the fear of people who differ from us.

Imagine how much more *care-full* Christian congregations would be if they caressed people with Paul's gracious words about love in 1 Corinthians 13 instead of battering them with his ungenerous words about gay and lesbian people in Romans 1. Furthermore, our neglect of another biblical "love note" has diminished our love life: "There is no fear in love, but perfect love casts out fear" (1 John 4:18). The cultural critic bell hooks observes:

> Fear is the primary force upholding structures of domination. . . . When we are taught that safety lies always with sameness, then difference, of any kind, will appear as a threat. When we choose to love we choose to move against fear—against alienation and separation. The choice to love is a choice to connect—to find ourselves in the other.[11]

Diversity is crucial for pursuing truth and making love. Consequently, there is no more pressing pastoral task than teaching people how to encounter diversity without the fear and fanaticism that terminate dialogue and destroy difference.

Studies indicate that personal experiences with loved ones or LGBT persons who are open about their sexual identity (i.e., "out" LGBT persons) significantly contribute to the development of "more inclusive perspectives regarding sexual differences."[12] This was true in my experience. While academic study facilitated my journey toward inclusive theology, the decisive moments involved friendships with "out" LGBT persons who challenged and expanded my theological and cultural boundaries. Warm relationships, not cold logic, transformed me. For example, at the covenant ceremony of two lesbian friends in Atlanta in 1996, the presence of grace and holiness in that ceremony and later at their dinner table was undeniable.

Additionally, in 2011 I facilitated the founding of the Open Church of Maryland, a congregation in Baltimore committed to radically inclusive love, courageous social justice activism, and compassionate interfaith collaboration. A gay friend accepted my invitation to serve as the first chair of the congregation's board of directors. He fulfilled the role ably for more than a year and has remained the vice-chair of the board for many years. Two lesbian friends also join him on the congregation's board. Thus, the six-person board is perfectly balanced between people who identify as LGBT and as heterosexual, respectively.

The anointed leadership and winsome interpersonal skills of these LGBT parishioners have facilitated the development of the congregation's worship life, community outreach, and governance structure. Witnessing their powerful ministries, I realized that right "heart orientation," not straight sexual orientation, is God's requirement for service in the church, and their hearts are rightly oriented toward God.

At the intersection of relationships, I made a U-turn and set my face toward inclusion. Human transformation has mysterious dimensions that transcend theoretical analysis and rationality. Stories go where statistics can't. People can easily ignore "facts," but human faces are not as easily dismissed. Faces are doorways to people's hearts. The adoption of more inclusive approaches will entail more than a mind game. It will require heart transplants—not on operating tables but around fellowship tables, as friends of diverse gender identities and sexual orientations recognize the face of God in one another.

Face-to-face encounters create vulnerability and blur the boundaries of neat theological doctrines and tidy ecclesial politics. These encounters are risky and do not always lead to positive outcomes. A 2007 controversy revealed the challenge and complexity of genuinely "facing" inclusion.

The Broadway Baptist Church, a moderate, predominantly white congregation in Fort Worth, Texas, was known for its quiet acceptance of lesbian and gay members. However, things became "noisy" as the congregation prepared for its 125th anniversary in 2007. In celebration of the historic moment, church leaders wanted to create a pictorial directory of congregants with photographs of families. Controversy erupted when gay couples in the congregation wanted to have their pictures in the directory. While some members welcomed the pictures of gay couples, others felt that placing these photographs in the directory crossed the line of welcome to the unacceptable position of actually affirming gay persons as *gay persons*.[13]

Eventually, church leaders resolved the dispute by creating a directory with photographs of church groups but not families. The pictures of gay couples would have placed an explicit frame around diversity. Such photographs for some congregants would have been too much *to face*. How often have congregations, irrespective of ethnicity or denomination, ignored or deleted sacred pictures of family because the photographs displayed diversity in all its stunning beauty?

Nearly a decade after this incident, I, too, experienced an episode illustrating the difficulty some people have facing inclusion. An association of African American ministers in Baltimore invited me in 2015 to facilitate a seminar at a local preaching conference. The president of the association is a long-time pastoral colleague. Although he is more moderate than I theologically, he is respectful of my progressive views on LGBT equality.

Our similarities or differences on LGBT issues were not germane to his invitation. The conference aimed to provide professional development resources to improve the preaching skills of a group of Baltimore ministers, some of who had not attended seminary. I readily accepted the invitation. News about my participation in the forthcoming conference circulated informally through the community.

A few weeks before the event, the president of the association asked for my headshot photograph to accompany my brief biography in the flyer announcing the event. I sent the photograph, and the flyer with my photograph was distributed to the wider membership of the association. Chaos erupted.

The informal circulation of my name had not ostensibly disturbed anyone. However, when the flyer associated my face with my name, apparently some ministers realized that the keynote presenter at the conference was going to be "that preacher—Brad Braxton—the one who started the Baltimore church with all the LGBT people."

Even though I am ordained in a Baptist denomination and have taught in seminaries for more than a decade, some of the Baptist ministers refused to attend a preaching conference where someone like me was a featured presenter. Their protest was swift and decisive.

Thus, a few days before the event, the president of the association called me and reluctantly rescinded the invitation. In 1949, the renowned theologian Howard Thurman wrote his influential book, *Jesus and the Disinherited*. I was honored in 2015 to join a distinguished group: *Jesus and the Disinvited*. If the promotion of radical inclusion in Jesus's name requires my name—and face—to be excluded from some "guest" lists, let it be so!

Many African Americans know the painful realities of racial politics where certain white people "welcome" African Americans as long as they reject or mute their cultural identity markers. In the face of this dehumanizing racism, James Brown declared these defiant lyrics, "Say it loud: I'm black and I'm proud!" The disruption of racism requires more than just black bodies. It requires *proud* black bodies.

Similarly, the disruption of dehumanizing heterosexism requires more than the quiet presence of LGBT bodies.[14] It, too, requires *proud* LGBT bodies. God's inclusive love calls LGBT persons to offer a creative remix: "Say it loud: I'm LGBT and I'm proud!" The courage and compassion needed for congregations to hear, face, and embrace this kind of diversity will surely make Jesus proud as well.

Preaching a Progressive Word: Sacred Use of the Sacred Desk

"Sticks and stones may break my bones, but words will never hurt me." This cute proverb cannot hide the ugly truth: words can hurt! Linguistic lacerations can inflict wounds on the psyche that linger beyond any physical fracture. Thankfully, however, words also can heal. For example, gracious, thoughtful sermons are acts of "linguistic hospitality." Through the creative use of language, sermons provide God a hospitable place to meet with and transform listeners. As a professor of homiletics—the art of sermon creation, delivery, and evaluation—words are my world. Thus, my question is: How might African American Christian preaching advance inclusive theologies of sexuality? A brief discussion of African American Christian preaching will facilitate answers to this question.

Preaching is a preeminent feature of African American Christianity. The poetic name describing the African American pulpit—*the sacred desk*—reveals the reverence that preaching commands. African American Christian preaching has provided some of the world's most powerful examples of rhetorical virtuosity.[15] Thus, it stands alongside other significant African American contributions such as spirituals, the blues, and jazz. I focus on two features of African American preaching: (1) the preacher's authority and (2) the preacher's style.

Typically, African American churches grant preachers a generous amount of authority. This authority consists of a communally derived sanction for preachers to speak on behalf of the congregation to the external "powers that be." African American congregations also expect their preachers to speak boldly to the congregation itself. Since spiritual authority comes through the congregation, humility in the preacher is appropriate. Yet most African American congregations have no tolerance for timidity in the pulpit. The preacher must wed a silver tongue to nerves of steel, taking parishioners to theological depths and heights they would not experience otherwise.

Philosophically, the authority given to the African American preacher reflects the primacy of the spoken word in many African rhetorical traditions. Certain African traditions emphasize *Nommo*. Nommo, a word from the African tribe Dogon, conveys "the generating and sustaining powers of the spoken word"—powers that permeate "every department of life."[16] Because of Nommo, "vocal expression reigns supreme" in most African cultures.[17]

Nommo requires the right persons and circumstances to convert its potential into power. In traditional African cultures, tribal chiefs and other religious leaders are catalytic agents. Since the preacher is the agent and embodiment of Nommo for many African American Christians, Nommo is conveyed to the community through the preacher's presence and words. The authority of the preacher is a rhetorical umbilical cord connecting African American ministers with Mother Africa.

Second, African American Christians believe that style is a central component of preaching.[18] Distinctive aspects of sermon delivery—gestures, tone of voice, rate of speech, picturesque language—are channels for Nommo and the gospel. Some preaching traditions regard the emphasis on style as an inappropriate focus on the messenger instead of the message. While it is true that a preacher can employ style for improper purposes, the lack of emphasis on style is also problematic.

The gospel transforms people in their emotional as well as their cognitive dimensions. The homiletician Henry Mitchell insists, "The opposite of 'entertaining' is not 'educational' but boring. Unless the gospel is engaging it is hardly heard, much less remembered."[19] Style is the preacher's antidote against sermonic amnesia, the inability of congregants to remember a sermon shortly after it is preached. In light of these two features of African American preaching, let us explore briefly (1) the ethics of preaching and (2) the potential of imaginative preaching to sponsor healthier conversations and progressive theologies of sexuality.

The Ethics of Preaching

The considerable authority enjoyed by many African American ministers should motivate them to achieve the highest standards of speech ethics. Since African American Christians revere sacred speech (Nommo), the pulpit microphone is arguably the most significant (and potentially dangerous) symbol of human power in congregations. An "open mic" should never be open season for preachers to take aim at persons with hatred and sarcasm, especially when addressing the mysteries of sexuality. For example, the crass phrase "God made Adam and Eve, not Adam and Steve" is undignified language unfit for any pulpit. Instead, care and compassion should characterize all sermons, regardless of preachers' theological perspectives.

The Bible is concerned about the ethics of how Christians communicate. For example, the Book of James warns believers, and especially leaders, about the lethal consequences of an unholy tongue:

> Not many of you should become teachers, my brothers and sisters, for you know that we who teach will be judged with greater strictness. . . . The tongue is a small member, yet it boasts of great exploits. How great a forest is set ablaze by a small fire! And the tongue is a fire . . . and is itself set on fire by hell (James 3:1, 5–6).

On those rare occasions when sexuality is addressed, too many sermons fuss about the sinful use of genitals, even as those sermons ironically ignore the sinful use of the tongue—the body part often injuring the body of Christ through callous discussions of sexuality. Jesus never condemned LGBT persons. He, however, was explicit about God's intolerance for careless speaking: "On the day of judgment you will have to give an account for every careless word you utter; for by your words you will be justified, and by your words you will be condemned" (Matthew 12:36–37). In light of Jesus's admonition, I present a sobering reminder to fledgling ministers in my preaching courses in seminary:

> There is a heavenly stenographer assigned to every preacher who records every word that comes from your mouth in the pulpit. At God's judgment bar, you will have to answer for every time you opened your mouth to bless or curse someone.

Many professions, such as medicine, law, and business, regulate the ethics of their practitioners. A failure to abide by the code of ethics can result in the loss of a license or disbarment. Preachers one day will stand before the Ultimate Chief Justice in Heaven's High Court. It would be tragic for any minister to be disbarred on judgment day for reckless endangerment with a lethal weapon—the tongue.

Preaching with Imagination

The emphasis on style should empower African American ministers to preach about sexuality with greater imagination. Sermons can facilitate constructive dialogue when preachers are "poets" and "spoken-word artists." The artistic genius Paul Robeson declared, "The purpose of art is not just to show life as it is, but to show life as it should be."[20] Poetic preaching can supply compelling images that exemplify the breadth of diverse forms of sanctified sexuality.

Jesus is an excellent tutor for homiletic creativity. He did not avoid sensitive, controversial subjects. He sometimes approached issues directly. For example, his initial sermon in Nazareth about justice and social boundaries incited a riot that nearly led to his death (Luke 4:16–30). However, on many occasions, Jesus's homiletic purposes were better served by the poetic indirection of parables—short stories with common elements that led to uncommon meanings. The pastor and theologian Eugene Peterson discusses the subversive nature of parables:

> Parables sound absolutely ordinary: casual stories about soil and seeds, meals and coins and sheep, bandits and victims, farmers and merchants. . . . As people heard Jesus tell these stories . . . they relaxed their defenses. They walked away perplexed, wondering what they meant, the stories lodged in their imagination. And then, like a time bomb, they would explode in their unprotected hearts. . . . Parables aren't illustrations that make things easier; they make things harder by requiring the exercise of our imaginations.[21]

Preachers should imitate Jesus's creative style when seeking to promote healthier dialogue concerning sexuality, especially given the discomfort and defensiveness caused by sexual topics. I offer two examples.

First, during a recent sermon to men about social justice engagement in Christian congregations, I inserted this sentence: "Let this be a house where heterosexual Christian men and gay Christian men can peacefully break bread even as they break down stereotypes." This sentence appeared to create a perceptible shift in the spiritual energy in the sanctuary. It was as if some congregants were asking, "Did he just put the words 'gay' and 'Christian' in the same sentence?" Some might have considered the reference about "breaking bread" as an invitation to think about Holy Communion and its implications for genuine hospitality. Like a poem or parable, that simple sentence was designed to imply as much and hopefully more. Amid a sermon of more than two thousand words, I smuggled in twenty-three words to explode preconceived assumptions about the boundaries of the church. It was not a frontal attack on exclusion, but instead guerilla warfare for an inclusive gospel.

A second example involves my experience of presiding at Holy Communion. The biblical scholar Margaret Aymer helped me recognize the profound theological connections between the symbolic "blood" at Holy Communion and the blood issues affecting millions through HIV-AIDS.[22] Now, when inviting persons to the Lord's Table, I remind them that the body of Christ has AIDS. Therefore, if they drink the "blood of Jesus," they, too, will have AIDS and must show compassion and solidarity with those infected with this disease that is spread frequently through heterosexual activity. Jesus's broken body becomes an instrument for further reflection and action concerning our sexualized bodies. The table in the church house and the beds in our houses are connected.

Rules of Engagement: Promoting "Public Safety"

Christians should seek to influence practices not only inside faith communities but also in the larger society. By referring to his followers as the "salt of the earth" and the "light of the world," Jesus believed that faith in God had consequences beyond religious borders (Matthew 5:13–16). The social dimensions of the gospel call persons in Christian circles to enter the public square. The goal is not to invade the public square with Christian imperialism disguised as evangelism. Rather, our calling as believers is to improve public conversation and conduct through distinctive, if not unique, values and practices.

The ethicist Ellen Marshall outlines the extensive and informal boundaries of the public square. "The 'public square' is not a neatly circumscribed area that we enter only at a specified time for a preplanned discussion. . . . [The public square] denotes a circumstance more than a place, a circumstance marked by a plurality of views and by discussion of issues that affect people beyond the discussants. In this sense, the public square is everywhere."[23] Diverse people with different perspectives who seek and even compete for seemingly dwindling resources are often a formula for social contexts that are contentious, inhospitable, and potentially violent. Many television news programs provide striking examples of public incivility. Inflammatory rhetoric from political opponents can heat up ratings but does little to illumine a path toward the transformation of public values and public policies.

Spirited debate and disagreement are signs of healthy public life in a congregation or an entire country. Yet when public arguments become arsenals for dehumanization, a "public safety" crisis emerges. We have witnessed in recent years horrific incidents where snipers shoot people in public places, such as churches, entertainment venues, and schools. Tragic examples include the shootings at Mother Emanuel AME Church in 2015 (Charleston, SC), Pulse nightclub in 2016 (Orlando, FL), and Marjory Stoneman Douglas High School in 2018 (Parkland, FL). The moral outrage at such events is swift and insistent.

We must become equally adamant about the safety of public conversations, refusing to tolerate character assassinations by the tongues of rhetorical snipers. The election of Donald Trump as president of the United States contributed to a downward spiral in our speech ethics. Rather than offer examples of the power of language to lift downtrodden hearts, then President Trump's divisive rhetoric fueled a cultural climate that normalizes character assassinations and other forms of hostility.[24]

Christian communities can aid and abet new life by promoting and demonstrating values that ensure safe spaces for public dialogue. If adopted more broadly, these values could transform the current climate of partisan rancor and move us toward more constructive discussions of important issues in the public square. Whether we are talking about human rights for LGBT persons, immigration reform, or national security strategies, we need an enhanced ability to air legitimate differences of opinion without the divisiveness that diminishes a sense of the common good. In this age of expanding social diversity, Christian congregations might best serve the body of Christ and the body politic by seeking to improve the character of public conversations. The way we talk in public about complex moral issues is itself a moral issue.

More Christian congregations might consider adopting three "rules of engagement" to govern their actions, especially in matters of significant public consequence. Typically, "rules of engagement" refer to the principles governing army or police use of violent force to subdue enemies or lawbreakers. I redeploy the term to depict principles for unleashing nonviolent "soul force" that triggers the retreat of hostility and the advancement of mutual understanding, even if genuine differences remain. These rules are not novel nor are they unique to Christianity. Their value lies in the ability to foster what the theologian Victor Anderson calls "creative exchange" or a deep commitment to religious and moral openness that enlarges the truths derived in our limited social contexts.[25]

Additionally, as a practical theologian, I value these rules because of their proven ability to promote safer conversations about sensitive topics like sexuality. The limitations of this chapter permit only a cursory presentation of the rules. Yet, when leading public discussions about sexuality and other sensitive topics, my brief presentation of these rules has inevitably produced a lasting positive effect on the conversation. Thus, these rules might possess a moral potency that transcends the ability to fully define them.

1. Demonstrate Intellectual Charity

The word *charity* is a synonym for unconditional love or *agape*. When expressing the demanding morality needed to foster the beloved community, Jesus said, "Love your enemies" (Matthew 5:44). In this verse, the Greek verb "to love" (*agapaō*) is used; hence the term *agape*. The true test of unconditional love is our ability to treat well those who are opposed to us. Removing love from the sphere of emotions and placing it in the sphere of the will, Jesus suggests that love for opponents is a love we have to think about. Thus, it is an intellectual form of love. This kind of love will neither come naturally nor will it necessarily "feel good." It is a love that we must will into existence. Intellectual charity requires a toughness of mind and a dogged determination that allow us to bestow goodwill on people without discrimination.

Furthermore, by intellectual charity, I also mean a generous attempt to understand and depict the perspectives of our opponents. Too often in public conversations, we listen superficially to the opinions of others just long enough to create a caricature that we dismiss with haste and hostility. The philosopher Iris Murdoch suggested that love is the "nonviolent apprehension of difference."[26] Consequently, we approach different perspectives not to do violence to those perspectives or the people holding them. Rather, we honor difference as a moral demonstration that something other than our perspective is also real.[27]

2. Show Compassion

The word *passion*—a significant part of the word *compassion*—is related to the Greek verb *paschō*, which means "to suffer" or "to endure." Compassion involves our willingness to endure vulnerability and enter imaginatively into the experiences of other people. Compassion often begins with a simple question: Why does this person or group hold certain perspectives? Compassion may not result in agreement about difficult topics, but it will produce kinder speech as people wrestle with those topics. As Mother Teresa insisted, "Kindness has converted more people than zeal, science, or eloquence."[28]

3. Practice Hospitality

Hospitality involves honoring one's neighbors. A compelling gesture of hospitality is contained in the Sanskrit greeting used in India when people meet one another, *Namaste*. This simple salutation carries a profound meaning: "The sacred in me greets the sacred in you." Even as people stand firm on their differences of opinions, their spirits can bow with reverent hospitality. When we encounter others, we host the sacred significance that God has deposited in every life.

The Conviction and Final Sentence

I hope that when Christian congregations come before God on the Day of Judgment, God will find irrefutable evidence that they aided and abetted new life. Based on the conviction, I pray that the Great Judge will mercifully toss out other offenses and sentence us to life eternal.

CHAPTER 12

An Experiment in Inclusion

A Conversation with Christine and Dennis Wiley

INTERVIEW BY DERRICK MCQUEEN

September 27, 2013, Washington, DC

This conversation has been edited for length and clarity.

DERRICK MCQUEEN (DM): You know, a major part of the foundation for our work together has been the idea, or goal, of having open and affirming churches in black communities—in historically black churches. And we just want to get your take on what was the journey, the process, like for you? Of moving your church into the position of being an "open and affirming" or "inclusive" ministry?

DENNIS WILEY (DW): It's been a journey. And just to go back a little bit, in terms of my own evolution to the position that I hold today of being supportive of *full* LGBT equality and inclusiveness in every aspect—not only in society but also within the church itself.

I guess my journey started, in a way, back when I was growing up in the segregated South in Winston-Salem, North Carolina, and getting some taste of what's it's like to be discriminated against based on what I would call "superficial differences." And drinking out of "colored" or "negro" water fountains and going to segregated bathrooms—movie theaters, restaurants, etc. And my parents being *very* active in the local Winston-Salem movement for civil rights and equality. So that, I think, is where the seed was planted for me to have an appreciation for the humanity of all human beings.

And then, later on, after moving to Washington, DC, and then going to Harvard, graduating from there and coming back home to work with my father, who pastored this very church—the Covenant Baptist Church (now known as the Covenant Baptist Church of Christ)—that I now pastor along with my wife.

He was called to pastor this white Southern Baptist Church in 1969. The community had begun to change, racially, after the 1954 Supreme Court decision, which was before our family moved to Washington in 1964. I was fourteen years old at the time. When we first came to the city, my father pastored another church—Springfield Baptist Church—an African American congregation in Washington. And then, after about five years there, when I was in college, he was called to *this* church. Membership was dwindling, and as the financial resources were *also* dwindling, the church could not pay a pastor. And my father, at the time, was working with the Southern Baptist Convention in their Department of Cooperative Ministries, which worked to foster better relations between blacks and whites. It was through that connection that his name came to the attention of this church. Now, most churches in this community who experienced this transition, where a lot of their members were moving out to the suburbs because this community was becoming more African American, most of them would sell the church to an African American or black congregation. But this church took the unusual step of saying, "No, we're going to stay in this community; we're going to serve this community." And when the members heard him preach, they decided they were going to call a black pastor. It was unprecedented, you know, for a white Southern Baptist Church to call an African American pastor.

So he began pastoring Covenant in 1969, and I returned home from college in 1972. And so, when I came in the early 1970s, I worked with him here at this church. I also was employed by an after-school program for District of Columbia junior and senior high school students that was called Workshops for Careers in the Arts, the precursor to what eventually became the Duke Ellington School of the Arts. I was a guidance counselor who also occasionally served as a musician for some of the performing arts productions. But in that capacity, I began to examine my own self in terms of some of the stereotypes and prejudices that I had.

When I was working here in the church with the youth, there was this young guy who was a part of our youth ministry. And when we were doing a play, I noticed that he loved to put on leotards. And he just seemed to be so *liberated*, and he would dance around and prance around. I kind of suspected that he might be struggling with his sexuality and, at one point, he came to me and shared with me that that was the case. So I counseled him and was very supportive of him. When I returned to the church as pastor, he eventually also returned as an openly gay young man who became involved in our HIV/AIDS ministry and really did a wonderful job. And he ultimately *died* of AIDS. I remember that when he was on his sickbed, Pastor Chris and I went to visit him in the hospital, and he just thanked us for allowing him to come back home where he was able to be himself in this church.

And even prior to pastoring Covenant, when I went to Union Theological Seminary, that experience also opened my mind and my heart, you know? Because New York is a very progressive city; and Union is a very progressive seminary and it had a gay caucus. That further expanded my perspective. Studying with James Cone, I began to understand that any of us who have been the victims of any kind of oppression ought to be the last ones in the world to oppress anybody else.

And then, last but not least, I did my dissertation on Howard Thurman. And, of course, Howard Thurman is known for dedicating his life to breaking down the barriers that divide us as human beings, one from the other. He did not deal directly with this issue because, during his time, issues of sexual orientation and gender identity/expression were not usually openly addressed. But he did deal with race and class, and religion, national origin, those kinds of things. But I don't think anybody can read Thurman's theology and *not* believe—that if he were alive today, he would be on the side of justice and freedom and equality for all people, including lesbian, gay, bisexual, and transgender persons.

CHRISTINE WILEY (CW): In terms of my background, I'm a military brat, and my mother was a first-generation, British-born black woman. Her mother, my grandmother, was from East Prussia. And her family migrated to London to escape discrimination as Jews. But my grandmother married a man from the Caribbean, so she experienced all kinds of discrimination from her family. I remember going to the market one day in London, and she said, "You see those two old ladies over there?" And I said, "Yeah." And she said, "Those are my sisters."

But she hadn't spoken to them in years because they disowned her. My grandmother told the story of an incident where she was walking down the street and had to go into the police station because people were harassing her and throwing horse manure at her. But the police would harass her *also*. Everybody on the block in the East End of London that they lived on, all the mothers were white, and all of the fathers were either African or Caribbean. So, one of the things my mother always instilled in me—and she said it very clearly—was, "Never think that you're better than anyone else." And then she said, "I want you to know that whores and funnymen are some of the nicest people you'll ever meet." I never forgot that.

DM: Wow.

CW: A major experience, for my part, was working in the Community Mental Health Center as a therapist. And I remember two things. One, [the receptionist] said, "Okay, Christine, you have a new client. Mr. George Somebody." So I looked in, and I said, "He's not in there." And she said, "Yes he is! Go in there."

I went in there, and I looked, and he wasn't in there. And she said, "Call out his name!" So I said, "Mr. George So-and-so." And this very tall woman got up. That was my real first experience with a transgender person.

I just remember working with that person and the extent of her pain. The extent of her discrimination. I don't even *know* if I really understood at that time the difference between trans* people and gay people, but I remember saying, "Okay, my job is to meet them where they are."

I worked with a couple shortly after that, a gay couple. And they had an argument. One partner was kind of overpowering the other one, you know? The other one just didn't have any power at all. There even got to be this argument about sex, regarding who's on the top and who's on the bottom. And I'm saying to myself, "What in the *heck* do I do with this?"

And again, I just kept getting, "Treat them as if you were just counseling any other couple." I had dealt with sexual issues before. And in that clinic, it wasn't just them. I was also meeting with poor people, people who were struggling, people who were sent by the courts. And so I just felt like I was meeting with all of the marginalized people and that this was what I was called to do.

Dennis is the one who really kind of brought me along theologically because we never talked about any of this stuff in seminary. I always had had the view that all people were the same in God's sight, but I also was aware of the stigma around it (sexual difference). So I remember, in the beginning, Dennis did a lot of preaching about telling the congregation that gay people were welcome here. Whenever he said it, it would just *jolt* me. And a lot of other people! Whenever he would preach or teach anything about being welcoming or affirming—well, not even welcoming or affirming, because we didn't use that language then—he opened the door for me to acknowledge, "That's what I believe also."

I would have this *long* line of gay men at my door to counsel with them. I hadn't said anything! *He* said everything, but they would be at *my* door. Finally, after taking some time with some of these men, what I realized was, even though Dennis was *saying* it, it was like they were projecting it onto me as if I said it. Because he was a straight black male, and they were afraid of straight black men, a number of gay men would come to me for counsel. So, that was very interesting.

DM: I'm going to ask one *small* question about assessing a bit about what you both just said. You've taken me along this track of evolution. How important do you think it is for people to examine their own evolutionary process and their thought process around this issue?

CW: I think it's very important. See, we were teaching and preaching this for twenty years, nineteen years, before we made a move as a church. To actually have the congregation embrace it.

DW: That's a good question. I have had to remind myself that I have not always been where I am now. Sometimes it's easy to be a little bit more judgmental when you forget that, "okay, well, I went through some of that process myself." And it allows you to be a little bit more patient with people. You really have to exercise patience when you see some of this. You have to fight the tendency to be kind of self-righteous, which is kind of hard to do sometimes, when you see all the vitriol and venom that people have who have not arrived at this point. I mean, I would love to say, "Okay, I've always been *right here*." But, if I'm honest, it's similar to racism: when you're growing up in a heterosexist society, it's difficult to escape.

We didn't have a handbook. We didn't have a manual when we did this. And I think that one of the things to help us in working with people—particularly in that movable middle—is to give people an opportunity to evolve. And give them that space to grow.

CW: But even as you say that we did come to a particular point where we said, "Now is the time." We actually used Martin Luther King's book, *Why We Can't Wait*. And we got to a point where this is it. The congregation had to *own* that this is who we are as a church. So even though it is necessary for people to have an evolution, we had been carrying this congregation and teaching the congregation for quite a long time. And so there became a point where regardless of whether you're with us or not, this is what it is! So, either you throw us out [as pastors]—which they were able to do; this is a Baptist church, and they throw out a lot of folks—*or* you understand what we're espousing here.

DW: One other thing I forgot to mention was that, when I first became pastor here in 1985, one of the first Bible studies I did was entitled "Money, Sex, and Power." So, one of the first things we have to understand is that sexuality, in and of itself, is a taboo subject within the black church and many churches. People just don't deal with the whole issue of sex and sexuality, much less homosexuality.

So in the mid- to late 1990s, we were trying to walk people through this, but Pastor Chris is right in referring to *Why We Can't Wait*. And Martin Luther King's "Letter from the Birmingham Jail." For him, waiting has always meant: Never. So if you're trying to *do* this, and you're trying to wait for the *right* time, the right time will probably never come. At a certain point, you have to go forward.

Part of this process that we were trying to model was moving towards the fact that we also realized that sexism and heterosexism are very closely related. We understood this instinctively before we really had processed it intellectually. But we realized that we had to model, as a couple, that kind of equality between men and women. That I'm not the head of the woman, and she doesn't serve me. [She does not have to] be obedient to me.

So we understood, in some kind of intuitive way, that this was integral to where God was helping us move this congregation. Of course, for the first eighteen years of my pastorate, I was the pastor, the senior pastor. Pastor Chris was assisting me, but we had been *talking* ever since day one about seeking formal approval and endorsement from this congregation to lead them through a process where they could call us to be co-pastors (i.e. co-equal pastors). We knew it was important that they called us as co-pastors, rather than our imposing that upon them.

Also, one other little point. Pastor Chris talked about the fact that we preached that we were an open and affirming church. I knew that if we were serious about *full* inclusion of LGBT persons, somewhere down the line, somebody was going to want to consecrate their relationship in the form of some kind of union ceremony.

I had to ask myself the question: What would I do? If a same-sex couple came to me and said, "We want to be married or we want to be united in the form of a union ceremony," what would I do? And my answer was that I would. I will unite them.

CW: There was a process. Because for the first union ceremony, you and I had a discussion about it. And determined that I would do it. Remember? I did it outside. And then, the next union ceremony, we determined it was time for *you* to do one. And you did one outside of the congregation.

DW: Now, let me just say a word about another thing that's critical. There was a young man that came to our church and was a part of a community outreach program that we were affiliated with. And he was a gay brother. He became very actively involved in our church, and he eventually became a minister. Chris really pushed him to go to seminary and everything. And he began to invite many of his friends. So he inadvertently helped to push us along, in terms of making sure that our walk matched our talk. And, he didn't come out (to the church), openly, himself, for quite a while.

CW: Like fifteen years.

DW: Right, quite a while, yeah. But we pretty much knew who he was. I think he played a role of a catalyst in terms of *escalating* this process for us. In terms of getting to that date where someone was going to come to us and want to be united in holy matrimony. And so, in the early twenty-first century, the first few years of the 2000s, we finally did come to the point of saying, "Okay, a lot of gay people are coming in." But some of our congregation were asking questions like, "Well, what direction are we going?"

CW: Oh, yeah, that was a big question.

DW: Which is really code language for: "Why are we letting all these gay people in? What's going on here?"

They didn't come out and say that directly, but that was what was underneath that question. What direction are we going in? And so it was around that same time that we began to develop information to share with the congregation about Chris and me becoming copastors. We had dialogue sessions in the church, and we looked at our constitution. We felt strongly that if we were going to present to the church this model of a copastorate, we needed to heed the seasoned counsel of my father to have the constitution revised in a way that would support that. And we developed a ten-point vision statement to put more flesh on this whole word, *inclusive*. It begins that Covenant Baptist Church will be served by a copastorate, including pastors Dennis and Christine Wiley. And then the second point is that Covenant will be an open and welcoming church where everyone is welcome. Regardless of race, class, gender, or sexual orientation. So, we tied that to the copastorate in such a way that we were trying to help people understand these two go together.

CW: And there was quite a bit of tension at that time. Some people did not support us. It brought a division within the church, you know? There were sides. Essentially, though, when it got to the point where we actually voted on becoming a copastorate and also open and affirming, it was an overwhelming majority.

Now, after that, we experienced a celebration—a year that was *great*. The church was growing, but *now*, more people were coming to the church who were gay. Before, there were mainly gay men who were coming. Now, there were women couples coming in droves. Some were bringing their children. And they were coming to talk beforehand to let us know. And they were open!

DM: Right.

CW: They were out. And so this young man that Dennis talked about, he was in the closet for about fifteen years while he was with us. So it was kind of like he was *forced*. And he came out over a period of five, seven years.

But it became clear that there was tension in the congregation. That some of the straight people were *tolerating* the gay people. They still thought it was a sin, you know?

DW: As more gay people were coming in, both male and female, we began to be very direct and truthful about who these people were. See, the thing is: in the black church we've always had gay people. The message was "don't flaunt it," so to speak. Which simply means, keep it quiet.

CW: Right. "Why do you have to say it?"

DW: Right. Don't name it. But we realized that if we're talking about full inclusion, we've got to be able to name it. And people are very uncomfortable with that. Let's say two same-gender loving people join the church at the same time, and I announce that they are partners!

You know? And then we hear mumblings about "why you got to say that?"

CW: [Or] "What's a *partner*?" That's one thing. The other thing was we heard some mumblings from, say for instance, the ushers. That two women were sitting *close together*. . . .

DW: Right. They had their arm around each other. Now they weren't saying this if there was a heterosexual [couple]. That would be just normal, you know? So we have learned that is what separates a lot of the churches, that *claim* to be open and affirming, from those that are really trying to live this thing out. And it's a whole 'nother ballgame. People were saying, "This is outrageous. That they would be sitting so close together in church. She had her hand on her knee."

So, that leads up to when the first couples started coming to you [Christine].

CW: Yeah, so. We had these two people who were in seminary. They wanted ecclesiastical endorsement, so I asked them about their life. Both of them had partners. The gay couple were living together, and both of them were members of our church. The lesbian woman's partner was not yet a member of the church. They weren't living together, but they were getting *ready* to live together.

So I told them, "Requirements for being a minister are the same for everybody. So we have to examine your life and see what it's like. And we can't just have you messing around here. I want to know what your intentions are. Is this a lifelong relationship for you? Do you intend to be partners for life? You know, what is it?" Neither of the couples were clear, so I wouldn't bring them forth. I said, "You need to be in counseling to figure out what that is." So, I did counseling with the gay couple. And then the lesbian couple got counseling from a female AME [African Methodist Episcopal] pastor who was in the closet.

Both of them saw counselors for about a year. And it just happened that both of them, around the same time, determined that they wanted holy union ceremonies. And they wanted it done in the church.

We told them, "This is going to be a process. We've got to take it to the congregation." Both of us had done union ceremonies before, but it was outside of the church. And so we brought it to the church. We had a lot of folk there. Might've been 150 to 200 people there that night, you know?

DW: Tell him about the process before we brought it to the church, in terms of the advice we had gotten.

CW: Oh yeah! At that time we were kind of courting the United Church of Christ (UCC) in terms of becoming a part of the UCC denomination. We had some mentors that were working with us, so we talked to them about it. And we also met with our deacons and all the ministers.

All of them recommended to us that it not be an up-and-down vote as to whether or not we should do this. That there needed to be consensus.

DW: It would be too divisive otherwise.

CW: So, Dennis said to the congregation—and they were there!—"These two people both want union ceremonies, and it is our intention to perform them. But we want to hear from you."

Except for one at the end, the majority [who spoke up] were straight people. And they were saying affirming kinds of things about their experiences with gay people.

DW: That was in April of 2007, which was two and a half years before Washington, DC, legalized marriage equality. At the end of that meeting, we kind of suspected that there were probably some people who had some concerns but were not expressing them. And so we said, "Okay, we realize that maybe some people have some questions. And, if you didn't speak up tonight, feel free to come to us. We'd be glad to meet with you." Maybe a handful of people took us up on that—at the most, maybe, five people or so.

DM: Right.

DW: But most of the people did not. And so, it was just eerily quiet, you know? And we thought, "Oh, well, I guess our congregation was further along than what we had realized." But then, as we got closer and closer to that first union ceremony, and we began to hear murmurings that had been under the surface. Those began to arise.

CW: We went on vacation to Atlantic City, and the associate dean at Howard was calling Dennis, asking about some course he was teaching. And he said, "Oh, I heard you're doing something different over at Covenant." And Dennis says, "Something different? Naw, Naw." "Oh yeah, yeah. I heard you're doing something different."

And he said, "Something about a union ceremony?" This was around the first of July. And he said he heard it at the Wednesday Clergy Fellowship. So, I said, "What in the world?"

DW: So now, which brings us to that first union ceremony in July of 2007. Wonderful, wonderful ceremony. We were pleasantly surprised to see some of our straight Covenant members there. That was nice to see. And the ceremony was beautiful. At the end of the ceremony, I noticed there was a member who was sitting in the back. And she was in a pretty intense conversation with the chairperson of our deacon board at that time, who's a woman. And, when I saw the member, I said, "Aw, okay. She's here!"

CW: That's because he's so gullible! I knew right away, she was mad as a mug!

DW: I said, "Oh boy! I didn't expect she would be here. But she's come to show her support, you know?" And so when I saw her, I kind of waved. But I noticed she didn't really wave back. I chalked it up to [her being] in such intense conversation that she probably didn't see me wave.

But finally, as the crowd began to thin out after the service, she came up. And she let me have it. She told me this was the most despicable—and these are not her exact words, but this is the gist of it, the essence of it—that this was the most despicable thing she'd ever seen. That we were desecrating the sanctuary. She may have said, "You could've done it in your office."

CW: There were a lot of people who said, "Well, why didn't you do it in your office?"

DW: Yeah! There was really something about that. That we would have the *audacity* not only to do this but to do it in the sanctuary. How could we dare? Especially, *this* holy union. In *this* sanctuary. And she made it clear she wasn't ever—

CW: Never—

DW: —going to set foot back in this church again.

CW: Although, she did.

DW: Yeah, she did come back. Because we had a meeting. And I'll tell you about that in a minute. But she wrote us letters. She wrote it to the deacons. And she even wrote to the Progressive National Baptist Convention! But she didn't quite understand Baptist polity.

CW: She got in touch with all the newspapers.

DW: She contacted the newspapers. Local newspapers, as well as the *Washington Post*. Etcetera. She was just upset. She wanted the deacons to do something about us.

CW: And she eventually sued us.

DW: And she threatened that she was going to demand her tithes for the previous two years be returned to her and that she would stop giving to the church. And yes, Chris is right. She sued us, but eventually dropped the case. Before that happened, when we realized that there was this undercurrent that was making itself known before the second union ceremony, we called another meeting of the church. We sent out a notice and said, "You know, we understand there are some concerns. And we want to give everyone a chance to express whatever their concerns are."

At this particular meeting, which was toward the end of July, the opposition did speak out. Although there were some people who spoke in support. But mainly, it was to give those who had not spoken earlier a chance. And, of course, this lady was there. She did set her foot back in the church to come to this meeting. And once again, she expressed how outraged she was. After we heard that, and the concerns of a few others, we said, "Well, all right, clearly we must have misread this congregation. We thought, from the other meeting, [where] the response was so positive and so supportive, that the church was on board. But in light of this meeting, what we will do is to call a moratorium on union ceremonies for a while." After we do the next one! Because we've committed ourselves to the lesbian couple in August. I said, "We've given our word. We're gonna honor that."

"But after that, we will have a moratorium regarding union ceremonies and allow the church to discuss this issue more and to hear the concerns. And to work through this together." So that's what we did. In October, we met and we appointed a task force. And we tried to make it representative of a cross-section of the congregation. In fact, we had asked people, "Who would like to serve on the task force?" We went over that list, and we made sure that it was balanced—people who were *for*, people who were *against*, and people who were undecided. That task force was charged with coming back to us with some recommendations as to how we should proceed from that point forward.

CW: The key piece is that the congregation determined that they didn't want to just say, "No, we're not going to do it anymore." *They* determined and voted that they wanted to study it for a year.

And that particular meeting on that night was a real turning point. Because now some of the gay people in the congregation who thought that these people were their friends—who had embraced them, and smiled at them, and all of that—now they're hearing them say, "This is a sin." So we lost some of the gay folk because this kicked up their stuff from other congregations they had been in. You know?

DW: And let me just throw in here: We lost *some* people, after the co-pastorate.

CW: Yeah, we did. Because they didn't want a woman pastor.

DW: They didn't want a woman pastor. So we lost *some* people after that. But, you know, comparatively speaking, it was a relatively small number. But after *this*, again, it wasn't a mass exodus all at once. It was kind of a trickling out. Some people said they were going to stick around until this task force gave its final report. To see what was going to happen.

CW: Well, the task force was to recommend the process for inquiry and education. They gave their recommendation for what the process would be. Then we dealt with the process in terms of movies. And Bible studies. And fishbowl discussions. And preaching. But then, after having done that, *then* we were to vote.

DW: Yes.

CW: When we came together after that year, Dennis and I were thinking: We're probably not ready to vote. So we even put it before them, to say, "Do you want to study it some more? Or do you want to vote regarding whether union ceremonies will be a part of the ministry of this church?" But they were ready to vote. By that time, the congregation had changed significantly. We had a good number of gay and lesbian persons that had joined the congregation. The congregation voted that union ceremonies would be part of our ministry.

DW: So that settled that. And the people who were waiting around for the final decision—we didn't see them anymore.

CW: Exactly! Not since that night.

DW: That was their last night, you know? They had stuck around a whole year, to see what was going down.

CW: But they were [only] coming to worship maybe once a month. They were just kind of hanging on by a thread. That night, we saw people we hadn't seen in fifteen years come to vote. And when I say that, I'm talking about straight folk who were against it.

DW: Right. And one of the things we should just mention is that in the midst of all this—I can't remember exactly where it came in the chronology—but, tell him about Mahan. What a blessing.

CW: Oh my gosh! Yes, such a blessing. In the midst of this, it was *so* painful. Members of the local, predominantly black, Baptist Convention of DC and Vicinity tried to put us out. I was getting accosted in the mall by people telling us they were going to get our church. Some members of the congregation were depressed because those that were with us and for us, their families were telling them, "You need to get out of that church." Their friends were saying, "You need to get out of that church." Their coworkers were telling them, "You need to get out of that church!"

But several things happened. One was that there was an organization called the Association of Welcoming and Affirming Baptists. [A man] got in touch with us and he said, was there anything that they could do? I said, "Tell your churches to pray for us." We got letters from all over the country. All. Over. The country. We read them in Bible study, and it was so affirming for us and also for the congregation.

DW: The letters were overwhelmingly from white—

CW: From white people, yeah. They weren't from black people. And a couple of Latinos.

And then. One of the books we used was called *Exile or Embrace? Congregations Discerning Their Response to Lesbian and Gay Christians* by a guy named Mahan Siler; former pastor of the progressive Pullen Memorial Baptist church in Raleigh, North Carolina. He wrote about his experiences of doing a union ceremony and the church becoming open and affirming. And they were a predominantly white Southern Baptist church. So, they really caught hell. I mean, the whole denomination put them out.

We used his book because he told his story, but he also put a process in. So we used his process in our task force. He heard we were using that book and we got an invitation from him. He was coming into town, and he wanted to take us to dinner. And he just ministered to us. Our hearts were broken. And he wanted us to know—this white man, you know?—"You're doing the right thing. It takes so much courage to do that." It was such a wonderful thing. And that's a whole piece about inclusion. We kept getting wonderful affirmation from people we were not in fellowship with, whereas the Black Church totally ostracized us. I had a meeting with Sam Lloyd, who was the dean of the Washington National Cathedral. Our community organizer happened to bring him by. He was new in town. We established a relationship with Sam [while] he developed a congregation because they actually hadn't had a congregation in the cathedral. And we ministered to each other.

Also, we went to our DC Baptist Convention and the very first African American executive minister they had. This was before our church had taken the vote for us to be copastors. [We wanted to know:] If we ever got thrown out, where was a good place to plant a church? So he talked to us for two hours and just talked about the fact that we were called to be right where we were. And we appreciated that so much. Do you know, he left that position and became the first African American pastor of First Baptist Church in Washington, DC? And in the last six months or so, they got rid of him. They were concerned because there were so many African Americans coming to this predominantly white church, and they were starting to have a more celebrative worship. And then they were concerned because now, there were gay people joining the church. So [there's] what the people *say* they want, and then, when you give it to them, they [blame you]. The same thing happened to a girlfriend of mine. This white congregation in Reston, Virginia, voted to be open and affirming, so they did outreach. She had them doing outreach to the LGBT community. And the people from her congregation *left*—to the point where they could no longer pay her salary. She had to leave as the pastor and go get a job.

DW: During this whole period, we began to explore [becoming] affiliated with the United Church of Christ. We realized that their theology was more consistent with who we are—not only in terms of supporting LGBT equality but also in terms of social justice ministry in general. And we were finding that we didn't have a lot of people in the black church that we could really talk with, you know?

CW: We were getting all kinds of awards from gay organizations—

DW: Yeah, certainly, the gay community has expressed a great deal of appreciation, both black and white, for who we are and what we've tried to do. Unfortunately, we have not received the same kind of appreciation from the black church, in general.

CW: We, along with another minister from All Souls Church, Unitarian, developed a group called DC Clergy United for Marriage Equality. We helped to build support for the passage of a law legalizing Marriage Equality in the District of Columbia. Within a three-week period, I think we had an interracial group of about 150 ministers who had signed on. There was this very *loud* group of African American ministers who were against marriage equality, but we had to show there was another face to that. And the fact that a traditional black Baptist church was leading the effort made it very significant.

DW: Just a side note. You know, a lot of other states now have kind of come on board with supporting marriage equality, but there are a lot more to go. What we've noticed is that, especially ever since President Obama came out with his statement of support, seemingly a growing number of progressive black ministers have come out in support of marriage equality as a *civil* right. And what was so interesting about that is that at one point, black folk didn't want to in any way suggest that gay rights and civil rights had anything in common. But I think it became politically advantageous in terms of passing these laws. People even in the black community began to emphasize that everyone is due equal protection under the law. So even though we're not trying to force our views on somebody else, and we're not asking the church and the state to blur those lines of separation, the church does have a responsibility to allow people to be true to their own beliefs and convictions.

Anyway, that has moved some people in the black community, in the black church, to be able to at least *vote* for marriage equality. But I think that we just have to be real clear about the distinction between marriage equality as a *civil* right versus marriage equality as a *moral* right.

What we have tried to do here at Covenant is to understand that we can't fight for LGBT equality outside the walls of the church if we're not willing to try to model it—and live it—inside the walls of the church. All the churches that claim to be open and affirming or whatever—perhaps they haven't been through what we have been through. And we can understand that. I mean, this is risky business. Would we wish on anybody what we've been through? But at the same time, the question becomes: If not me, then who? How does this happen? That you move this push for equality beyond something that is a legalized, civil issue rather than a real genuine, human, and moral issue. That really makes a difference.

DM: Because that's been a line. Many people, especially listening to some of the pastors in Maryland, what they were saying was: "Well, I believe in the civil [rights]. I'll fight for it, for the civil nature of it. But it's not gonna happen in my church. We don't have to do it."

DW: Yeah, [the idea is that] we can fight for this out there, but don't bring that up in here. So, yeah. I just think that is a nuance. There's a film out called *The New Black* that kind of lifts that up. You have to be aware of that nuance, in terms of understanding what's going on. Please understand, I'm not trying to say anything negative about anyone else who has taken that stance. I'm just saying there's a clear difference between *that* on the one hand and what we've tried to do *here*.

Which is to really change the culture of the church, itself. For instance, Martin Luther King used to say you can't legislate morality. He would say, "Legislation can't make you love me, but it can keep you from lynching me." At some point, if we're really talking about moving beyond legally appropriate acts of behavior—if we're really talking about changing hearts—then we as the church have a responsibility to go beyond just fighting for it as a civil right. At some point, we as the church have to figure out how to teach our people to respect all human beings. And to love all human beings equally, regardless of their sexual orientation.

CW: And you can't do that without taking risks. So many people want to know how they can do it without taking risks.

DM: You can't.

CW: We have some friends who started a church as an open and affirming congregation. However, their people were tentative about gay people. And so, now, they're thinking about connecting with UCC. But, they're not sure: "If we connect with UCC, how deep does that take us into the open and affirming piece, you know?" They only have one gay person in their congregation. Well, you never know—there could be some other people, we never know—but as far as they know, there's one gay person who's the *child* of somebody.

But those people would be hesitant if you told them to go do some outreach to the gay community. And I've said to the pastors, several times, "If you want your people to get to know some gay people, then you need to have them come over and fellowship at my church." In their head, they want to do the right thing, but it's kind of like when I was a kid. When we were in Germany, the Germans always kept looking at the back of us, because they had always been told black people had—

DM: Tails, yeah.

CW: Yeah. So, you know. I don't know if they think gay people have tails, but there's this real fear. And it's because of the whole stigma that has been placed. But it's relationships that change hearts. It's relationships. You have to put yourself in an arena where you're going to have the opportunity to have a relationship with someone who's different.

DW: And here's what's ironic. The lady who I mentioned in the first union ceremony came up to me—

CW: [The one] who sued us for back tithes.

DW: Yeah. She said the reason we were doing this was because we knew gay people had a lot of money, and we wanted to grow our church.

CW: And remember her nephew from Florida?

DW: Oh yeah. Yes.

CW: He had run away, and she was so worried about him. She left a message that she thought he would come to our church because he was gay. And she knew we would take care of him.

DW: And she wanted us to be on the lookout for him. She wanted him to come to our church.

DM: I think that another thing we've identified and hit upon, is that even these *hard* moments—and this is what I put to the Holy Spirit again—people don't recognize that the Spirit has a way of creating evolutionary moments for you.

CW: Watching my LGBT brothers and sisters has been so helpful for me in this journey. In the midst of it, I get mad as a mug. But they don't ever get mad. And if *they* aren't mad—and they have it worse than I do, you know?—I guess I need to be all spiritual, too. I mean, it has really been a help to me. It wasn't really so much a process for me. I think it was just early on. My mother's statement to me—I didn't know what it meant at that time, but it was a powerful thing for me. And then, I didn't have the experience of growing up in the black church.

DW: Let me just say two things. We're still struggling in many ways, especially financially. Our congregation lost a lot of people, but we gained a lot of people, as well.

CW: And many of them don't have deep roots in the church.

DW: Yeah. As far as their being in the habit of supporting the church financially, we've got a lot of work to do. As it relates to that, we have definitely felt it personally as well as institutionally.

CW: Somewhere in that process, we didn't get a salary for four months.

DW: Right. And even now, it cut very deeply into our giving. So it is understandable why some people, even if they're really in favor of LGBT equality, if they're pastoring or trying to build a big church or whatever, would have some trepidation about treading in this area. Because this is not the way to build a thriving church, necessarily. I think that one day, it will be, but I don't know if we're quite there yet.

I'll also say this though. Even as we share our setbacks and our disappointments and that kind of thing, it has been a blessing. It has been a blessing; we have learned so much. And we have gained so much. Most recently, we have started a couples ministry. And we've had the couples over at our house; we've had functions here at the church, like for Valentine's. And we make it clear: when we invite couples, we're not saying "straight couples" or "gay couples," we're just saying "couples." And it's so beautiful to see these couples—some straight, some gay and lesbian—coming together.

CW: There's a good mix.

DW: We're playing games. We're telling stories. We're developing relationships. And we realize that we're all the same. You know? I mean, [there are] a lot of rumors about us. We don't even know what people are saying about Covenant Church.

CW: They think we're having orgies.

DW: But I think if people could really see us. . . . Recently, on the fiftieth anniversary of the Birmingham Bombing, we had a special Sunday to commemorate the four innocent girls who lost their lives while attending Sunday School at the 16th Street Baptist Church on that fateful day. We had a lot of guests that came to our church on that sacred anniversary occasion. I don't know what those people may have heard about Covenant. But I think they are beginning to see that we're a church just like any other church. There's no real difference. We aren't over here having orgies, or anything. We are simply trying to be the church. And it has never been our intention to be a gay church or a straight church. We just want to be—

DM: In Christ's church.

DW: Right. That's what we're trying to do. That's our story.

DM: Well, thank you so much.

Epilogue

JOSEF SORETT

This book began as an idea that grew from a 2010 event organized in response to a set of public debates. More surprising is that the substance of what it presents to readers, albeit with a bunch of updating, is no less relevant and insightful today, even as the social context and conversations taking place around the book's subject have significantly changed.

At the time of the book's genesis, the push to legalize same-sex marriage was building steam but had only won a legal victory in the state of Massachusetts. Then came the election cycle of 2008, which at the national level ushered Barack Obama, the first black president of the United States, into the White House. Yet, amid a new wave of postracial euphoria occasioned by Obama's election, the nation's progressive bona fides were put in relief when, simultaneously, the third-largest state in the union (and what is generally considered one of its most liberal) passed legislation, in the form of Proposition 8, which outlawed same-sex marriage.

There's no need to recount the details of the 2008 election cycle further here. The book's introduction has already done this and captured how "gay vs. black" became a popular caption. Frankly, it's a story that is now well-known and more than twice-told. But, to the point, black churches were blamed for this blemish on the body politic, and with this scapegoating came a new wave of interest in this seemingly foreign institution that has long stood center stage in the history of American culture and politics.

Indeed, this contradiction—black church as problem and promise—created the conditions of possibility for a project that became the context for this book, including the convening transcribed in its first chapter. The assumption, better understood as a question, then: Were black churches a formidable problem for a growing marriage equality movement?

To be sure, black churches proved not to be too much of an impediment, as Proposition 8 was overturned a handful of years later. In 2021, marriage equality is almost an afterthought, even as the years since produced a steady stream of pushback against protections for LGBTQ citizens. Marriage was the issue then, and now debates swirl around the Equality Act. But, as was clear then, black churches and the communities they serve were never the real obstacles to achieving marriage equality, just as winning marriage equality was never the solution to the range of problems that constrained black life—and black LGBTQ lives, in particular—in the twenty-first century. This awareness lent an of unevenness to the first conversations where the ideas for this book took shape. Marriage was *the* major political issue driving the national dialogue on sexual and gender equality. Still, it was not identified as *the* primary concern shaping discussions about the inclusion of black LGBTQ folk within the context of black churches and communities, or into the body politic, in general. This disconnect is only all the more clear after close to a decade of a #BlackLivesMatter movement that developed in response to a steady stream of anti–black violence broadcast across the airwaves, and on the heels of four years of a Trump presidency.

Recognizing that debates about marriage equality provided the context, if not the motivation, for this anthology still raises questions that animate the book's chapters. If not election cycles, one might ask, what are the best terms or better contexts in which to understand the sexual politics of black churches? Certainly, the controversy that developed around Kim Burrell's 2016 antigay sermon, also detailed in the book's introduction, fails to provide a much more helpful frame. That said, the outing of Burrell's homophobic preaching (and her subsequent partial canceling) does provide us with another common lens through which the sexual politics of black churches garners attention beyond that of the congregations or communities they serve; namely, a scandal. One thinks immediately of another (even more) popular gospel artist and preacher, Donnie McClurkin. He made similar headlines in 2007 for declaring that he had been healed of homosexuality, not long before appearing at a campaign rally for then-presidential candidate Barack Obama. Ex-gay speeches and antigay sermons of this sort led to the "gay vs. black" storyline. Notably, McClurkin's testimony of professed healing once again made headlines in 2021, following an interview on TV One's *Uncensored*, just as this anthology was going to production.[1]

Even still, the scandal that is the antigay sermon or the ex-gay confession is a relatively recent phenomenon compared to a much longer history of sex scandals that have turned black churches into fodder for media spectacles. Here one thinks immediately of the story of Clarence Cobbs, detailed by Wallace Best in chapter 5 of this volume. Yet a much longer list of examples would include names like Adam Clayton Powell Jr., C. L. Franklin, Prophet James Jones, Henry Lyons, and much more recently, Bishop Eddie Long; but also, perhaps, the postmortem fascination with the sex lives of Malcolm X and Martin Luther King Jr., still by far the nation's two most readily recognized black religious leaders.

The point here is not that black (male) clergy are exceptional in their capacity for sexual transgression. One could quickly call up a list of white counterparts—from Henry Ward Beecher to Jimmy Swaggart, Jim Bakker, Ted Haggard, and Jerry Falwell Jr.—with their own scandals. Rather, my point here is to call attention to the points at which the sexual politics of black churches—be it a clergyperson or a member of the rank and file—tend to become a national preoccupation. Indeed, public concern with black sexuality or black religion is generated, on the one hand, by election cycles and sex scandals, on the other. To put the matter another way (and to restate something from the introduction), black churches' political or public significance ought not to be confused with the sexual politics of black churches. In the case of both election cycles and scandal, public discourse tends to presume a certain black pathology (e.g., cultural backwardness and/or sexual transgression) even as it obscures any substantive attention to the complicated religious, cultural, and political histories and contemporary contexts in which black sexual politics take shape. Never mind the actual lives of black LGBTQ persons and communities.

The point here has also not been to suggest an exceptional or celebratory story of black churches. It has been, instead, to recognize the significance of an evolving national context while also shifting more attention to how the sexual politics of black churches are shaped by but also depart from and exceed the national storyline—be it a growing marriage equality movement or the latest sexual scandal. In helping to facilitate this shift of gaze, the chapters in this volume raise as many new questions as they have answered. This is precisely the point, which is to say, what do we learn and what additional questions emerge when neither scandal nor election cycle is driving the conversation? What are the cultural contexts, discursive frames, and languages around and through which black churches, and the communities they serve, have cultivated a set of practices for negotiating the normative religious and civic logics of sex and sexuality (and gender) of the nation? And how have such negotiations created space for affirming black sexual difference (and black LGBTQ lives, specifically) *and* reinscribed, deepened, and amplified longstanding practices of exclusion? What are the constraints and possibilities that shape black (LGBTQ) lives after (marriage) equality?

Just as scholars have noted that "there is no such thing as the "Black Church," there is similarly no singular sexual politics of black churches that can be discerned as unifying the observations and analyses made by the contributors to this volume. That said, I'll highlight a couple of general observations here in place of a larger set of conclusions. First, in focusing on the sexual politics of black churches, with the backdrop of LGBTQ equality and inclusion, we are already and necessarily thinking about gender. This is perhaps especially apparent in part 3 of this anthology. Jonathan Lee Walton captures how a longstanding investment in a certain kind of black masculinity, what he calls "Afrophallic Protestantism," has been valorized by black churches and communities. Wallace Best's chapter on Clarence Cobbs also affirms as much even as it reveals that so-called nonnormative sexualities have coexisted along with this black masculinist norm and, in different historical moments, have even found public affirmation. Monique Moultrie, in turn, unveils the other side of these gender logics in her account of how media ministries for and by black women both embrace and complicate the desire for a certain kind of black man(hood) that is hard to come by. This gender logic is also on view in part 5, when Dennis and Christine Wiley note that the question of women serving as pastors was no less fraught than their efforts to move a black Baptist congregation toward being "open and affirming" in its inclusion of black LGBTQ members and clergy. Yet each of these poignant observations still leave open the question of how black trans men and women fare in the face of binary gender logics that persist, often with theological sanction.

Another observation worth noting concerns the Bible's arguably oversized role in both national discussions of homo/sexuality and within black churches. To be sure, there are distinct traditions of scriptural interpretation within black churches, as well as different strategies for reading with and against popular (or normative) interpretations of the Bible. However, in chapter 3, Michael Brown offers readers a portrait of early Christian communities (the context in which the New Testament was written) that is critical for anyone, Christian or otherwise, who would try to understand "what the bible says about (homo) sexuality" in the present moment. One might also rightfully conclude from Brown's essay that black Christians, like all Christians and religious communities (irrespective of racial identity), read and interpret scripture in different ways and debate and weigh its significance differently given the subject at hand. This truth is just as apparent in Nyasha Junior's treatment in chapter 2 of #SayHerName, which also illumines how certain practices of scriptural interpretation can abet or counter the erasure of black women in both church and society. Junior's chapter further confirms that the authority afforded to the linked logics of gender and sexuality apparent in the more recent historical record (e.g., American history) are often just as an important source of authority as the Bible itself, as a sacred text produced during a different historical moment.

An observation that emerges primarily in part 3 centers around the degree to which black churches have or have not provided a space of belonging and inclusion across lines of sexual difference and for black LGBTQ folks, specifically. One might note here that Wallace Best's example of Clarence Cobb already brought this matter to the fore. Accordingly, within the context of a heteronormative, masculinist norm, black churches have allowed for a certain measure of (gender and sexual) difference to abide—except when they have not. And that continues to be the case. As Melynda J. Price points out in chapter 7, there is a range of kinship structures (including ones that center black women's authority) that have long been valued within black churches, the communities they serve, and even in the face of a public avowal of a certain vision of the nuclear family. At the same time, it is relatively difficult to find black churches, at either the local or denominational level, that abide by official policies and/or practices that openly affirm the presence and full inclusion of black LGBTQ persons within the life and leadership of the congregation. Recognizing this, Valerie Purdie Greenaway and colleagues identify the experience of "intersectional invisibility" and "ontological exclusion" still faced by LGBTQ black Christians (chapter 8).

Invisibility and exclusion continue to be a reality for LGBTQ persons within the context of many Christian churches, including those that fall under the rubrics of the "Black Church," which raises several important questions concerning the impact of marriage equality on African American communities. How many black LGBTQ-identified people have exercised the legal right to marriage? How have black churches become accommodated to the reality of marriage equality? Have a significant number of black churches embraced marriage equality and allowed for same-sex unions within the context of their congregations? How have the experiences of black LGBTQ couples who have married with their churches changed? Are those churches, assuming they are black churches, publicly affirmative of their unions? Or does a climate and culture of "don't ask, don't tell" still order the sexual politics of black churches? As Dennis and Christine Wiley note in chapter 12, many black clergy stepped up to support of marriage equality as a legal or civil right, but very few did so on theological or moral grounds or moved their congregations and/or denominations to ordain LGBTQ members or perform same-sex unions. In certain instances, some black denominations and congregations responded to the public debate around marriage to draft statements and policies that disciplined clergy and congregations that engaged in such practices. In fact, the African Methodist Episcopal denomination debated this very question at its General Conference in July of 2021.[2] As federal and state policy campaigns (e.g., the Equality Act) continue to be waged around a broader set of LGBTQ protections, will black clergy once again step up as advocates and allies under the rubrics of "civil rights"? Or will they align themselves with more conservative strands of American Christianity that consider such legislation to be a threat to their faith under the veil of religious freedom? Ultimately, one wonders about the larger implications of how black clergy and churches have drawn lines, porous as they may be, between civil equality and theological inclusion. Together, these concerns suggest the metaquestion of how (or how much) things have changed since marriage equality has been achieved. And what might all of this mean for a new generation of young people, along a spectrum of gender expressions and sexual orientations, coming of age within black churches and the communities they serve?

What is clear is that marriage equality was never a panacea for a range of social arrangements and structural inequalities that continue to constrain black life (and black LGBTQ lives, specifically) and fracture black communities across lines of racial, gender, and sexual difference. If nothing else, the ongoing reality of exclusion and invisibility clarifies the stakes for the kinds of constructive and practical work put forward in part 5 of this volume. Even if one remains offended or unpersuaded by the suggestion that "gay is the new black," Monica Coleman (chapter 9) provides a clear set of categories to facilitate a space for what one might identify as intersectional theological reflection—that is, thinking theologically across the lines of race, gender identity, and sexual orientation. In chapter 10 by Luke A. Powery, readers (be they preachers or not) are invited to recognize that a reckoning with the historical and contemporary violence done to black bodies is the condition of possibility for the valuing of spirit so central to black church traditions. Moreover, Powery's homiletic seems to suggest that lingering with the idea of the black body as sacred text is a prerequisite for a vision of preaching that would align itself with #BlackLivesMatter, even as it also highlights how black preaching has long availed itself of a set of extra-canonical sources—be it the physical black body or the broader body of black literature (e.g., Toni Morrison's Baby Suggs "in the clearing"). Taking Powery's centering of the black body a step further, in chapter 11, Brad Braxton calls for a brand of preaching that is deliberately "sexually explicit" with the goal of undoing practices that exclude and render invisible. That is, Braxton lauds a model of preaching that counters a prevailing culture of silence and shame regarding *sexual* bodies, in general, and one which is often openly and explicitly antagonistic toward LGBTQ bodies. By way of personal disclosure and provocation, creating discomfort figures here as a strategy for tackling taboo, shifting the terms of stigma and sexual violence, and inviting an open conversation from the pulpit that is, ultimately, concerned with imagining new life in the pews and beyond.

There is perhaps no cultural practice as central to the history of black churches as the tradition of call and response. This tradition, which evokes a conversation between the pulpit and the pews—preacher and congregation, soloist and choir—to make something new possible, provides the context, most obviously, for the chapters on preaching in the book's final section. The conversation occasioned by the exchange that is call and response also provides a certain organizing principle for this entire anthology. We began, in chapter 1, with a public discussion in a packed classroom on a hot summer night. Our final chapter brings things to a close with a conversation between two copastors who also happen to be husband and wife. Moreover, each chapter in this book began as a series of brief, informal presentations around a conference table that took the shape of a day-long conversation. And each chapter grew out of that gathering in July of 2010, which convened in response to a national debate about marriage. And, now, as an extended reflection on the sexual politics of black churches, this book stands as yet another call—to more research, to further conversation. Yes, about the sexual politics of black churches, but even more with an eye toward affirming black life and the fullness thereof.

Notes

Introduction

1. Her comments are viewable at https://www.youtube.com/watch?v=nmLHh-RwGWU.
2. Michael Joseph Gross, "Gay Is the New Black: The Last Great Civil Rights Movement," *Advocate*, December 16, 2008, http://www.advocate.com/news/2008/11/16/gay-new-black.
3. In 2017, Pew found that 51 percent of African Americans supported same-sex marriage, which was nearly twenty points higher than their support when measured in 2001 (32 percent). The same study showed that 62 percent of white Americans supported same-sex marriage, up from 34 percent in 2001. "Attitudes on Same-Sex Marriage by Race," Pew Research Center, May 14, 2019, http://www.pewforum.org/fact-sheet/changing-attitudes-on-gay-marriage/.
4. Gross, "Gay Is the New Black."
5. I recognize that gender identity and sexual orientation are deeply complex, but these terms (LGBT, LGBTQ, LGBTQ+) have been used throughout for this audience by the discretion of each author. No one has been intentionally left out.
6. Adam Serwer, "You Can't Equate Your Sin With My Skin," *Mother Jones*, September/October 2012, http://www.motherjones.com/politics/2012/07/you-cant-equate-your-sin-my-skin.
7. Jonathan L. Walton, "Gay Ain't the New Black, But . . .," *Religion Dispatches*, June 26, 2009, http://religiondispatches.org/gay-aint-the-new-black-but/.

8. John McWhorter, "Gay Really Is the New Black: African-Americans Have a Special Responsibility to Fight for Equality," *New York Daily News*, January 24, 2013, http://www.nydailynews.com/opinion/gay-new-black-article-1.1246187.
9. Yoruba Richen made these comments on the "Representing Religion, Contesting Sexuality" film screening and directors' panel as part of the conference, "Are the Gods Afraid of Black Sexuality? Religion and the Burdens of Black Sexual Politics" (Columbia University, New York, October 25, 2014).
10. Wallace Best, "The Right Achieved and the Wrong Way Conquered: J. H. Jackson, Martin Luther King, Jr., and the Conflict over Civil Rights," *Religion and American Culture: A Journal of Interpretation* 16, no. 2 (2006): 195–226.
11. Randall Balmer, "The Real Origins of the Religious Right," *Politico*, May 27, 2014, http://www.politico.com/magazine/story/2014/05/religious-right-real-origins-107133.
12. "Many Americans Uneasy with Mix of Religion and Politics," Pew Center for People and the Press, Pew Forum on Religion in Public Life, April 24, 2006. According to this survey, in response to the question "Does your clergy address laws regarding homosexuality from the pulpit?" black Protestants were the highest group reporting yes, at 62 percent, while the overall total was 52 percent. Just outpaced by white evangelicals in this last question, the study shows black Protestants as ranking near the top in each category.
13. The following article draws on the data from the Associated Press poll: "Exit Poll Shows Blacks, Hispanics Overwhelmingly Backed Prop. 8," accessed April 21, 2009, https://latimesblogs.latimes.com/lanow/2008/11/70-of-african-a.html.
14. Patrick J. Egan and Kenneth Sherrill, "California's Proposition 8: What Happened, and What Does the Future Hold?" commissioned by the Evelyn & Walter Haas, Jr., Fund in San Francisco. Released under the auspices of the National Gay and Lesbian Task Force Policy Institute, January 6, 2009.
15. Mark Schoofs, "Mormons Boost Antigay Marriage Effort," *Wall Street Journal*, September 20, 2008, https://www.wsj.com/articles/SB122186063716658279.
16. For a quick example of this logic, see "Political Animal: No, Blacks Did Not Destroy Gay Marriage," *Washington Monthly*, accessed April 24, 2009, https://washingtonmonthly.com/2009/01/08/no-blacks-did-not-destroy-gay-marriage/.
17. For recent treatments of marriage in the context of African American history and contemporary life, see: Ralph Richard Banks, *Is Marriage for White People? How the African American Marriage Decline Affects Everyone* (New York: Penguin, 2011); Tera Hunter, *Bound in Wedlock: Slave and Free Black Marriage in the Nineteenth Century* (Cambridge: Belknap Press of Harvard University); Katherine Franke, *Wedlocked: The Perils of Marriage Equality* (New York: New York University Press, 2015); Dawn Mouzon, "Why Has Marriage Declined Among Black Americans," Scholars Strategy Network, September 26, 2013, https://scholars.org/brief/why-has-marriage-declined-among-black-americans;

and Joy Jones, "Marriage is for White People," *Washington Post*, March 26, 2006, https://www.washingtonpost.com/archive/opinions/2006/03/26/marriage-is-for-white-people/095b1136-1440-4380-ac23-64beeeac3df4/.
18. Fredrick C. Harris, *Something Within: Religion and Political Activism* (New York: Oxford University Press, 2000).
19. Barbara Savage, *Your Spirits Walk Beside Us: The Politics of Black Religion* (Cambridge, MA: Belknap Press of Harvard University, 2008).

2. Jephthah's Daughter and #SayHerName

1. Some scholars have chosen to give Jephthah's Daughter a name. For example, Mieke Bal names her "Bath" as a shortened form of "Bath-Jephthah" (daughter of Jephthah). Consult Mieke Bal, *Death and Dissymmetry: The Politics of Coherence in the Book of Judges* (Chicago: University of Chicago Press, 1988), 43. J. Cheryl Exum names her "Bat-jiftah" (daughter of Jephthah). Consult J. Cheryl Exum, "Feminist Criticism," in *Judges and Method: New Approaches to Biblical Studies*, 2nd ed., ed. Gale A. Yee, (Minneapolis: Fortress, 2007), 74. She is named "Seila" in Pseudo-Philo (40:2).
2. Abraham has another son, Ishmael, who was expelled along with his mother Hagar (Genesis 21). The Qur'an also includes this near sacrifice episode. Consult John Kaltner, *Ishmael Instructs Isaac: An Introduction to the Qur'an for Bible Readers* (Collegeville, MN: Liturgical Press, 1999). On racialized interpretations of Hagar, consult Nyasha Junior, *Reimagining Hagar: Blackness and the Bible* (New York: Oxford University Press, 2019).
3. Although they may differ on the helpfulness of the comparison, recent examples include Daniel I. Block, *Judges, Ruth* (New American Commentary 6; Nashville: B and H, 1999), 371–372; Victor A. Matthews, *Judges and Ruth* (New Cambridge Bible Commentary; Cambridge: Cambridge University Press, 2004), 126; Susan Niditch, *Judges: A Commentary* (Old Testament Library; Louisville, KY: Westminster John Knox, 2008), 133; Jack M. Sasson, *Judges 1–12: A New Translation with Introduction and Commentary* (Anchor Yale Bible 6D; New Haven, CT: Yale University Press, 2014), 445–448; Susanne Scholz, "Judges," in *Women's Bible Commentary: Twentieth-Anniversary Edition*, revised and updated 3rd ed., ed. Carol A. Newsom, Sharon H. Ringe, Jacqueline E. Lapsley, (Louisville, KY: Westminster John Knox, 2012), 120; J. Alberto Soggin, *Judges: A Commentary*, trans. J. S. Bowden (Old Testament Library: Philadelphia, 1981), 215; and Phyllis Trible, *Texts of Terror: Literary-Feminist Readings of Biblical Narratives*, (Philadelphia: Fortress, 1984), 105.
4. I would like to thank Stephen C. Russell and Jeremy Schipper for their input on earlier drafts of this essay.

5. For biblical scholarship on Judges, consult Susan Ackerman, *Warrior, Dancer, Seductress, Queen: Women in Judges and Biblical Israel* (New York: Doubleday, 1998); David M. Gunn, *Judges Through the Centuries* (Malden, MA: Blackwell, 2005); Gregory Mobley and Joanna Kline, "Book of Judges" in *Oxford Bibliographies in Biblical Studies* (New York: Oxford Bibliographies), doi: 10.1093/obo/9780195393361-0115; Susan Niditch, *Judges: A Commentary*; Sasson, *Judges 1–12*; Susanne Scholz, "Judges," in *Women's Bible Commentary: Twentieth-Anniversary Edition*, ed. Carol A. Newsom, Sharon H. Ringe, Jacqueline E. Lapsley, rev. and updated 3rd ed. (Louisville, KY: Westminster John Knox, 2012), 113–141; and Gale Yee, ed., *Judges and Method: New Approaches to Biblical Studies*, 2nd ed. (Minneapolis: Fortress Press, 2007). For a bibliography covering recent scholarship on Judges 11, consult Serge Frolov, *Judges* (Forms of Old Testament Literature; Grand Rapids, MI: Eerdmans, 2013), 226–229.
6. All biblical translations come from the New Revised Standard Version.
7. The narrator focuses on Jephthah and obfuscates the horror of the father's sacrifice of Jephthah's Daughter. Often, the literature regarding the text fixates on the alleged sacrifice of Jephthah's Daughter might that Jephthah killed his daughter or fulfilled his vow through some other means. Sacrificialists argue that Jephthah offered his daughter as a burnt offering. Conversely, nonsacrificialists argue that Jephthah obliged his daughter to remain a virgin and to dedicate herself to religious service. Consult John L. Thompson, *Writing the Wrongs: Women of the Old Testament Among Biblical Commentators from Philo Through the Reformation*, (Oxford: Oxford University Press, 2001). Esther Fuchs argues that, in doing so, these commentators preserve the narrator's focus on Jephthah and maintain the victimization of Jephthah's Daughter. They focus on Jephthah at the expense of his daughter by looking at her compliance or his foolishness in making the vow. Consult Esther Fuchs, "Marginalization, Ambiguity, Silencing: The Story of Jephthah's Daughter," in *A Feminist Companion to Judges*, vol. 4, *Feminist Companion to the Bible*, ed. Athalya Brenner (Sheffield, England: Sheffield Academic Press, 1993), 130.
8. Consult Patrisse Khan-Cullors and Asha Bandele, *When They Call You a Terrorist: A Black Lives Matter Memoir*, (New York: St. Martin's, 2018).
9. On Black women's leadership in social media innovation and activism, consult Feminista Jones, *Reclaiming Our Space: How Black Feminists Are Changing the World from the Tweets to the Streets* (Boston: Beacon, 2019).
10. Many have noted parallels between contemporary murders and the 1955 lynching of fourteen-year-old Emmett Till. His mother, Mamie Till Bradley, insisted on an open casket funeral. Approved by his mother, the public viewing of his body and the subsequent publication of the photographs of Till's brutalized body served to garner attention for his murder and those of other

Black Americans. On Till's lynching and subsequent action, consult Mamie Till-Mobley and Christopher Benson, *Death of Innocence: The Story of the Hate Crime that Changed America* (New York: One World/Ballantine, 2003); and Christopher Metress, *The Lynching of Emmett Till: A Documentary Narrative* (Charlottesville: University of Virginia Press, 2002). Also, the Smithsonian's National Museum of African American Museum of History and Culture in Washington, DC has a poignant Emmett Till exhibition that includes Till's casket: https://nmaahc.si.edu.

11. Consult the African American Policy Forum #SayHerName campaign website: https://www.aapf.org/sayhername.
12. Sasson, *Judges 1–12*, 447.
13. Niditch, *Judges: A Commentary*, 133.
14. Soggin, *Judges: A Commentary*, 215.
15. Trible, *Texts of Terror*, 105.
16. In biblical texts, women characters are often unnamed. Examples include the wife of Noah (Genesis 7:13), the mother of Samson (Judges 13:2, 24), and the wife of Job (Job 2:9).
17. Niditch, *Judges: A Commentary*, 133. For a recent and detailed study of warrior culture in ancient Israel and related cultures, consult Mark S. Smith, *Poetic Heroes: Literary Commemorations of Warriors and Warrior Culture in the Early Biblical World* (Grand Rapids, MI: William B. Eerdmans, 2014).
18. Since the #SayHerName campaign recognizes that contemporary police violence against Black women and girls involve domestic violence as well as state-sanctioned violence, one could also use the prism of #SayHerName to read Jephthah's actions as an act of domestic violence.
19. By comparison, Judges 11:30 reads, "And Jephthah made a vow to the Lord, and said, 'If you will give the Ammonites into my hand . . .'"
20. This is an excellent example of victim-blaming. Hebrew Bible scholar Renita Weems remarks, "In a perfect example of what is known as blame the victim, Jephthah lashed out at his only begotten daughter. . . . Jephthah talked as though he were the victim when, in fact, it was his unnamed daughter who would become the victim of his foolish vow." Renita J. Weems, *Just a Sister Away: A Womanist Vision of Women's Relationships in the Bible* (San Diego, CA: LuraMedia, 1988), 56.
21. To be precise, the Hebrew word that the New Revised Standard Version translates as "vow" in Judges 11:30, 25, 39 is different than the Hebrew word that it translates as "oath" in 1 Samuel 14:26–28.
22. Audre Lorde, "A Litany for Survival," in *The Black Unicorn: Poems* (New York: Norton, 1978), 32.

3. An Inconsistent Truth: The New Testament, Early Christianity, and Sexuality

1. Roger Bagnall and Bruce Frier, *The Demography of Roman Egypt* (Cambridge: Cambridge University Press, 1994), 76.
2. Bagnall and Frier, *The Demography of Roman Egypt*, 105.
3. Craig Williams, *Roman Homosexuality: Ideologies of Masculinity in Classical Antiquity* (Oxford: Oxford University Press, 1999), 138, 141.

4. "Have the Sons of Africa No Souls?" Manliness, Freedom, and Power in the Cultural Roots of Afro-Phallic Protestantism

1. Donald E. Hall, *Muscular Christianity: Embodying the Victorian Age* (Cambridge: Cambridge University Press, 1994); Tony Ladd and James A. Mathisen, *Muscular Christianity: Evangelical Protestants and the Development of American Sport* (Grand Rapids, MI: Baker, 1999); John J. MacAloon, *Muscular Christianity in Colonial and Post-Colonial Worlds* (London: Routledge, 2008); Clifford Putney, *Muscular Christianity: Manhood and Sports in Protestant America, 1880–1920* (Cambridge, MA: Harvard University Press, 2001); Gail Bederman, *Manliness & Civilization: A Cultural History of Gender and Race in the United States, 1880–1917* (Chicago: University of Chicago Press, 1995); Gail Bederman, "The Women Have Had Charge of the Church Work Long Enough: The Men and Religion Forward Movement of 1911–1912," *American Quarterly* 41, no. 3 (1989): 432–65; Stephen D. Johnson, "Who Supports the Promise Keepers?" *Sociology of Religion* 61, no. 1 (2000): 93–104; and Becky Beal, "The Promise Keepers' Use of Sport in Defining 'Christlike' Masculinity," *Journal of Sport and Social Issues* 21, no. 3 (1997): 274–84.
2. Cheryl Gilkes, *If It Wasn't for the Women: Black Women's Experience and Womanist Culture in Church and Community* (Maryknoll, NY: Orbis, 2001); Evelyn Brooks Higginbotham, *Righteous Discontent: The Women's Movement in the Black Baptist Church, 1880–1920* (Cambridge, MA: Harvard University Press, 1993); and Anthea D. Butler, *Women in the Church of God in Christ: Making a Sanctified World* (Chapel Hill: University of North Carolina Press, 2007).
3. Julius Bailey, *Around the Family Altar: Domesticity in the African Methodist Episcopal Church, 1865–1900* (Gainesville: University Press of Florida, 2005); and David W. Wills, "Womanhood and Domesticity in the A.M.E. Tradition: The Influence of Daniel Alexander Payne," in *Black Apostles at Home and Abroad: Afro-Americans*

and the Christian Mission from the Revolution to Reconstruction, ed. Richard Newman and David W. Wills (Boston: G. K. Hall, 1982), 133–146.
4. As particular Enlightenment thinkers like Immanuel Kant politically organized the European world in general, and European interiority in particular, over against racialized others. This project, argues Carter, was tied to a reconstitution of Christianity as "modernity's supreme rational religion" grounded in Christian supersessionism. J. Kameron Carter, *Race: A Theological Account* (Oxford: Oxford University Press, 2008).
5. Putney, *Muscular Christianity*, 1.
6. See Ann Douglas, "Ministers and Mothers," in *The Feminization of American Culture* (New York: Knopf, 1977).
7. Bederman, *Manliness & Civilization*.
8. Bederman, "The Women Have Had Charge of the Church Work Long Enough."
9. Luther Halsey Gulick, *Philosophy of Play* (New York: Charles Scribner's Sons, 1920), 92.
10. David Walker, *David Walker's Appeal, in Four Articles; Together with a Preamble to the Coloured Citizens of the World, but In Particular, and Very Expressly, to Those of the United States of America*, rev. ed., introduction by Sean Wilentz (New York: Hill and Wang, 1995), 71, 70.
11. Frederick Douglass, William L. Andrews, and William S. McFeely, *Narrative of the Life of Frederick Douglass, an American Slave, Written by Himself: Authoritative Text, Contexts, Criticism*, 1st ed. (New York: Norton, 1996), 15.
12. Jenny Jenny Franchot, "The Punishment of Esther: Frederick Douglass and the Construction of the Feminine," in *Frederick Douglass: New Literary and Historical Essays*, ed. Eric Sundquist (Cambridge: Cambridge University Press, 1990), 149.
13. Eddie S. Glaude, *Exodus! Religion, Race, and Nation in Early Nineteenth-Century Black America* (Chicago: University of Chicago Press, 2000), 144.
14. Henry Highland Garnet, "An Address to the Slaves of the United States of America (Rejected by the National Convention, 1843)" https://digitalcommons.unl.edu/cgi/viewcontent.cgi?article=1007&context=etas. The quote appears on pp. 5–6.
15. Julius Bailey, *Around the Family Altar*, 44.
16. Bailey, *Around the Family Altar*, 45. Historian David Wills notes the connection between Payne's efforts to improve the educational standards of the clergy and opposition to female evangelist Jarena Lee. "There surely can be little doubt," Wills writes, "that the segment of the city's A.M.E. community that wished to push Jarena Lee out significantly overlapped with the segment that would shortly draw Daniel Alexander Payne in." Wills, "Womanhood and Domesticity," 138.
17. Editorial, "Manliness in Preaching," *Christian Recorder* (1861)

18. Douglas, *The Feminization of American Culture*. Edward J. Blum and Paul Harvey, *The Color of Christ: The Son of God & the Saga of Race in America* (Chapel Hill: University of North Carolina Press, 2012).
19. Franchot, "The Punishment of Esther," 144.
20. James Jasinski, "Constituting Antebellum African Identity: Resistance, Violence, and Masculinity in Henry Highland Garnet's (1843) 'Address to the Slaves,'" *Quarterly Journal of Speech*, 93 (2007): 27–57.

    James Jasinski argues that Garnet's address "negotiated the disjunctive logics of submission/resistance, emasculation/brutish violence, and 'suffering servant'/'avenging messiah' by drawing on and exploiting the resources of these and other performative traditions in order to fashion a tertium quid, a middle course of action capable of constituting a new mode of African American agency" (27). In this way, Jasinksi builds upon Glaude's argument by priviliging the ways agency and masculinity were inextricably linked in this mid-nineteenth-century discourse.
21. Lois E. Horton and James Oliver Horton, "Violence, Protest, and Identity: Black Manhood in Antebellum America," in *Free People of Color: Inside the African American Community*, ed. James Oliver Horton (Washington, DC: Smithsonian Institution Press, 1993), 80.
22. Maria W. Stewart and Marilyn Richardson, *Maria W. Stewart, America's First Black Woman Political Writer: Essays and Speeches* (Bloomington: Indiana University Press, 1987), 57.
23. David Ruggles, "National Reform Convention," *Liberator* (Boston) August 13, 1841.
24. Ruggles, "National Reform Convention."
25. Jasinski, "Consituting Antebellum African Identity."

5. Everybody Knew He Was "That Way": Chicago's Clarence H. Cobbs, American Religion, and Sexuality During the Post–World War II Period

1. "Mac Jones' Widow to Wed Rev. Cobbs," *Chicago Defender*, January 13, 1945; *The Pittsburgh Courier*, January 20, 1945.
2. Mac Jones was one-third of the infamous Jones brothers, a trio of African American businessmen/mobsters who built a financial empire on Chicago's South Side during the 1920s and 1930s. The Jones brothers, however, did not care much for the black Chicagoans from which they amassed their fortunes. Their businesses did not employ blacks, and all those in key positions in their empire were white. See John William Touhy and Ed Baker, "The Legend of Tommy Roe," *Chicago Defender*, July 29, 1944.

3. Davarian L. Baldwin, *Chicago's New Negroes: Modernity, the Great Migration, and Black Urban Life* (Chapel Hill: University of North Carolina Press, 2007), 50.
4. The unsavory incident was undoubtedly the one in which a young man allegedly had to undergo reconstructive surgery on his genitals after an encounter with Cobbs. The rumor quickly spread that Cobbs had severely bitten the young man's penis. Some accounts even state that the young man died from his injuries. "State's Attorney Probes Scandal on Rev. Cobbs," *Chicago Defender*, November 25, 1939; "Six Sleuths Put on Trial of Shocking Rumors in Rev. Cobbs Scandal," *Chicago Defender*, December 2, 1939; *Pittsburgh Courier*, January 27, 1940; and David Jones, independent scholar, phone interview, Princeton University, October 27, 2010.
5. David Jones, phone interview, Princeton University, February 14, 2011.
6. "Radio Pastor Sues *Defender* for $250,000," *Chicago Defender*, December 9, 1939; "Cobbs Settles Libel Suit," *Chicago Defender*, March 22, 1941; St. Sukie de la Croix, *Chicago Whispers: A History of LGBT Chicago Before Stonewall* (Madison: University of Wisconsin Press, 2012), 157.
7. Michael Musto, "The Glass Closet: Why the Stars Won't Come Out and Play," *Out*, October 2007.
8. Jim Elledge, *The Boys of Fairy Town: Sodomites, Female Impersonators, Third-Sexers, Pansies, Queers, and Sex Morons in Chicago's First Century* (Chicago: Chicago Review Press, 2018), xviii.
9. bell hooks, *Talking Back: Thinking Feminist, Thinking*, 2nd ed. (New York: Routledge, 2014), 126.
10. *Chicago Defender*, January 18, 1965.
11. James R. Grossman, *Land of Hope: Chicago, Black Southerners, and the Great Migration* (Chicago: University of Chicago Press, 1991); Nicholas Lemann, *The Promised Land: The Great Migration and How It Changed America* (New York: Vintage, 1992); and Wallace D. Best, *Passionately Human, No Less Divine: Religion and Culture in Black Chicago, 1915–1952* (Princeton, NJ: Princeton University Press, 2005).
12. Although the precise origins of the church remain unclear, its origins in Chicago most likely came by way of a woman named Mother Leafy Anderson, the pioneering Spiritual teacher who is most noted for establishing the Spiritual church in New Orleans in 1920. This is why Horace Cayton and St. Clair Drake's assertion that "the spiritualist [*sic*] denomination seems to have been born in New Orleans and transplanted to [Chicago's] Bronzeville," is incorrect. In actual fact, beginning in 1913, Mother Leafy Anderson spent a number of years in Chicago, where she established Spiritual churches and missions before heading to New Orleans. A woman by the name of Mother Della Hedgepath introduced Cobbs to the Spiritual church not long after his arrival in Chicago, and she had most likely come to the church through Mother Leafy Anderson. Horace Cayton and St. Clair Drake, *Black Metropolis: A Study of Negro Life in*

a *Northern City* (Chicago: University of Chicago Press, 1993); Claude F. Jacobs and Andrew J. Kaslow, *The Spiritual Churches of New Orleans: Origins, Beliefs, and Rituals of an African-American Religion* (Knoxville: University of Tennessee Press, 1991), 33.

13. Bailey's design was a ground-hugging, expansive structure of simple lines, flat roofs, rounded edges, and no ornamentation. The exterior material was glazed terra cotta, which as a relatively inexpensive material had become popular during the difficult economic times of the 1930s. It would be Bailey's last major project. He died in 1941. See *African American Architects: A Biographical Dictionary, 1865–1945* (New York: Routledge, 2004), 23–25; Lee Bey, "Black Designer All But Forgotten," *Chicago Sun Times*, February 9, 1998.
14. *Chicago Defender*, July 5, 1953.
15. "Preach, Sing, and Praise the Lord," *Chicago Tribune*, June 11, 1972.
16. Hans A. Baer, "The Limited Empowerment of Women in Black Spiritual Churches: An Alternative Vehicle to Religious Leadership," *Sociology of Religion* 54, no. 1 (1993): 71.
17. "Metropolitan Spiritual Churches of Christ, Inc. Chicago, Illinois, Forty-Fifth Annual Congress, President's Annual Message," 1970. Document in possession of author.
18. O. Winkfield, "The First Church of Deliverance (Spiritualist)," WPA Files, Federal Writers Project, Box A125, Library of Congress.
19. David Jones, interview with the author, February 14, 2011.
20. Patricia Anne Smothers, "History and Beliefs of the Metropolitan Spiritual Church of Christ, Incorporated" (MDiv thesis, Ashland Theological Seminary, 1987), 9–11.
21. *Chicago Defender*, June 4, 1938.
22. "Preach, Sing, and Praise the Lord," *Chicago Tribune*, June 11, 1972.
23. "Preliminary Staff Summary of Information," First Church of Deliverance, Chicago Commission on Landmarks, 1994. Document in possession of author.
24. "Interview: Rev. Cobbs," Illinois Historical Library, Federal Writers' Project, Box 187, Springfield, IL.
25. "Noted Chicago Pastor, Clarence Cobbs, 71, Dies," *Jet*, July 19, 1979.
26. "Metropolitan Spiritual Churches of Christ, Inc. Chicago, Illinois, Forty-Fifth Annual Congress, President's Annual Message," 1970. Document in possession of author.
27. Robert M. Marovich, *A City Called Heaven: Chicago and the Birth of Gospel Music* (Urbana: University of Illinois Press, 2015), 64–70.
28. Some sources give Cobbs credit for composing this song, but he clearly did not write it. It was composed by Rev. Herbert W. Brewster in 1949, made famous, first, by Clara Ward and then immortalized by Mahalia Jackson, who sang it at

the 1963 March on Washington. Anthony Heilbut, author interview, New York City, January 6, 2014.
29. "Noted Chicago Pastor, Clarence Cobbs, 71, Dies," *Jet*, July 19, 1979.
30. *Chicago Defender*, April 11, 1942.
31. "Preliminary Staff Summary of Information, First Church of Deliverance, Chicago Commission on Landmarks, 1994." Document in possession of author.
32. "First Church of Deliverance (Spiritual) Interview: Rev. Cobbs," Illinois Historical Library, Federal Writers Project, Box 187, Folder "First Church of Deliverance (Ed. Copy1)"; *Chicago Defender*, December 2, 1939.
33. "A Challenge by Lloyd Davis," *Chicago Defender*, November 30, 1946.
34. Sukie de la Croix, "Cobbs and First Church of Deliverance" document in possession of author.
35. "Interview: Rev. Cobbs," Illinois Historical Library, Federal "Writers' Project, Box 187, Springfield, IL; Best, *Passionately Human, No Less Divine*, 43; *Chicago Defender*, September 2, 1939; *Chicago Defender*, December 6, 1940.
36. "Praises Rev. Cobb," *Chicago Defender*, January 25, 1947; "Doing an Excellent Job," *Chicago Defender*, February 22, 1947.
37. David Jones, phone interview, Princeton University, February 14, 2011.
38. Steven Seidman, *Beyond the Closet: The Transformation of Gay and Lesbian Life* (New York: Routledge, 2003), 25 and 30; and Eve Kosofsky Sedgwick, *Epistemology of the Closet* (Oakland: University of California Press, 2008), 71 and 68, respectively.
39. Musto, "The Glass Closet," 52–54.
40. Sukie de la Croix, from email document compiled from *Chicago Whispers* and *Black Pearls*. Document in possession of author.
41. George Chauncey, *Gay New York: Gender, Urban Culture, and the Making of the Gay Male World, 1890–1940* (New York: Basic Books, 1994), 3; David K. Johnson, "The Kids of Fairytown: Gay Male Culture on Chicago's Near North Side in the 1930s," in *Creating a Place for Ourselves: Lesbian, Gay, and Bisexual Community Histories*, ed. Brett Beemyn (New York: Routledge, 1997), 101; and Allen Drexel, "Before Paris Burned: Race, Class, and Male Homosexuality on the South Side of Chicago, 1935–1950," in Beemyn, *Creating a Place for Ourselves*, 121.
42. Best, *Passionately Human, No Less Divine*, 188, 8n; Hans A. Baer, "The Limited Empowerment of Women in Black Spiritualist Churches," *Sociology of Religion* 54, no. 1 (1993): 76; Mick Dumke, "Give Us Our Daley Bread," *Chicago Reader*, November 8, 2007; and "Bishop Lucius Hall Elevated to Archbishop," *Chicago Crusader*, July 24, 2010.
43. David Jones, phone interview with the author, Princeton University, March 28, 2011.
44. Sukie de la Croix, "Excerpts from an Interview with a 67-Year-old African American Gay Man," document in possession of the author.
45. Chauncey, *Gay New York*, 53; *Chicago Defender*, April 11, 1942.

46. Hans A. Baer, "The Metropolitan Spiritual Churches of Christ: The Socio-Religious Evolution of the Largest of the Black Spiritual Associations," *Review of Religious Research* 30, no. 2 (December, 1988): 142.
47. In February 1940 police arrested William F. Taylor who had been found in a parked car with a "24-year-old male companion" in a secluded area in Kansas City. After questioning the young man, police went to Taylor's home where they found Boswell, arresting him and another young man. The two young men, members of Metropolitan Spiritualist, confessed (perhaps under duress) that they had been paid between $2.50 and $5 each time to "consort" with Taylor and Boswell and had been doing so for a number of years. Taylor, they said, had threatened them with death if they told anyone about it. While Taylor was being held, police found what they determined to be suicide notes in Taylor's cell. Both men were eventually paroled on two-year sentences. See *Chicago Defender*, February 24, 1940; *Afro-American* February 24, 1940; *Chicago Defender*, March 2, 1940; *Chicago Defender*, March 28, 1942.
48. United States Census, 1930; Annie Turnbo Malone, *Madam C. J. Walker's Role Model: Entrepreneur, Annie Malone* (Gambrills, MD: Freeman, 2014).
49. *Chicago Defender*, February 16, 1946.
50. *Pittsburgh Courier*, January 21, 1939; IHL, FWP, Box 187.
51. *Pittsburgh Courier*, January 23, 1943. The article states that Cobbs was taking the trip with his "Boxer Secretary" Nate Bolden, mistaking Edward Bolden for the Chicago-area middleweight boxer by that name.
52. David Jones, interview with the author, March 28, 2011; *The Chicago Defender*, May 24, 1958.
53. *New York Amsterdam News*, December 15, 1945.
54. "Coast Notes," *Afro-American*, December 4, 1943.
55. Stephanie Coontz, *Marriage, A History: How Love Conquered Marriage* (New York: Penguin, 2006); and Nancy F. Cott, *Public Vows: A History of Marriage and the Nation* (Cambridge, MA: Harvard University Press, 2002).
56. Stephanie Coontz, *The Way We Never Were: American Families and the Nostalgia Trip* (New York: Basic, 1992), 24.
57. Margot Canaday, *The Straight State: Sexuality and Citizenship in Twentieth-Century America* (Princeton, NJ: Princeton University Press, 2009), 95.
58. Coontz, *The Way We Never Were*, 25.
59. Coontz, *The Way We Never Were*, 25.
60. John D'Emilio, *Sexual Politics, Sexual Communities: The Making of a Homosexual Minority in the United States, 1940–1970* (Chicago: University of Chicago Press, 1983), 24. See also Allan Berube, *Coming Out Under Fire: A History of Gay Men and Women in World War Two* (New York: Penguin, 1990).
61. Neil Miller, *Out of the Past: Gay and Lesbian History from 1869 to the Present* (New York: Vintage, 1995), 247.

62. Seidman, *Beyond the Closet*, 14–15.
63. D'Emilio, *Sexual Politics, Sexual Communities*, 17.
64. Miller, *Out of the Past*, 247.
65. Kinsey's two groundbreaking studies on male and female sexuality were published in 1948 and 1953 respectively. See Jonathan Gathorne-Hardy, *Kinsey: Sex the Measure of All Things* (Bloomington: Indiana University Press, 2004); James H. Jones, *Alfred C. Kinsey: A Life* (New York: Norton, 2004).
66. John D'Emilio and Estelle Freedman, *Intimate Matters: A History of Sexuality in America* (New York: Harper and Row, 1988), 288.
67. Seidman, *Beyond the Closet*, 26.
68. David Johnson, *Buying Gay: How Physique Entrepreneurs Sparked a Movement* (New York: Columbia University Press, 2019).
69. St. Clair Drake, Horace R. Clayton, and Mary Pattillo (foreword), *Black Metropolis: A Study of Negro Life in a Northern City* (Chicago: University of Chicago Press, 2015); Baer, "The Metropolitan Spiritual Churches of Christ," 146.
70. Sukie de la Croix, "The Mark IV in the Early 70s, by Ray Thomas as told to Sukie de la Croix." Document in possession of author.
71. Sukie de la Croix, "Young, Black and Gay in the 1960s," and "Anonymous Man." Documents in possession of author.
72. Sukie de la Croix, "Excerpts from an Interview with Chicago Drag legend, Ebony Carr" and "The Alley." Documents in possession of author.
73. Marybeth Hamilton, "Sexual Politics and African American Music: Or, Placing Little Richard in History," *History Workshop Journal* 46 (1998): 160–176; Horace Griffin, "Their Own Received Them Not: African American Lesbians and Gays in Black Churches," in *The Greatest Taboo: Homosexuality in Black Communities*, ed. Delroy Constantine-Simms (New York: Alyson, 2000), 110.
74. Thomas B. Romney, "Homophobia in the Black Community," *Blacklight* 1(1980), 4; Michael Long, "Stop the Silence, Bernice King," *Washington Blade*, October 14, 2010, www.washingtonblade.com/2010/10/14/stop-the-silence-bernice-king.

6. Interrogating the Passionate and the Pious: Televangelism and Black Women's Sexuality

Selections in this chapter appeared in Monique Moultrie, *Passionate and Pious: Religious Media and Black Women's Sexuality* (Durham: Duke University Press, 2017).

1. Beyoncé, "Single Ladies (Put a Ring on It)," CD, track 8, on *I Am . . . Sasha Fierce*, Sony BMG Music Entertainment, 2008.

2. Kimberly Davis, "Sex and the Spirit: SOS for Single Christian Sisters," *Ebony*, January 2005, 108. See also Julie Zauzmer, "ChristianMingle Now Allows Gays Dating, After a Lawsuit," *Washington Post*, July 7, 2016. According to a Sparks Network press release, the founder of Christian Mingle and J-Date has recently merged with Elite Singles and Zoosk, Inc., to become the second-largest online dating provider in North America. "Press Release," Sparks Network, March 21, 2019, https://www.spark.net/news-releases/news-release-details/spark-networks-se-enters-definitive-agreement-acquire-zoosk-1.
3. Most recent texts exploring religious media do not address sexuality, with the exception of Marla Frederick, *Colored Television: American Religion Gone Global*. (Stanford, CA: Stanford University Press, 2016); and Monique Moultrie, *Passionate and Pious: Religious Media and Black Women's Sexuality* (Durham, NC: Duke University Press, 2017). For example, contemporary scholarship on televangelism neglecting to address faith-based sexuality ministries includes Denis Bekkering, *American Televangelism and Participatory Cultures: Fans, Brands, and Play with Religious Fakes* (New York: Palgrave Macmillan, 2018); Paula McGee, *Brand New Theology: The Wal-Martization of T. D. Jakes and the New Black Church* (Maryknoll, NY: Orbis, 2017); Phillip Luke Sinitiere, *Salvation with a Smile: Joel Osteen, Lakewood Church, and American Christianity* (New York: New York University Press, 2017); and Carolyn Rouse, John Jackson, and Marla Frederick, *Televised Redemption: Black Religious Media and Racial Empowerment* (New York: New York University Press, 2016).
4. Marla Frederick, "'But It's Bible': African American Women and Television Preachers," in *Women and Religion in the African Diaspora*, ed. R. Marie Griffith and Barbara Dianne Savage (Baltimore: Johns Hopkins University Press, 2006), 283.
5. Jonathan L. Walton, "Response to Joseph de León," in *Creating Ourselves: African Americans and Hispanic Americans on Popular Culture and Religious Expression*, ed. Anthony Pinn and Benjamin Valentin (Durham, NC: Duke University Press, 2009), 272.
6. Rosalind Bentley, "For 'Prophetess' of True Romance, Marriage a Mess," *Atlanta Journal-Constitution*, August 26, 2007, http://www.religionnewsblog.com/19144/juanita-bynum-8. According to the 2000 U.S. Census, just 31 percent of black women were married, the lowest proportion of all races. Jesse D. McKinnon and Claudette E. Bennett, "We the People: Blacks in the United States," Census 2000 Special Reports, August 2005, http://www.census.gov/prod/2005pubs/censr-25.pdf, 5. By the 2010 census, the percentage of black women who were married had declined still further, to 26 percent. "African American Women," Black Demographics, accessed June 1, 2021, http://blackdemographics.com/population/black-women-statistics/.
7. Pat Burson, "Evangelist with a Big Stick," *Newsday*, October 23, 2004, http://www.religionnewsblog.com/9080/evangelist-with-a-big-stick.

8. *No More Sheets*, DVD, produced by Juanita Bynum (Waycross, GA: Juanita Bynum Ministries, 1998).
9. John Storey, "Introduction to Part Three: Structuralism and Poststructuralism," in *Cultural Theory and Popular Culture: A Reader*, ed. John Storey (New York: Prentice Hall, 1998), 97.
10. Juanita Bynum, *No More Sheets: The Truth About Sex* (Lanham, MD: Pneuma Life, 1998), 157.
11. Frederick, "'But It's Bible,'" 283.
12. Ty Adams, *Single, Saved, and Having Sex* (New York: Walk Worthy, 2006), 19.
13. Adams, *Single, Saved, and Having Sex*, 26. Ty Adams, "Sexual Sin," UnitedToDance, June 16, 2016, 13:24, https://www.youtube.com/watch?v=NCvggXQ3i7w.
14. Adams, *Single, Saved, and Having Sex*, 18–19.
15. Adams, *Single, Saved, and Having Sex*, 24–25.
16. Adams, *Single, Saved, and Having Sex*, 98.
17. This is an ongoing process as they both continue to share their testimonies. For example, in July 2012, Juanita Bynum redefined her sexual testimony to include having had sexual relationships with women. During February 2019, Ty Adams used her YouTube channel to chronicle single dating adventures. See https://www.huffpost.com/entry/juanita-bynum-ive-been-with-women_n_1683529 and https://www.youtube.com/watch?v=kYq9rXdhyGg.
18. Bobby Chris Alexander, *Televangelism Reconsidered: Ritual in the Search for Human Community*, American Academy of Religion Studies in Religion (Atlanta, GA: Scholars Press, 1994), 23.
19. Jacqueline Bobo, "The Color Purple: Black Women as Cultural Readers," in Storey, *Cultural Theory and Popular Culture*, 312.
20. Marla Frederick, *Between Sundays: Black Women and Everyday Struggles of Faith* (Berkeley: University of California Press, 2003), 196.
21. Tricia Rose, *Longing to Tell: Black Women Talk about Sexuality and Intimacy* (New York: Farrar, Straus and Giroux, 2003), 395.
22. Frederick, *Between Sundays*, 194.
23. Renita J. Weems, *What Matters Most: Ten Lessons in Living Passionately from the Song of Solomon* (New York: Walk Worthy, 2004), 17–18.
24. Traci West, "A Space for Faith, Sexual Desire, and Ethical Black Ministerial Practices," in *Loving the Body: Black Religious Studies and the Erotic*, ed. Anthony B. Pinn and Dwight Hopkins (New York: Palgrave Macmillan, 2004), 39.
25. Robert Michael Franklin, *Another Day's Journey: Black Churches Confronting the American Crisis* (Minneapolis: Fortress, 1997), 79–80.
26. Katie Cannon, "Sexing Black Women: Liberation from the Prisonhouse of Anatomical Authority," in Pinn and Hopkins, *Loving the Body*, 17.

7. The Self-Interested Politics of Collective Religious Transformation: Issues of Family Definition and LGBT Inclusion in Black Churches

1. The legal scholar Catherine Smith uses theories from social psychology to explore the concerns of black LGBT people in her article, "Queer as Black Folk?" *Wisconsin Law Review* 379 (2007). She points to the ways that discrimination based on intersecting identities can be missed by each of the communities that black LGBT should find themselves in solidarity. Smith's primary examples of the ways in which black LGBT find themselves particularly disadvantaged draw from family law issues and other legal areas where the definition of *family* condition who receives state benefits.
2. Jane Mansbridge and Katherine Tate, "Race Trumps Gender: The Thomas Nomination in the Black Community," *PS: Political Science and Politics* 25, no. 3 (September 1992): 488–492. Gay and Tate "Doubly Bound", Cohen and Dawson work looking at poor blacks
3. Katherine Tate, *From Protest to Politics: The New Black Voters in American Elections* (Cambridge, MA: Harvard University Press, 1993).
4. Katherine Tate, "1996 National Black Election Study: Survey Respondents Report," typescript, 1996
5. Michael C. Dawson, *Behind the Mule: Race and Class in African-American Politics* (Princeton, NJ: Princeton University Press, 1994).
6. Cathy J. Cohen, *The Boundaries of Blackness: AIDS and the Breakdown of Black Politics* (Chicago: University of Chicago Press, 1999).
7. This quotation is drawn from Booker T. Washington's famous speech at the Cotton States Exchange and International Exposition in 1895. It would later come to be known as the Atlanta Compromise Speech because of the location of the gathering and Washington's call for accommodation rather than resistance to the white supremacist racial order.
8. Cohen, *The Boundaries of Blackness*, 75
9. Allison Calhoun-Brown, "African American Churches and Political Mobilization: The Psychological Impact of Organizational Resources," *Journal of Politics* 58, no. 4 (November 1996): 935–953.
10. Melanye T. Price, *Dreaming Blackness: Black Nationalism and African American Public Opinion* (New York: New York University Press, 2009), 5. More recently, the Pew Research Center has published some research about the percentage of African Americans who support marriage equality (2015 and 2017: http://www.people-press.org/2017/06/26/support-for-same-sex-marriage-grows-even-among-groups-that-had-been-skeptical/), and in 2017 PRRI found that blacks had the highest recognition of LGBT discrimination of any racial group. Daniel

Cox, Rachel Lienesch, Robert P. Jones, "Who Sees Discrimination? Attitudes on Sexual Orientation, Gender Identity, Race, and Immigration Status: Findings from PRRI's American Values Atlas," PPRI, June 21, 2017, https://www.prri.org/research/americans-views-discrimination-immigrants-blacks-lgbt-sex-marriage-immigration-reform/.

11. Survey results from 2017 show that nearly three-quarters of black Americans believe that gays and lesbians (73 percent) and transgender persons (72 percent) "face a lot of discrimination" as compared to whites who believe that gays and lesbians (54 percent) and transgender people (59 percent) face a significant amount of discrimination. Cox, Lienesch, and Jones, "Who Sees Discrimination?"
12. Cox, Lienesch, and Jones, "Who Sees Discrimination?" African Americans having the highest opposition to allowing small business owners to discriminate against gays and lesbians was found in the 2015 survey and in 2017.
13. Krissah Williams, "Politics of Race and Religion: Moral Issues Leave Black Evangelicals Between Parties," *Washington Post*, November 26, 2007.
14. Allison Calhoun-Brown, "African American Churches and Political Mobilization: The Psychological Impact of Organizational Resources" *Journal of Politics* 58, no. 4 (November 1996): 935–953.
15. Calhoun-Brown defines a political church as a church distinct from others because of its provision of space where politicization can take place and because political ministers largely lead them. Calhoun-Brown measures political churches by whether or not respondents recalled having heard political announcements at church. Calhoun-Brown, "African American Churches," 941, 951.
16. Michael Gryboski, "United Methodist Megachurch in Texas May Leave UMC Over Ongoing Internal Debates," *Christian Post*, July 12, 2018, https://www.christianpost.com/news/united-methodist-megachurch-in-texas-may-leave-umc-over-ongoing-internal-debates.html.
17. Linda Young, "High-Achieving Black Women and Marriage: Not Choosing or Not Chosen," *Psychology Today*, June 14, 2010, https://www.psychologytoday.com/us/blog/love-in-limbo/201006/high-achieving-black-women-and-marriage-not-choosing-or-not-chosen.
18. Melynda J. Price, "As Marriage Expands, So Does Singlehood," *New York Times*, July 6, 2015, https://www.nytimes.com/roomfordebate/2015/07/06/has-being-single-in-america-changed/as-marriage-expands-so-does-singlehood.

8. Intersectional Invisibility and the Experience of Ontological Exclusion: The Case of Black Gay Christians

1. Cara Mia DiMassa and Jessica Garrison, "Why Gays, Blacks Are Divided on Prop 8," *Los Angeles Times*, November 8, 2008.

2. Karl Vick and Ashley Surdin, "Most of California's Black Voters Backed Gay Marriage Ban," *Washington Post*, November 7, 2008.
3. Kimberle Crenshaw, "Mapping the Margins: Intersectionality, Identity Politics, and Violence against Women of Color," *Stanford Law Review* 43, no. 6 (1991): 1241–1299.
4. Mignon R. Moore, "Articulating a Politics of (Multiple) Identities," *Du Bois Review* 7, no. 2 (2010): 1–20.
5. Michael Eric Dyson, "When you Divide Body and Soul Problems Multiply: The Black Church and Sex," in *Traps: African American Men on Gender and Sexuality*, ed. Rudolph Byrd and Beverly Guy-Sheftall (Bloomington, IN: Indiana University Press, 2001), 308–326.
6. Crenshaw, "Mapping the Margins."
7. Mignon Moore, *Invisible Families: Gay Identities, Relationships, and Motherhood among Black Women* (Berkeley: University of California Press, 2011).
8. Moore, *Invisible Families*.
9. William G. Hawkeswood and Alex. W. Costley, *One of the Children: Gay Black Men in Harlem* (Oakland: University of California Press, 1996), 107.
10. Quoted in Gary D. Comstock, *A Whosoever Church: Welcoming Lesbians and Gay Men into African American Congregations* (Louisville, KY: Westminster John Knox, 2001), 62.
11. Cathy J. Cohen, *The Boundaries of Blackness: AIDS and the Breakdown of Black Politics* (Chicago: University of Chicago Press, 1997), 285.
12. Quoted in Keith Boykin, *One More River to Cross: Black and Gay in America* (New York: Doubleday, 1996), 119.
13. Boykin, *One More River to Cross*, 285.
14. Hawkeswood and Costley, *One of the Children*, 39.
15. For a pioneering psychological study in this regard, see Patricia Devine, "Stereotypes and Prejudice: Their Automatic and Controlled Components" *Journal of Personality and Social Psychology* 56, no. 1 (1989): 5–18.
16. Ian Hacking, *Historical Ontology* (Cambridge, MA: Harvard University Press, 2002).
17. Cohen, *The Boundaries of Blackness*, 12.
18. Sandra Lipsitz Bem, *The Lenses of Gender: Transforming the Debate on Sexual Inequality* (New Haven, CT: Yale University Press, 1991).
19. Adrienne Rich, *Blood, Bread, and Poetry: Selected Prose, 1979–1985* (New York: Norton, 1986).
20. Allan Bérubé, *Coming Out Under Fire: The History of Gay Men and Women in World War 2* (New York: Free Press, 2000), 246.
21. Steven Seidman, *Beyond the Closet: The Transformation of Gay and Lesbian Life* (New York: Routledge, 2002), 41–42.
22. Cohen, *The Boundaries of Blackness*, 14.

23. Seidman, *Beyond the Closet*, 42. See also Elizabeth A. Armstrong, *Forging Gay Identities: Organizing Sexuality in San Francisco, 1950–1994* (Chicago: University of Chicago Press, 2002).
24. Seidman. *Beyond the Closet*, 42.
25. Seidman. *Beyond the Closet*, 43.
26. Roy F. Baumeister and Mark R. Leary, "The Need to Belong: Desire for Interpersonal Attachments as Fundamental Human Motivation," *Psychological Bulletin* 117, no. 3 (1995): 497.
27. Armstrong, *Forging Gay Identities*.
28. Audre Lorde, *Sister Outsider: Essays and Speeches* (Berkeley, CA: Crossing Press, 1989), 120.
29. A. Sedlovskaya, V. Purdie-Vaughns, R. Eibach, M. LaFrance, R. Romero-Canyas, and M. Camp, "Internalizing the Closet: Stigma Concealment Heightens the Cognitive Distinction Between Public and Private Selves," *Journal of Personality and Social Psychology* 104, no. 4 (2013): 695–715.
30. Valerie Purdie-Vaughns, Claude M. Steele, Patricia G. Davies, Ruth Ditlmann, and Jennifer R. Crosby, "Social Identity Contingencies: How Diversity Cues Signal Threat or Safety for African Americans in Mainstream Institutions," *Journal of Personality and Social Psychology* 94, no. 4 (2008): 615.
31. Purdie-Vaughns, et al., "Social Identity Contingencies."
32. Amin Ghaziani, *The Dividends of Dissent: How Conflict and Culture Work in Lesbian and Gay Marches on Washington* (Chicago: University of Chicago Press, 2008).
33. Ghaziani, *The Dividends of Dissent*, 266, 267.
34. Moore, *Invisible Families*.
35. Robert D. Putnam and David E. Campbell, *American Grace: How Religion Divides and Unites Us* (New York: Simon and Schuster, 2010), 137.
36. Putnam and Campbell, *American Grace*, 278.
37. Edwin Sanders, "New Folks Say, 'I Got Here and I Just Felt Like No One Was Looking at Me Strange, No One Was Treating Me Different, I Was Just Able to Be Here,'" in *A Whosoever Church: Welcoming Lesbians and Gay Men into African American Congregations*, ed. Gary D. Comstock (Louisville, KY: Westminster John Knox, 2001), 139–151.
38. Bayard Rustin, "Time on Two Crosses: An Interview with George Chauncey, Jr.," in *Time on Two Crosses: The Collected Writings of Bayard Rustin*, ed. Devon W. Carbado and Donald Weise (Paris: Cleis, 2003), 299–305.

9. Gay *Is* the New Black, Theologically Speaking

1. Other issues include school choice, affordable health care, and "wealth creation." Ellen Barry, "Atlanta 'Legacy' March Troubles Rights Leaders; King's Daughter in

Anti-Gay Marriage Protest," *San Francisco Chronicle*, December 11, 2004, http://www.sfgate.com/cgi-bin/article.cgi?f=/c/a/2004/12/11/MNGPDAAEJ01.DTL.
2. Many people attribute this phrasing to fashion designer Gianfranco Ferre when quoted in a March 1983 article in the *Los Angeles Times*.
3. James H. Cone, *A Black Theology of Liberation* (Maryknoll, NY: Orbis, 1990).
4. Victor B. Anderson, *Beyond Ontological Blackness: An Essay in African American Religious and Cultural Criticism* (New York: Continuum, 1995).
5. By July 2019, these issues were cause for a major split with the United Methodist Church. No historically black denomination has an inclusive approach to the ordination of openly GLBTQI clergy nor do they sanction same-gender marriages performed by their ordained clergy.
6. Horace L. Griffin, *Their Own Receive Them Not: African American Lesbians and Gays in Black Churches* (Cleveland, OH: Pilgrim, 2006).
7. M. H. Morton, A. Dworsky, and G. M. Samuels, *Missed Opportunities: Youth Homelessness in America. National Estimates* (Chicago: Chapin Hall at the University of Chicago, 2017).
8. "Preventing Suicide: Facts About Suicide," Trevor Project, accessed July 24, 2019, https://www.thetrevorproject.org/resources/preventing-suicide/facts-about-suicide/
9. "Preventing Suicide: Facts About Suicide," Trevor Project.
10. That is, it's hard to go back and "prove" someone was GLBTQ-identified or practicing if that person never made public or written declarations of such. There is also little evidence that there is a direct relationship between knowledge of significant GLBTQ African American historical figures and openness to the full inclusion of GLBTQ persons in African American churches and society. See Roger Sneed, "Beyond 'The Down Low': Constructing Black Gay Male Identity Beyond Problem and Plague," Men's Studies in Religion Group and Black Theology Group and Womanist Approaches to Religion and Society Group, Annual Meeting of the American Academy of Religion, Chicago, IL, November 1, 2008.
11. Dwight Hopkins, *Being Human: Race, Culture, and Religion* (Minneapolis: Fortress Press, 2005); Emilie M. Townes, *Womanist Ethics and the Cultural Production of Evil* (New York: Palgrave Macmillan, 2006); Victor Anderson, *Creative Exchange: A Constructive Theology of African American Religious Experience* (Minneapolis: Fortress Press, 2008); and Brian Bantum, *Redeeming Mulatto: a Theology of Race and Christian Hybridity* (Waco, TX: Baylor University Press, 2010).
12. See Monica A. Coleman, *The Dinah Project: a Handbook for Congregational Response to Sexual Violence*, 2004 (Eugene, OR: Wipf and Stock, 2010).
13. Justin Edward Tanis, *Trans-Gendered: Theology, Ministry and Communities of Faith* (Cleveland, OH: Pilgrim, 2003).

14. "Mission and Vision," Reconciling Ministries Network, accessed September 15, 2010, http://www.rmnetwork.org/about/who-we-are/.
15. Also known as "gay pride parades," "pride events," and "pride festivals," pride parades celebrate GLBTQ cultures. They often also highlight legal issues that concern GLBTQ communities. They usually occur annually.
16. Two examples include City of Refuge United Church of Christ, founded by Bishop Yvette Flunder and Unity Fellowship Church Movement by Rev. Carl Bean.

10. Flesh That Needs to be Loved: Wounded Black Bodies and Preachin' in the Spirit

1. Cheryl Townsend Gilkes, "The 'Loves' and 'Troubles' of African-American Women's Bodies," in *A Troubling in My Soul: Womanist Perspectives on Evil and Suffering*, ed. Emilie M. Townes (Maryknoll, NY: Orbis, 1993), 242.
2. M. Shawn Copeland, *Enfleshing Freedom: Body, Race, and Being* (Minneapolis: Fortress Press, 2010), 7.
3. Darnell L. Moore, "Theorizing the 'Black Body' as a Site of Trauma: Implications for Theologies of Embodiment," *Theology and Sexuality* 15, no. 2 (2009): 176.
4. Thomas H. Troeger, "Emerging New Standards in the Evaluation of Effective Preaching," *Worship* 64, no. 4 (1990): 294.
5. Richard F. Ward, *Speaking of the Holy: The Art of Communication in Preaching* (St. Louis: Chalice, 2001), 19.
6. Jon Michael Spencer, "Folk Preaching (African-American)," *Concise Encyclopedia of Preaching*, ed. William H. Willimon and Richard Lischer (Louisville, KY: Westminster John Knox, 1995), 142.
7. Throughout this article, "body" may refer to the black body as metaphor or the material reality of the black body. I say "basically" regarding the somatic silence because black homiletician Teresa Fry Brown deals with the body in a significant way in two important works related to the body and embodiment: *Weary Throat and New Songs: Black Women Proclaiming God's Word* (Nashville, TN: Abingdon, 2003) and *Delivering the Sermon: Voice, Body, and Animation in Proclamation* (Minneapolis: Fortress, 2008). Also, the more recent work of homiletician Lisa L. Thompson takes up the topic of the body, particularly related to the black woman's body. See her *Ingenuity: Preaching as an Outsider* (Nashville, TN: Abingdon, 2018).
8. Toni Morrison, *Playing in the Dark: Whiteness and the Literary Imagination* (Cambridge, MA: Harvard University Press, 1992), 10.
9. Anthony B. Pinn, *Embodiment and the New Shape of Black Theological Thought* (New York: New York University Press, 2010), 3.

10. Pinn, *Embodiment*, 4.
11. Barbara Brown Taylor, *An Altar in the World: A Geography of Faith* (New York: HarperCollins, 2009), 48.
12. Pinn, *Embodiment*, 97.
13. Copeland, *Enfleshing Freedom*, 1.
14. JoAnne Marie Terrell, *Power in the Blood? The Cross in the African American Experience* (Maryknoll, NY: Orbis, 1998), 34.
15. James Cone, "Strange Fruit: The Cross and the Lynching Tree," *African American Pulpit* 11, no. 2 (Spring 2008): 24.
16. See "Were You There?" in *Songs of Zion*, ed. Jefferson Cleveland (Nashville, TN: Abingdon, 1982), 126; James Weldon Johnson, "The Crucifixion," in *God's Trombones: Seven Negro Sermons in Verse* (New York: Penguin, 1927), 42.
17. N. Lynne Westfield, *Dear Sisters: A Womanist Practice of Hospitality* (Cleveland, OH: Pilgrim, 2007), 86.
18. See Luke 1:26–2:21.
19. W. E. B. DuBois, *The Souls of Black Folk* (New York: Penguin, 1969[orig. 1903]), 275.
20. Louis-Marie Chauvet, *The Sacraments: The Word of God at the Mercy of the Body* (Collegeville, MN: Liturgical Press, 2001), 114.
21. Louis-Marie Chauvet, "Editorial: Liturgy and the Body," in *Liturgy and the Body*, ed. Louis Chauvet and Francois Kabasele Lumbala (Maryknoll, NY: Orbis, 1995), viii.
22. Copeland, *Enfleshing Freedom*, 2.
23. Robert E. Hood, *Must God Remain Greek? Afro Cultures and God-Talk* (Minneapolis: Fortress, 1990), 204, 193.
24. Luke A. Powery, *Spirit Speech: Lament and Celebration in Preaching* (Nashville, TN: Abingdon, 2009), 10–14.
25. Joseph Murphy, *Working the Spirit: Ceremonies of the African Diaspora* (Boston: Beacon, 1995), 169–170, 173–174.
26. W. E. B. DuBois, *The Souls of Black Folk*, 211; Melva Costen, *African American Christian Worship* (Nashville, TN: Abingdon, 1993), 48–49.
27. Albert Raboteau, *Slave Religion: The "Invisible Institution" in the Antebellum South* (New York: Oxford University Press, 1978), 61–62.
28. Allen Dwight Callahan, *The Talking Book: African Americans and the Bible* (New Haven, CT: Yale University Press, 2008), 62.
29. C. Eric Lincoln and Lawrence Mamiya, *The Black Church in the African American Experience* (Durham, NC: Duke University Press, 1990), 6.
30. Callahan, *The Talking Book*, 62.
31. Anthony B. Pinn, *Terror and Triumph: The Nature of Black Religion* (Minneapolis: Fortress, 2003), 98.

32. Zora Neale Hurston, *The Sanctified Church* (Berkeley, CA: Turtle Island, 1983), 79.
33. Pinn, *Terror and Triumph*, 99.
34. Pinn, *Terror and Triumph*, 100.
35. Dolan Hubbard, *The Sermon and the African American Literary Imagination* (Columbia: University of Missouri Press, 1994), 2.
36. Anthony Pinn, "Reading the Signs: The Body as Non-Written Text," in *Being Black, Teaching Black: Politics and Pedagogy in Religious Studies*, ed. Nancy Lynne Westfield (Nashville, TN: Abingdon, 2008), 85.
37. Raboteau, *Slave Religion*, 237.
38. James Forbes, *The Holy Spirit and Preaching* (Nashville, TN: Abingdon, 1989), 19.
39. Pinn, "Reading the Signs," 87.
40. Taylor, *An Altar in the World*, 40.
41. James L. Empereur, "The Physicality of Worship," in *Bodies of Worship: Explorations in Theory and Practice*, ed. Bruce T. Morrill (Collegeville, MN: Liturgical Press, 1999), 145.
42. Anthony B. Pinn, "Black Theology, Black Bodies, and Pedagogy," *Cross Currents* 50, nos. 1/2(2000): 200; Teresa Fry Brown, *Delivering the Sermon: Voice, Body, and Animation in Proclamation* (Minneapolis; Fortress, 2008), 2.
43. Brown, *Delivering the Sermon*, 77.
44. Elochukwu E. Uzukwu, *Worship as Body Language: Introduction to Christian Worship, An African Orientation* (Collegeville, MN: Liturgical Press, 1997), 6.
45. Thomas G. Long, "And How Shall They Hear? The Listener in Contemporary Preaching," in *Listening to the Word: Studies in Honor of Fred B. Craddock*, ed. Gail R. O'Day and Thomas G. Long (Nashville, TN: Abingdon, 1993), 178.
46. Charles Rice, *The Embodied Word: Preaching as Art and Liturgy* (Minneapolis: Fortress, 1991), 135.
47. Alla Renee Bozarth, *The Word's Body: An Incarnational Aesthetic of Interpretation* (Lanham, MD: University Press of America, 1997), 1.
48. Albert Raboteau, *Fire in the Bones: Reflections on African-American Religious History* (Boston: Beacon, 1995), 142.
49. Raboteau, *Slave Religion*, 235.
50. Particularly see chapter 1 in Mark L. Knapp and Judith A. Hall, *Nonverbal Communication in Human Interaction* (Boston: Thomson Learning, 2002).
51. Raboteau, *Fire in the Bones*, 144. Italics mine.
52. Johnson, *God's Trombones*, 6–7.
53. DuBois, *The Souls of Black Folk*, 211.
54. Todd Farley, "The Use of the Body in the Performance of Proclamation," in *Performance and Preaching: Bringing the Sermon to Life*, ed. Jana Childers and Clayton J. Schmit (Grand Rapids, MI: Baker Academic, 2008), 117.

55. Lorna Marshall, *The Body Speaks: Performance and Expression* (London: Methuen, 2001), xi, xii, 21.
56. Toni Morrison, *Beloved* (New York: Vintage, 2004 [1987]), 102–104.
57. Copeland, *Enfleshing Freedom*, 51–52.
58. Stephanie Paulsell, "Honoring the Body," in *Practicing Our Faith: A Way of Life for a Searching People*, ed. Dorothy C. Bass (San Francisco: Jossey-Bass, 1997), 14–15.
59. Pinn, *Terror and Triumph*, 102.
60. Copeland, *Enfleshing Freedom*, 104.
61. Paulsell, "Honoring the Body," 15.
62. Paulsell, "Honoring the Body," 16.
63. Taylor, *An Altar in the World*, 41.
64. Paulsell, "Honoring the Body," 18.
65. Troeger, *Preaching and Worship*, 85.
66. Troeger, *Preaching and Worship*, 86.
67. Wallace Best, "The Spirit of the Holy Ghost is a Male Spirit: African American Preaching Women and the Paradoxes of Gender," in *Women and Religion in the African Diaspora: Knowledge, Power, and Performance*, ed. R. Marie Griffith and Barbara Dianne Savage (Baltimore, MD: John Hopkins University Press, 2006), 127.
68. Uzukwu, *Worship as Body Language*, ix.
69. Pinn, *Embodiment*, 74; Best, "The Spirit of the Holy Ghost," 111.
70. Lee Butler, "The Spirit is Willing and the Flesh is Too: Living Whole and Holy Lives Through Integrating Spirituality and Sexuality," in *Loving the Body: Black Religious Studies and the Erotic*, ed. Anthony B. Pinn and Dwight Hopkins (New York: Palgrave Macmillan, 1007), 120.
71. Taylor, *An Altar in the World*, 40.
72. Taylor, *An Altar in the World*, 42.

11. Aiding and Abetting New Life: "Sex-Talk" in the Pulpit, Pew, and Public Square

1. Dorothy C. Bass, "Introduction," in *Practicing Theology: Beliefs and Practices in Christian Life*, ed. Miroslav Volf and Dorothy C. Bass (Grand Rapids, MI: William B. Eerdmans, 2002), 3.
2. Kathleen A. Cahalan and James R. Nieman, "Mapping the Field of Practical Theology," in *For Life Abundant: Practical Theology, Theological Education, and Christian Ministry*, ed. Dorothy C. Bass and Craig Dykstra (Grand Rapids, MI: William B. Eerdmans, 2008), 79.
3. *Kin-dom* is a term coined by feminist theologians to disrupt the unjust assumption that God is "male."

4. Peter J. Gomes, *The Scandalous Gospel of Jesus: What's So Good About the Good News?* (New York: HarperOne, 2007), 196–97.
5. Samuel D. Proctor and Gardner C. Taylor with Gary V. Simpson, *We Have This Ministry: The Heart of the Pastor's Vocation* (Valley Forge, PA: Judson, 1996), 20–21.
6. Teresa Fry Brown, "Avoiding Asphyxiation: A Womanist Perspective on Intrapersonal and Interpersonal Transformation," in *Embracing the Spirit: Womanist Perspectives on Hope, Salvation, and Transformation*, ed. Emilie M. Townes (Maryknoll, NY: Orbis, 1997), 81.
7. Zora Neale Hurston, *The Sanctified Church: The Folklore Writings of Zora Neale Hurston* (Berkeley, CA: Turtle Island Foundation, 1981), 49–50.
8. Martha Simmons, personal conversation with author, circa 2009.
9. G. Lee Ramsey Jr., *Care-Full Preaching: From Sermon to Caring Community* (St. Louis: Chalice, 2000), 31–58.
10. Emmanuel Y. Lartey, *Pastoral Theology in an Intercultural World* (Cleveland, OH: Pilgrim, 2006), 136.
11. bell hooks, *All About Love: New Visions* (New York: William Morrow, 2000), 93.
12. Josef Sorett and Renata Cobbs Fletcher, *Religion, Sexuality and Black Culture Project: A Final Report* (New York: Public/Private Ventures, 2009), 28.
13. Bob Allen, "Baptist Church Postpones Vote on Including Gays in Church Directory (Updated)," *Good Faith Media*, December 3, 2007, https://goodfaithmedia.org/baptist-church-postpones-vote-on-including-gays-in-church-directory-updated-cms-11969/.
14. Heterosexism is "an ideology and system of power that defines what constitutes normal and deviant sexuality and distributes social rewards and penalties based on this definition." Patricia Hill Collins, *Black Sexual Politics: African Americans, Gender, and the New Racism* (New York: Routledge, 2005), 351.
15. Martha Simmons and Frank A. Thomas, eds., *Preaching with Sacred Fire: An Anthology of African American Sermons, 1750 to the Present* (New York: Norton, 2010).
16. Arthur L. Smith (also known as Molefi Kete Asante), "Socio-Historical Perspectives of Black Oratory," *Quarterly Journal of Speech* 56 (1970): 264.
17. Smith, "Socio-Historical Perspectives," 264.
18. James Henry Harris, *The Word Made Plain: The Power and Promise of Preaching* (Minneapolis: Fortress, 2004), 77–94.
19. Henry H. Mitchell, "African-American Preaching: The Future of a Rich Tradition," *Interpretation* 51 (October 1997): 378.
20. Quoted in Cornel West and Kelvin Shawn Sealey, *Restoring Hope: Conversations on the Future of Black America* (Boston: Beacon, 1997), 4.
21. Eugene H. Peterson, *The Contemplative Pastor: Returning to the Art of Spiritual Direction* (Grand Rapids, MI: William B. Eerdmans, 1989), 32–33.
22. Margaret Aymer, personal conversation with author, circa 2008.

23. Ellen Ott Marshall, *Christians in the Public Square: Faith that Transforms Politics* (Nashville, TN: Abingdon, 2008), xxi.
24. Ben Kesslen, "Anti-Semitic Assaults in U.S. More than Doubled in 2018, ADL Reports," NBC News, April 30, 2019, https://www.nbcnews.com/news/us-news/anti-semitic-assaults-u-s-more-doubled-2018-adl-reports-n1000246; and Leila Fadel, "U.S. Hate Groups Rose Sharply in Recent Years, Watchdog Group Reports," NPR, February 20, 2019, https://www.npr.org/2019/02/20/696217158/u-s-hate-groups-rose-sharply-in-recent-years-watchdog-group-reports.
25. Victor Anderson, *Creative Exchange: A Constructive Theology of African American Religious Experience* (Minneapolis: Fortress, 2008), 3–4.
26. Iris Murdoch, *Existentialists and Mystics: Writings on Philosophy and Literature*, ed. Peter Conradi (New York: Penguin, 1997), 218.
27. Murdoch, *Existentialists and Mystics*, 203.
28. Mother Teresa, *Love: The Words and Inspiration of Mother Teresa* (Boulder, CO: Blue Mountain, 2007), 87.

Epilogue

1. Donnie McClurkin, "Gospel Singer Donnie McClurkin Speaks of Mateless Future, Says He's 'Got Joy,'" Religion News Service, April 2, 2021, https://religionnews.com/2021/04/02/gospel-singer-donnie-mcclurkin-speaks-of-mateless-future-says-hes-got-joy/.
2. Kathryn Post, "AME General Conference Debate on same-sex marriage continues after bill is voted down," Religion News Service (July 7, 2021). https://religionnews.com/2021/07/07/the-ame-general-conference-will-consider-bill-on-same-sex-marriage/.

Contributors

Victor Anderson is Oberlin Theological School Professor of Ethics and Society at Vanderbilt University, the Divinity School and College of Arts and Sciences. He is the author of *Beyond Ontological Blackness: An Essay in African American and Cultural Criticism* (2016); *Pragmatic Theology: Negotiating the Intersections of an American Philosophy of Religion and Public Theology* (1998), and *Creative Exchange: A Constructive Theology of African American Religious Experience* (2008).

Wallace Best is the Hughes-Rogers Professor of Religion and African American Studies at Princeton University. He is the author of *Langston's Salvation: American Religion and the Bard of Harlem* (2017), winner of the 2018 Award for Excellence in the Study of Religion in Textual Studies from the American Academy of Religion, as well as *Passionately Human, No Less Divine: Religion and Culture in Black Chicago, 1915-1952* (2005), winner of the 2006 Illinois State Historical Society Award, Publications Category. He has also published in *Religion and American Culture*, *Religion and Politics*, *Fides Et Historia*, *U.S. Catholic Historian*, *Callaloo*, the *Huffington Post*, *Reuters*, and the *Washington Post*. He has held fellowships at the Center for the Study of Religion at Princeton University and the W. E. B. Du Bois Research Institute at the Hutchins Center, Harvard University.

Brad R. Braxton is the Chief Diversity, Equity, and Inclusion Officer at St. Luke's School in New York. He also is the Founder of The Open Church in Baltimore, MD, and is a curatorial adviser for "Creative Encounters:

Living Religions in the United States," the 2023 Smithsonian Folklife Festival on religious diversity. He holds a Ph.D. in New Testament studies from Emory University and was a Rhodes Scholar at the University of Oxford.

Michael Joseph Brown is the president of Payne Theological Seminary, professor of New Testament and Christian Origins, and the author of numerous publications. Dr. Brown's work focuses on the intersection between literary and material cultures. An ordained minister in the African Methodist Episcopal Church, he works closely with ecclesial and social leaders to advance social justice and the dignity of all humankind.

Nick Camp is an assistant professor of organizational studies at the University of Michigan, with a courtesy appointment in psychology. He has authored publications in the *Journal of Personality and Social Psychology* and *Social Psychology*, and his work has been supported by numerous grants and fellowships, including from the National Science Foundation.

Cathy Cohen is the David and Mary Winton Green Distinguished Service Professor at the University of Chicago. She is the author of *The Boundaries of Blackness: AIDS and the Breakdown of Black Politics* (1999) and *Democracy Remixed: Black Youth and the Future of American Politics* (2012). Cohen is also coeditor of the anthology *Women Transforming Politics: An Alternative Reader* (1997) with Kathleen Jones and Joan Tronto. Her articles have been published in numerous journals and edited volumes including the *American Political Science Review*, *NOMOS*, *GLQ*, *Social Text*, and the *DuBois Review*. Cohen is the founder and director of two public-facing research projects: the Black Youth Project and the GenForward Survey.

Monica A. Coleman is Professor of Africana Studies at the University of Delaware. She is the author or editor of six books, including *Making a Way Out of No Way: A Womanist Theology* (2008) and *Bipolar Faith: A Black Woman's Journey with Depression and Faith* (2016). Coleman's research includes process, liberation, and womanist theologies; Black religious traditions; and theories of religious pluralism.

Richard Eibach is an associate professor of psychology at the University of Waterloo. Eibach's research has been published in a range of scientific journals and edited volumes, including *Psychological Science*, the *Journal of Personality and Social Psychology*, and *Sex Roles*.

Serene Jones is a highly respected scholar and public intellectual. The Rev. Dr. Serene Jones is the sixteenth president of the historic Union

Theological Seminary in the City of New York. The first woman to head the 182-year-old institution, Jones occupies the Johnston Family Chair for Religion and Democracy. She is a past president of the American Academy of Religion, which annually hosts the world's largest gathering of scholars of religion. Jones also spent seventeen years at Yale University, where she was the Titus Street Professor of Theology at the Yale Divinity School and chair of the Women, Gender and Sexuality Studies Program. She is the author of several books, including *Trauma and Grace* (2009) and, most recently, her memoir *Call It Grace: Finding Meaning in a Fractured World* (2019). A popular public speaker, Jones is sought by media to comment on major issues impacting society because of her deep grounding in theology, politics, women's studies, economics, race studies, history, and ethics.

Nyasha Junior is an associate professor in the Department of Religion at Temple University in Philadelphia. Her research and teaching focus on religion, race, and gender. She is the author of *An Introduction to Womanist Biblical Interpretation* (2015) and *Reimagining Hagar: Blackness and Bible* (2019) and coauthor of *Black Samson: The Untold Story of an American Icon* (2020).

Derrick McQueen earned his Ph.D. in homiletics and the New Testament from Union Theological Seminary. Rev. Dr. McQueen is the associate director for community partnerships at the Columbia University Center on African-American Religion, Sexual Politics and Social Justice. A sought-after thought partner, he serves on several boards and is a consultant to congregations, communities, and organizations on racial equity and healing rituals. A strong voice for the African American LGBTQ movement, he is also the pastor of St. James Presbyterian Church in Harlem, the oldest African American Presbyterian Church in New York City.

Monique Moultrie is an associate professor of religious studies at Georgia State University. Her scholarly interests include sexual ethics, African American religions, and gender and sexuality studies. She is the author of *Passionate and Pious: Religious Media and Black Women's Sexuality* (2017), and her forthcoming manuscript *Hidden Histories: Faith and Black Lesbian Leadership* will be published by Duke University Press.

Luke A. Powery is the dean of Duke University Chapel and an associate professor of homiletics at Duke Divinity School. He has also served on the faculty of Princeton Theological Seminary.

Melynda J. Price is University Research Professor and the William L. Matthews, Jr. Professor of Law at the University of Kentucky. She is the author of *At the Cross: Race, Religion and Citizenship in the Politics of the Death Penalty* (2015). Her work has been published in peer-reviewed social science and law journals, newspapers, and literary journals. Her research focuses on race, gender, and citizenship; the politics of punishment; and the role of law in the politics of race and ethnicity in the United States and at its borders.

Valerie Purdie Greenaway is an associate professor of psychology and an instructor at Columbia Business School at Columbia University. She has authored numerous publications that have appeared in journals such as *Science, Science Advances, Psychological Science,* and *Journal of Personality and Social Psychology*. She is an associate editor for *Psychological Review*, and her work has been featured in the *New York Times, Fortune* magazine, the *Atlantic, Scientific American, NBCUniversal,* and *NPR*.

Barbara Savage is the Geraldine R. Segal Professor Emerita of American Social Thought in the Department of Africana Studies at the University of Pennsylvania. Her books include *Your Spirits Walk Beside Us: The Politics of Black Religion* (2008), which won the Grawemeyer Prize in Religion. She also coedited *Women and Religion in the African Diaspora: Knowledge, Power, and Performance* (2006). She holds an undergraduate degree from the University of Virginia, a law degree from Georgetown University, and a doctorate in history from Yale University.

Josef Sorett is professor of Religion and African American and African Diaspora Studies at Columbia University. Sorett is currently the chair of the Department of Religion and directs the Center on African-American Religion, Sexual Politics and Social Justice. He is the author of two books, *Spirit in the Dark: A Religious History of Racial Aesthetics* (2016) and the forthcoming *The Holy Holy Black: The Ironies of an American Secular*.

Jonathan Lee Walton is dean of the School of Divinity at Wake Forest University where he also holds the Presidential Chair in Religion and Society. Trained as a social ethicist, he is the author of two books, *Watch This! The Ethics and Aesthetics of Black Televangelism* (2009) and *A Lens of Love: Reading the Bible in Its World for Our World* (2018).

Christine Y. Wiley is pastor emerita of Covenant Baptist UCC in Washington, DC. She has been a significant leader for justice in the Washington, DC, community and the country. Rev. Dr. Wiley serves as an adjunct professor at Howard University School of Social Work and is the director of Pastoral Clinical Services, a counseling and consultation center. She consults with churches, the academy, and government entities. She has three wonderful adult children and six adorable grandchildren.

Dennis W. Wiley is pastor emeritus of the trailblazing Covenant Baptist United Church of Christ in Washington, DC, and a former adjunct professor of theology at the Howard University School of Divinity. A black liberation theologian, prominent civic activist, and gifted musician, Rev. Dr. Wiley has rendered theological lectures and presentations throughout the nation and has been published in several major religious books, magazines, and journals. As a practical theologian devoted to bridging the gap between church, academy, and community, he is in the vanguard of African American clergy committed not only to the *particular* goal of black liberation but also to the *universal* quest for radical inclusion. His progressive, groundbreaking ministry is a model for the effective integration of theory and praxis.

Index

abolitionism, 72, 74
Abraham (biblical figure), 45–48, 219n2
abstinence, 59, 111, 112, 113
abuse: from church, 34; marital, 109
acceptance, 21, 139
activism: for black women, 42; gay, 100; LGBTQ, 7, 30
Adam and Eve, 151
Adams, Ty, 106, 109–111, 115, 231n17
"Address to the Slaves of the United States of America" (Garnet), 73–74
adoption, of children, 130
adultery, 53, 62
Africa, 183
African American Christians, 183
African American church liberation tradition, 157
African American identity, 77
African American Pentecostals, 25
African American Protestants, 5–6, 25, 68, 131, 143
African Americans, 2, 72; Christian historical perspective of, 152–153; equality of, 152–153; gay, 19, 22, 131–133; GLBTQ, 150; homiletics of, 159–160, 164, 172; homophobia and, 102–103; politics and, 6
African evangelists, 36
African Methodist Episcopal (AME), 75, 214, 223n16
Afro-phallic Protestantism, 68–72
Afro-Protestantism, 2, 5
AIDS. *See* HIV/AIDS
Alexander, Bobby, 111–112
AME. *See* African Methodist Episcopal
Amendment 1, 7
American culture: black congregations and, 11; race, religion, sexuality in, 5–8
Anderson, Mother Leafy, 225n12
Anderson, Victor, 18, 148–149
androcentrism, 134, 135
anthropology, theological, 151–155, 156
antiblack police violence, 7
anti-gay sermons, 211
antiviolence, 127
arrest, for homosexuality, 228n47

Association of Welcoming and Affirming Baptists, 202–203
athletics, 71
Atlanta Compromise Speech, 232n7
Aymer, Margaret, 186

Baby Suggs (fictional character), 159, 166–171
Bailey, Walter T., 84, 226n13
Barnes, Sandra, 9
Bass, Dorothy, 173
Battle, Juan, 9
beholding, 165
bell hooks, 37, 99, 179, 195
belonging, 139, 141
Beloved (Morrison), 166–167, 168–170
Bérubé, Allan, 137
Between Sundays (Frederick), 112–113
Beyoncé, 104
"Beyond 'The Down Low'" (Sneed), 236n10
Bible, 33, 63–64, 178, 212–213; Genesis 22, 41–42, 44–45; interpretation of, 112, 114; John 1:1, 14, 159; Judges 11, 41–42, 44–45; Matthew 25, 35; New Testament, 52, 58–59, 63; Old Testament, 59, 60; violence in, 46–47; warrior culture in, 48, 221n17; women in, 221n16
biblical canon, 41
Biden, Joe, 6
bishops, 56–57
"black, versus gay," 2–3
black bodies, 237n7; as practical progress, 166–171; preaching, 160, 163–166, 172; spirit and material, 162–163; as theological possibility, 160–166
black caucus, 24
black Christian identity, 131

black church, 10; inclusion in, 123, 124, 195; intersectional invisibility and, 141–144; white evangelicals and, 31–32. *See also specific churches and topics*
"black church effect," 26
black clergy, 7, 13, 21, 140, 169
black congregations, 11
black family, definition of, 130
black freedom, 3
black gay Christians, invisibility of, 129–130
black gospel music, 88
black lesbians, 135, 140
black LGBT agenda, 22–23
#BlackLivesMatter movement, 7, 43, 210
black masculinity, 23, 76
black men, 76–77; gay, 132; murders of, 43
blackness, 148–149, 152, 154
black people: oppression of, 148; salvation of, 21
black politics, 121
Black Sexualities (Barnes and Battles), 9
black sexuality, 21, 212
black southern migrants, 87
black theology, 23, 160
black women, 23, 112; activism for, 42; churchwomen, 104, 105, 113; discrimination against, 136–137; faith-based sexuality ministries and, 105–106; hypersexualization of, 110; marriage and, 107, 126; naming of, 45, 48–49; police violence against, 43–44, 45, 46; sexuality and, 105–106, 116; single, 107, 108; televangelism and, 105–108; underrepresentation of, 135; victimization of, 44
black youth, 26–27

Black Youth Project, 26
blood, of Christ, 186
blood banks, 88
Bobo, Jacqueline, 112
bodies, 159–160, 167, 237n7; Christianity and, 172; of women, 170. *See also* black bodies
"body talk," 176
Bolden, Richard Edward, 94–95, 228n51
Book of James, 184
born-again Christians, 26
Boswell, Leviticus, 93–94
Boundaries of Blackness, The (Cohen), 9, 121–122
Bowie, William N., 90
Bradden, William S., 89
Brewster, Herbert W., 88, 227n28
Broadway Baptist Church, 180
Brown, James, 176, 181
Brown, Teresa Fry, 237n7
Burrell, Kim, 1–2
Bush, George W., 123–124
Butler, Lee, 171
Bynum, Juanita, 106–109, 111, 231n17

call and response tradition, 215–216
Cannon, Katie, 115
canon, biblical, 41
capitalism, 70
Carr, Ebony, 102
Carter, J. Kameron, 68
Catholics, 6
caucus, black, 24
caucus, LGBTQ, 24
charity, intellectual, 188
Charleston, 11
Chauncey, George, 143–144
Chicago, 78–81, 82–83, 84–85, 103, 224n4; gay culture in, 91–92, 101–102

Chicago Defender (newspaper), 80
choice, religion and, 33–34
Christian churches, 5
Christianity, 150; bodies and, 172; enslaved people and, 74; GLBTQ and, 152–155; historical perspective of African Americans, 152–153; inconsistency in, 63–64; interpretation of, 112; marriage and, 55–56; muscular, 67, 69; sexuality and, 50–51, 55–61; sexual practices and, 63–64; sexual visions in, 61–63
Christian Mingle, 105
Christian ministry, 87
Christians, 53; African American, 183; black gay, 129–130; born-again, 26; second and third generation, 55–58
Christian theology, 151
churches: abuse from, 34; black LGBTQ community and, 120–121, 123, 124; culture at, 205; gay community in, 197; growing up in, 18–19; homophobia in, 83; as inclusive, 142, 143, 195; political, 233n15; Spiritual, 82, 84, 85, 86, 100–101; women in, 69. *See also* black church
church leaders, 157
Cicero, 56–57
civilization, savagery and, 71
civil rights movement, 3, 5, 148, 149–150, 190; LGBTQ rights movement and, 27–29; religion and, 28, 29–30
Clayburn, Ryllar Jeannette, 90
Clement of Alexandria, 51, 59, 60–61
clergy, black, 7, 13, 21, 140, 169
closet, glass, 81, 90–100
closeted, 20, 90–91
clothing, white, 87

Cobbs, Clarence H., 78–81, 82, 89–90, 100–101, 103; early life of, 83–84, 225n12; First Church of Deliverance and, 84, 85, 86–88; glass closet and, 91–92, 93–95; sex scandal, 80–81, 86, 225n4
Cohen, Cathy, 9, 18, 120, 121–122, 132
colorblind ideology, 137
Color Purple, The (film), 112
communication theory, 164
Community Mental Health Center, 193
compartmentalization, identity, 140
compassion, 188–189
compulsory heteronormativity, 27
Cone, James H., 148
conformity, sexual, 82
congregational recommendations, 156–157
conservatism, 2, 26
"Constituting Antebellum African Identity" (Jasinski), 224n20
contraception, 111
Cooper, Jack, 84–85
copastorate, 196–197
1 Corinthians, 52, 178
Costley, Alex. W., 131, 132–133
counseling: for couples, 198; mental health, 193–194
couples ministry, 207–208
Covenant Baptist Church, 191, 200–205, 208
creation, 150–155, 156
Crenshaw, Kimberlé Williams, 44
criminal justice reform, 43
critical race theory, 154
cross: lynching and, 161; symbol of, 144
culture: Chicago gay, 91–92, 101–102; of churches, 205; postwar, 99; of silence, 9. *See also* American culture

danced religion, 159–160
Day of Judgment, 189
deacons, 56–57
death, 21, 35
death penalty, 127
Defense of Marriage Act, 1996, 4
dehumanization, 181
D'Emilio, John, 98
demographic shifts, in religion, 24–25
desire, 60, 61
discrimination, 158, 192; against black LGBTQ communities, 123, 127, 232n10–12; against black women, 136–137; against intersectional identities, 232n1
dis-ease, 161
diversity, 178, 179, 180; religious, 85
divine, 162
divorce, 30, 97
domesticity, 69, 71–72
domestic violence, 58
dominance: heterosexual, 91; white masculine, 73
Don't Ask, Don't Tell policy, 7, 28
Dorsey, Thomas Andrew, 88
Douglas, Kelly Brown, 8
Douglas Memorial Community Church, 177
Douglass, Frederick, 72–73, 74
Du Bois, W. E. B., 165

ecclesiology, 151–155
economic outreach, 88
"effect, black church," 26
effeminism, 61–63, 75, 92
Egypt, exodus from, 42
ekklesia (church), 51
election trends, 136
electoral politics, 8
embodiment, 159, 162, 170–171, 237n7
Emmanuel AME Church, 11

enfleshment, 162
enslaved people, black, 134; Christianity and, 74
equality: of African Americans, 152–153; LGBTQ, 4, 5, 180, 212; marriage, 2–7, 14, 150, 204–205, 210, 214; of women, 73
Equality Act, 210
eroticism, 25
Esther (Douglass aunt), 72, 75–76
ethics: of preaching, 183–184; womanist sexual, 113–116
ethnocentrism, 134, 135, 137
evangelicals: African, 36; black churches and, 123–124
evangelism, 11, 31–32, 68–69. *See also* televangelism
every-body, 166–171
evolutionary process, 194
exclusion, 141, 213–214; ontological, 134
exile, from church, 36
Exile or Embrace? (Siler), 203
Exodus, story of, 29
expansionism, 36
expendability, of women, 43

face-to-face encounters, 180
faculty, racial diversity within, 24
"fairies," 92
faith-based sexuality ministries, 104–106
familial rejection, 154
families, 56–58; black, 130
fate, linked, 121–123
Fellowship of Affirming Ministries, 33
First Church of Deliverance, 84, 85, 86–88, 92
fluid gender identities, 67–68
Flunder, Yvette, 33
followers, of Jesus, 50
Franklin, Robert, 114–115
Frederick, Marla, 105, 112–113

freedom: masculinity and, 72–74, 76; religious, 33
Freud, Sigmund, 99
Fuchs, Esther, 220n7
fundamentalism, 32, 33
funerals, for gay people, 34

Garnet, Henry Highland, 73–74, 76, 77
Garrison, Lloyd, 74
gay, lesbian, bisexual, transgender, and queer (GLBTQ), 148, 149–151; Christianity and, 152–155
"gay, versus black," 2–3
gay African Americans, 19, 22; intersectional invisibility of, 131–133
gay and lesbian rights movement, 22
gay black men, 132
gay black ministers, 81
gay community: black, 137–139, 140, 141; in church, 196; white, 137–138
gay culture, Chicago, 91–92, 101–102
"gaydar," 19
gay identity, 100
"Gay is the new Black," problem with, 147–150
gay liberation movement, 3, 17
gay oppression, 100, 127
gay revolution, 1960s, 92–93
gender, race and, 68, 135
gender hierarchies, 67
gender identities, 63; fluid, 67–68; sexual identity and, 125
generational shift, 26
Genesis 22, 41–42, 46; #SayHerName campaign and, 44–45
Gilkes, Cheryl Townsend, 159
glass closet, 81, 90–100
Glaude, Eddie, 76
GLBTQ. *See* gay, lesbian, bisexual, transgender, and queer
globalization, 36–37

God, 44, 46, 99, 109, 151, 240n3; creation and, 152, 156–157
Gomes, Peter, 174–175
gospel, inclusive, 174–175
gospel music, black, 88
Great Depression, 87
Great Migration, 79, 83
Griffin, Horace, 153, 154, 155
Gross, Michael Joseph, 2–3
growing up, in churches, 18–19
guilt, 31
Gulick, Luther Halsey, 71

Hall, G. Stanley, 70–71
Hall, Lucius, 92
Hammon, Jupiter, 74
Harding, Vincent, 29
harmonization, of community, 168
Hawkeswood, William G., 131, 132–133
"head of the household," 56
heart orientation, 179
heterocentrism, 131, 134, 135, 137–138
heteronormativity, compulsory, 27
heterosexism, 181, 195, 241n14
heterosexual couples, 97
heterosexual dominance, 91
hierarchies, gender, 67
hip-hop, 26
history, 22
HIV/AIDS, 9, 20, 21, 122, 192; blood of Christ and, 186; church ignoring, 132
Holy Communion, 186
Holy Spirit, 50
homelessness, 154–155
homiletics, African American, 159–160, 164, 172
homo-intolerance, 31
homophobia, 5, 9, 31; in African American religious communities, 102–103; in churches, 83; hyper-, 8; sexuality and, 35
homosexuality, 1, 26, 31, 61–62, 110; arrest for, 228n47; Cobbs and, 90; curing, 125; laws on, 98–99, 218n12; medicalization of, 98–100; military and, 98; in 1940s, 80–81, 91–92; religion and, 98–99; stereotypes of, 93
hooks, bell, 37, 99, 179, 195
hope, theological, 157–158
Hope and History (Harding), 29
Hopkins, Dwight, 9
Horton, Lois E., 76–77
hospitality, 189
"household, head of," 56
"How I Got Over," 88
Hughes, Thomas, 69
human rights, 28
human sacrifice, 44–46
Hurston, Zora Neale, 176
hyperhomophobia, 8
hypermasculine social movements, 67
hypersexualization of black women, 110

identities: African American, 77; black Christian, 131; gay, 100; gender, 63, 125; intersectional, 129, 135–136, 144; masculine, 70; overlapping political, 120; racial, 2, 3, 138–139; religious, 119; sexual, 91, 96, 125
identity compartmentalization, 140
imagination, preaching with, 184–186
incarceration, rates of, 156
incarnation, 160–161
inclusion, 179–180, 190; in black churches, 123, 124, 195; in gospel, 174–175
intercourse, Christianity and, 60

interpretations: biblical, 112, 114; of scripture, 133, 212–213
intersectional identities, 129, 135–136, 144, 232n1
intersectional invisibility, 130–131, 134–136; in black gay community, 137–139; in black religious community, 131–133; consequences of, 139–144
intersectionality, 129
intimacy, public, 19–21
invisibility, 213–214; of black gay Christians, 129–130. *See also* intersectional invisibility
Isaac (biblical figure), 45, 46
Israel, ancient, 44–45

Jakes, T. D., 102, 103, 106
Jasinski, James, 224n20
Jephthah (biblical figure), 42–43, 45–48, 220n7
Jephthah's Daughter (biblical figure), 41, 42–43, 45–49, 219n1, 220n7
Jesus, 20, 30, 161, 174–175, 185; as effeminate, 75–76; followers of, 50; race and, 31; Second Coming of, 51, 52
Jesus and the Disinherited (Thurman), 181
John 1:1, 14, 159
Johnson, James Weldon, 165
Johnson, Luke Timothy, 50
Johnson, Lyndon, 150
Jones, McKissack McHenry "Mac," 78, 224n2
Jones, Serene, 18
Judges 11, 41–42, 46, 221n19; #SayHerName campaign and, 44–45, 48
judgment, 35
Judgment, Day of, 189
Julian Laws, 58

justice: criminal justice reform, 43; racial, 43; sexual, 115

Kant, Immanuel, 70, 223n4
kin-dom, 240n3
King, Bernice, 102–103, 147–148
King, Martin Luther Jr., 4–5, 28, 147–148, 194–195, 205
Kingsley, Charles, 69
Kinsey, Alfred, 99, 229n65

language: of sermons, 182–183; on sin, 30; theological, 25
Lartey, Emmanuel, 178
"Last Great Civil Rights Movement, The" (Gross), 2–3
Latino Pentecostals, 25
laws: on homosexuality, 98–99, 218n12; on marriage equality, 6; on same-sex marriage, 130, 148, 209
leaders, church, 157
Lee, Jarena, 223n16
lesbian and gay rights movement, 22
lesbian relationships, 114
lesbians, 109; black, 135, 140
letters, from Paul, 52, 61
LGBTQ activism, 7, 30
LGBTQ agenda, black, 22–23
LGBTQ caucus, 24
LGBTQ communities, black, 7; black churches and, 120–121, 123, 124; discrimination against, 123, 127, 232n10–12; HIV/AIDS and, 122–123; migratory path of, 125–126
LGBTQ equality, 4, 5, 180, 212
LGBTQ rights movement, 3; civil rights movement and, 27–29
LGBTQ students, 24
liberation tradition, African American church, 157
life expectancy, 59

linked fate theory, 121–123
"Litany for Survival, A" (Lorde), 49
liturgy, of Spirit, 167
Lloyd, Sam, 203
Long, Eddie, 147–148
Lorde, Audre, 49, 139–140
love: making, 178–179; unconditional, 188
Love and Liberty Fellowship Church International, 1
Loving the Body (Hopkins and Pinn), 9
lynching, 143, 220n10; cross and, 161

magazine covers, 135
making love, 178–179
malakos (solf man), 61, 62
male prostitutes, 61–62
manhood, 74–75
manliness, 74, 75, 87, 88, 91
marginalization, 122–123, 130
"Marginalization, Ambiguity, Silencing" (Fuchs), 220n7
marital abuse, 109
marriage, 33, 57, 104, 112, 214; age of, 59–60; black women and, 107, 126; Christianity and, 55–56; New Deal and, 97–98; rates of, 96–97; re-, 58; sexuality and, 54–55. *See also* same-sex marriage
marriage equality, 2–7, 14, 150, 204–205, 210, 214
marriage patterns, 59
Marshall, Ellen, 186
Marshall, Lorna, 159
masculine ideals, 77
masculine identity, 70
masculinity, 61–63, 68, 69; black, 23, 76; freedom and, 72–74, 76; hyper-, 67; moral agency and, 72–77; race and, 71–72; sports and, 71; white dominant, 73

mass shootings, 187
masturbation, 70, 109, 110
Matthew 25, 35
McClurkin, Donnie, 210–211
media, religious, 229n3
mediums, 85
men: effeminate, 61–63; family role of, 56–57; white, 69, 70. *See also* black men
mental health counseling, 193–194
Metropolitan Spiritual Churches of Christ, Inc. (MSCC), 84
middle-class, 69–70
migrants, black southern, 87
military: Don't Ask, Don't Tell policy, 7, 28; homosexuality and, 98
Millennium March on Washington (MMOW), 142
ministers, gay black, 81
ministries, faith-based sexuality, 104–105
ministry, couples, 207–208
minorities, 143–144
"miracles," 85
mistrust, 141
Mitchell, Henry, 183
MMOW. *See* Millennium March on Washington
monastic movement, 62
monogamy, 63
Monroe, Irene, 131–132
Moody Bible Institute, 32
moral agency, masculinity and, 72–77
morality, 59, 67
Mormons, 6
Morrison, Toni, 166–167, 168–170
Mother Teresa, 189
MSCC. *See* Metropolitan Spiritual Churches of Christ, Inc.
multi-racial, 154
murders, of black men, 43

Murdoch, Iris, 188
muscular Christianity, 67, 69
music, black gospel, 88
mysticism, 85, 93

naming, of black women, 45, 48–49
National Baptist Convention, 5
National Black Election Study (NBES), 121
National Organization for Marriage, 3
negotiated reading, 111–113
New Black, The (film), 4, 205
New Deal, marriage and, 97–98
New Testament, 52, 58–59, 63
New Thought philosophy, 86
Nommo (sacred speech), 182–183
No More Sheets (sermon), 107
Numbers 21, 47

Obama, Barack, 2, 6, 17, 124–125, 128, 148; election of, 209–210; on marriage equality, 204
Obergefell v. Hodges, 150
Old Testament, 59, 60
Oliver, James, 76–77
"one-drop rule," 149, 154
ontological exclusion, 134
ontology, 148; racial, 153–154, 155; sexual orientation and, 153–154; social, 129–130, 133–134
Open Church of Maryland, 179
oppression: of black people, 148; gay, 100, 127; racial, 4
"other-ing," 127
out, 90–91
outreach: economic, 88; for LGBTQ community, 126

passing, 154
passion, self-mastery and, 71
pastoral theology, 175–181

pastors: African American, 191; copastorate, 196–197
patristic period, 59
Paul (apostle), 51–55, 61
Payne, Daniel, 75, 223n16
Pentecostalism, 84
Pentecostals: African American, 25; Latino, 25
personhood, dimensions of, 133–134
Peterson, Eugene, 185
Philosophy of Play (Gulick), 71
Pilgrim Baptist, in Chicago, 83–84
Pinn, Anthony, 9
pneumatic possession, 163
police violence, 47–48; antiblack, 7; against black women, 43–44, 45, 46
political church, 233n15
political identities, overlapping, 120
political schizophrenia, 124
politics, 211; African Americans and, 6; black, 121; black churches and, 124; electoral, 8; identity compartmentalization and, 140; progressive, 2; racial, 181; of recognition, 129; of resistance, 33
porneia (sexual immorality), 52–53
possession, pneumatic, 163
postracial society, 28, 29
postwar culture, 99
power, 72–77
practical theology, 173–174
preaching, 161, 182; black body and, 160, 163–166, 172; ethics of, 183–184; with imagination, 184–186; on premarital sex, 114–115; of progressive word, 182; sexuality and, 171
prejudice, 191
premarital sex, 27, 106–107, 110; study on preachers and, 114–115

INDEX [257]

Price, Fred, 157
pride parade, 173, 237n15
privilege, 27; of recognition, 134; white, 138
procreation, 60, 63, 151
Proctor, Samuel, 175
progressive politics, 2
Proposition 8, 4–5, 6, 8, 128–129, 210
prostitution, 53–54, 61–62
Protestantism: Afro-, 2, 5; Afro-phallic, 68–72
Protestants, African American, 5–6, 25, 68, 131, 143
public intimacy, 19–21
public safety, 186–188
public square, 186

"Queer as Black Folk?" (Smith, Catherine), 232n1
Queer Eye (show), 149
Queer Eye for the Straight Guy (show), 149
queer theology, 23
queer theory, 9
Qur'an, 219n2

Raboteau, Albert, 164
race, 73, 137; in American culture, 5–8; critical race theory, 154; gender and, 68, 135; Jesus and, 31; masculinity and, 71–72; multi-racial, 154; religion, sexuality and, 19, 22, 128, 158
racial diversity, within faculty, 24
racial identity, 138–139; sexual orientation and, 2, 3, 154
racial justice, 43
racial ontology, 153–154, 155
racial oppression, 4
racial politics, 181
racism, 149, 194

Rado, Sandor, 99
rates, of marriage, 96–97
reading, negotiated, 111–113
recognition: politics of, 129; privilege of, 134
Reconciling Ministries Network, 157
"Reigniting the Legacy" march, 148
rejection, familial, 154
religion: in American culture, 5–8; black politics and, 10; choice and, 33–34; civil rights movement and, 28, 29–30; danced, 159–160; demographic shifts in, 24–25; homosexuality and, 98–99; race and, 19, 22, 128; sexuality and, 19, 22, 82, 128; slavery and, 163; studying, 8–10
religious affiliations, switching, 143
religious diversity, 85
religious experience, 25
religious freedom, 33
religious identity, 119
religious leaders, black, 124
religious media, 229n3
remarriage, 58
representation, 142
resistance, politics of, 33
revolution, gay, 92–93
Rich, Ann, 27
rights, human, 28
Robeson, Paul, 185
Roman Catholics, 25
Rose, Tricia, 113–114
Rosie the Riveter, 97
Ruggles, David, 77
rules, of engagement, 187
Russell, Stephen C., 219n4
Rustin, Bayard, 3, 143–144

sacred desk, 182
sacred speech (Nommo), 182–183
sacrifice, 220n7; human, 44–46

safe spaces, in communities, 142
safety, public, 186–188
Salvation (book), 21
salvation, of black people, 21
same-sex marriage, 2, 5, 6, 7, 17, 126; ban on, 147–148; legalization of, 130, 148, 209; support for, 217n3
same-sex union ceremony, 196, 199–203
Samuel 14, 47
"Sanctified Sexuality" sermon, 177
Sanders, Edwin II, 143
Satan, 109
Savage, Barbara, 10, 18–19
savagery, civilization and, 71
#SayHerName campaign, 42, 43, 49, 212n18; Genesis 22 and Judges 11 and, 44–45, 48; Jephthah and Abraham and, 45–48
scandal, Cobbs, 80–81, 86
Schipper, Jeremy, 219n4
schizophrenia, political, 124
Scripture, 35
scripture, interpretations of, 133, 212–213
Second Coming of Jesus, 51, 52
Sedgwick, Eve, 91
segregation, 190, 191
Seidman, Steven, 91, 138–139
self-control, 50, 54, 61–62, 64
self-mastery, passion and, 71
sermons, 164, 166–167, 169; anti-gay, 211; language of, 182–183; about sexuality, 177, 184
sex: premarital, 27, 106–107, 110; as taboo, 107
sexism, 170, 195; hetero-, 181, 195, 241n14
sex manuals, evangelical, 107
sex scandal, Cobbs, 80–81, 86
sexual conformity, 82

sexual health, community, 20
sexual identities, 91, 96
sexual immorality (*porneia*), 52–53
sexuality, 4, 9, 192; in American culture, 5–8; black, 21, 212; black women and, 105–106, 116; Christianity and, 50–51, 55–61; fear of, 169; homophobia and, 35; marriage and, 54–55; Paul and, 51–55; preaching and, 171; race and, 19, 22, 128, 158; religion and, 19, 22, 82, 128; self-control and, 63; sermon about, 177, 184; singles, 106–107; Spiritual churches and, 93; as taboo, 32, 195; talking about, 32–33; theology and, 25, 158; urban, 81. *See also* faith-based sexuality ministries; homosexuality
Sexuality and the Black Church (Douglas), 8
sexual justice, 115
sexual orientation, 152, 155–156; gender identity and, 125; ontology and, 153–154; racial identity and, 2, 154
sexual sin, 110
sexual violence, 72, 157
sexual visions, in Christianity, 61–63
shame, 31, 110–111
shootings, mass, 187
silence, culture of, 9
Siler, Mahan, 203
Simmons, Martha, 176
sin, 30–31, 77, 151–155; embracing of, 86–87; redefining, 156; sexual, 110
Single, Saved, and Having Sex (Adams), 109–111
Single, Saved, and Having Sex 2 (Adams), 111
single black women, 107, 108
"Single Ladies," 104
singleness, 97

singles sexuality, 106–107
"sisterspeak," 176
slavery, 72–76, 149, 152, 168–169; religion and, 163. *See also* enslaved people
Smith, Catherine, 232n1
Smith, Christine Marie, 173
Sneed, Roger, 236n10
social justice, 204
social media, 43
social ontologies, 129–130, 133–134
social sciences, 9
Soggin, J. Alberto, 44–45
some-bodies, 160–166
Song of Solomon, 114
Songs of Songs, 177
Souls of Black Folk, The (Du Bois), 165
Southern Baptist Convention, 191
Spirit, 162, 163, 167, 168, 171, 207
spirit and material black body, 162–163
Spiritual churches, 82, 84, 85, 86, 100–101
sports, masculinity and, 71
Starr-Jones, Jean, 78–81, 82, 95, 100
stereotypes, 191; of black men, 77; homosexual, 93; masculine, 62; racial, 8–9
Stewart, Maria W., 77
stigma, 130
strategic planning, 22
"street level" teaching, 177
Stromata III, 51
student body, 24
students, LGBTQ, 24
suffrage movements, women, 69
suicide, 31, 154–155
symbol, of cross, 144

taboo: sex as, 107; sexuality as, 32, 195
Tanis, Justin Edward, 156

Taylor, William F., 93–94, 228n47
teaching, "street level," 177
televangelism, 104, 105, 111–112, 115; black women and, 106–109
Their Own Receive Them Not (Griffin), 153
theological anthropology, 151–155, 156
theological hope, 157–158
theological possibility, black bodies as, 160–166
theological recommendations, 155–156
theological statements, 157
theology: black, 23, 160; Christian, 151; liberal, 87; pastoral, 175–181; practical, 174; queer, 23; sexuality and, 25, 158; Western, 8
Thompson, John L., 220n7
Thompson, Lisa L., 237n7
Thornton, Maggie, 84
Thurman, Howard, 181, 192
Till, Emmett, 220n10
Timothy 3:1-13, 56
tokenism, 141–142
Trans-Gendered (Tanis), 156–157
transgender people, 193
transgression, 31
transvestite, 102
Trump, Donald, 6, 187
Truth, Sojourner, 135

UCC. *See* United Church of Christ
unconditional love, 188
union ceremony, same-sex, 196, 199–203
Union Theological Seminary, 18, 23–24, 25, 192
United Church of Christ (UCC), 198, 204, 206
United Methodist Church, 157, 236n5
urban sexuality, 81
Uzukwu, Elochukwu, 164

victim-blaming, 221n20
violence: anti-, 127; in Bible, 46–47; domestic, 58; sexual, 72, 157. *See also* police violence
voting patterns, black, 8
Voting Rights Act of 1965, 4, 150

Walker, David, 72, 77
Walton, Jonathan, 106
warrior culture, in Bible, 48, 212n17
Washington, Booker T., 232n7
Weems, Renita, 114, 221n20
West, Traci, 114
Western theology, 8
Whipper, William, 74
white clothing, 87
white evangelicals, black churches and, 31–32
white gay community, 137–138
white male power, 70
white men, 69
white masculine domination, 73
white power structures, 76

white privilege, 138
white women, 135
Why We Can't Wait (King, M.), 194–195
Wiley, Dennis W., 3
Williams, Luella, 83
womanist sexual ethics, 113–116
women, 45, 70; in Bible, 221n16; bodies of, 170; church and, 69; equality of, 73; expendability of, 43; family roles of, 57–58; fear of, 169; suffrage movements of, 69; white, 135. *See also* black women
Works Progress Administration (WPA), 85
World War II, 96
worship, 85, 163
WPA. *See* Works Progress Administration
Writing the Wrongs (Thompson, J.), 220n7

Your Spirits Walk Beside Us (Savage), 10
youth, black, 26–27

RELIGION, CULTURE, AND PUBLIC LIFE
Series Editor: Matthew Engelke

After Pluralism: Reimagining Religious Engagement, edited by Courtney Bender and Pamela E. Klassen
Religion and International Relations Theory, edited by Jack Snyder
Religion in America: A Political History, Denis Lacorne
Democracy, Islam, and Secularism in Turkey, edited by Ahmet T. Kuru and Alfred Stepan
Refiguring the Spiritual: Beuys, Barney, Turrell, Goldsworthy, Mark C. Taylor
Tolerance, Democracy, and Sufis in Senegal, edited by Mamadou Diouf
Rewiring the Real: In Conversation with William Gaddis, Richard Powers, Mark Danielewski, and Don DeLillo, Mark C. Taylor
Democracy and Islam in Indonesia, edited by Mirjam Künkler and Alfred Stepan
Religion, the Secular, and the Politics of Sexual Difference, edited by Linell E. Cady and Tracy Fessenden
Boundaries of Toleration, edited by Alfred Stepan and Charles Taylor
Recovering Place: Reflections on Stone Hill, Mark C. Taylor
Blood: A Critique of Christianity, Gil Anidjar
Choreographies of Shared Sacred Sites: Religion, Politics, and Conflict Resolution, edited by Elazar Barkan and Karen Barkey
Beyond Individualism: The Challenge of Inclusive Communities, George Rupp
Love and Forgiveness for a More Just World, edited by Hent de Vries and Nils F. Schott
Relativism and Religion: Why Democratic Societies Do Not Need Moral Absolutes, Carlo Invernizzi Accetti
The Making of Salafism: Islamic Reform in the Twentieth Century, Henri Lauzière
Mormonism and American Politics, edited by Randall Balmer and Jana Riess
Religion, Secularism, and Constitutional Democracy, edited by Jean L. Cohen and Cécile Laborde
Race and Secularism in America, edited by Jonathon S. Kahn and Vincent W. Lloyd
Beyond the Secular West, edited by Akeel Bilgrami
Pakistan at the Crossroads: Domestic Dynamics and External Pressures, edited by Christophe Jaffrelot
Faithful to Secularism: The Religious Politics of Democracy in Ireland, Senegal, and the Philippines, David T. Buckley
Holy Wars and Holy Alliance: The Return of Religion to the Global Political Stage, Manlio Graziano
The Politics of Secularism: Religion, Diversity, and Institutional Change in France and Turkey, Murat Akan
Democratic Transition in the Muslim World: A Global Perspective, edited by Alfred Stepan
The Holocaust and the Nakba, edited by Bashir Bashir and Amos Goldberg
The Limits of Tolerance: Enlightenment Values and Religious Fanaticism, Denis Lacorne
German, Jew, Muslim, Gay: The Life and Times of Hugo Marcus, Marc David Baer
Modern Sufis and the State: The Politics of Islam in South Asia and Beyond, edited by Katherine Pratt Ewing and Rosemary R. Corbett
The Arab and Jewish Questions: Geographies of Engagement in Palestine and Beyond, edited by Bashir Bashir and Leila Farsakh
At Home and Abroad: The Politics of American Religion, edited by Elizabeth Shakman Hurd and Winnifred Fallers Sullivan

GPSR Authorized Representative: Easy Access System Europe, Mustamäe tee
50, 10621 Tallinn, Estonia, gpsr.requests@easproject.com

www.ingramcontent.com/pod-product-compliance
Lightning Source LLC
Chambersburg PA
CBHW022043290426
44109CB00014B/959